GURU ANGAD DEV

THE GREAT GURUS OF THE SIKHS SERIES

GURU ANGAD DEV

Editor-in-Chief

O. P. RALHAN

ANMOL PUBLICATIONS PVT. LTD.
NEW DELHI-110002 (INDIA)

ANMOL PUBLICATIONS PVT. LTD.
4374/4B, Ansari Road, Daryaganj
New Delhi-110 002

Guru Angad Dev Etc.

First Edition 1998

ISBN 81-7488-671-0

PRINTED IN INDIA

Published by J. L. Kumar for Anmol Publications Pvt. Ltd., New Delhi-110 002 and Printed at Mehra Offset Press, Delhi.

Preface

'Great Gurus of the Sikhs' in six volumes is a monumental work by the editor drawing every succinct information on each of the ten Gurus from unapproachable historical and religious sources.

These volumes should not be treated simply in biographical sketches of their lives or travelogue of their lives, but an account of their teachings, philosophies, travelogue, their sufferings and sacrifices for the country, their mythological and theological aspects, socio-economic reforms, their political contention and wars with the autocracy at their times and many more touching incidents of their lives, miracles which they manifested on several occasions—all have been contained in them. These volumes are treasures of religious wealth enshrined in their sacred *Vanis*—viz. Guru Granth Sahib and on political scenario of their times.

The sufferings of the Gurus were immense during Mughal period. Guru Arjun Dev, Guru Teg Bahadur and Guru Gobind Singh sacrificed every thing for the sake of their sincere love for humanity and reforming zeal. Repressive policies and numerous maneuvre could not bend them, instead. The rulers have to bow before them for their unparallelled and unmatched chivalry shown by them in spite of great emotional hurdles.

These volumes are faithful and sincere narration of the political conditions, social conditions, religious fanaticity of the rulers, prevailing at that times and how all those Great Gurus not only fought against heavy odds but simultaneously never allowed to fade away the spiritual lamp lighted by them which even today imparts eternal peace to thousands of people not only of Sikh people but all other religions.

These volumes on Great Gurus of the Sikhs advocate tenaciously a superb, enchanting study for each and every one. Highly recommended for teachers, students, social reformers, historians. A useful and worthy of acquisition for each library. Section of Sikh history in each library remain incomplete without such a marvellous set.

Contents

1

Guru Angad Dev

(b. 1539; d. 1552)

Lehna to Angad

Bhai Lehna, who became Guru Angad, was the son of a petty trader, named, Pheru. Born on March 31, 1504 in the village named Harike in the Ferozepur district, he grew to be a man of religious disposition under the influence of his mother, Dayabai and took special pleasure in his devotion to Durga, the Goddess of Shakti, and consort of Lord Shiva. When he came of age, he was married to a lady called Khivi. The lady belonged to matte-di-Sarai, the ancestrol village of Pheru. After some time, Angad's father having grown weary of his native village, decided to move to matte-di-Sarai. Shortly after the village was sacked by the Moghuls and Baloches who had come with Babur, and the family had to shift to Khadur beside the Beas, near Tarn Taran. Soon after, Pheru passed away and the entire burden of the family fell on Guru Angad.

While still a pious worshipper of Durga, he was once incharge of a group of pilgrims intent on visiting Jawala Mukhi, or 'Fire Mouth' a volcanic vent in the lower neighbouring Himalayas, from which flame came consecrated to the Goddess Durga. He was to have led Durga dance around the fire clad in a robe of office and in a harness of jingling bells. According to Archer, it seems Nanak, Then living—had gone to firemouth to preach his Gospel to the Durga Devotees on this festival occasion and Angad listened to the serman. He had known something of the Sikhs before this, in his own village and had been favourably impressed by a certain Jodha, a conscientious devotee very zealous at his 'morning prayer' and at quotations from the 'Jap ji.' He met Nanak himself at fire mouth and there and then he became a convert. The Sikh Sakhikars, however, say that Angad met Guru Nanak while on his way to Jawala Mukhi.

Whatever the case might have been, Bhai Lehna was altogether a changed man after his meeting with the Guru. He henceforward dedicated himself to the service of Guru Nanak and began to live at Kartarpur. Soon he succeeded in attaching himself to Nanak's personal staff. His devotion to Guru Nanak was so great that Budha, Sudhara, and others of Nanak's small community looked upon him as a good example. The whole hagiographical literature is replete with anecdotes bringing out his humility, spirit of service and that unquenchable thirst for truth and reighteousness which must mark one on whom the holy office was to devolve. No dates can be ascertained as to when Bhai Lehna came to the Guru but obviously it must have been during the last few years of the Guru's life when his thoughts must have constantly turned on finding a proper successor to himself. From the accounts which have come down, the Guru's sons, esteemable men in a general way, did not come upto the measure of greatness and holiness requisite in a fit successor to him. Bhai Gurdas has left an impression of the situation in the following lines of his poem:—

> 'The sons did not fulfil the Guru's behests.
> They proved untractable and dis-obedient.'

The Guru's choice, therefore, fell on Bhai Lehna who had proved to be the fittest. Various tests to which Bhai Lehna was put to by Guru Nanak displayed his unshakable faith in the Guru and the three cardinal principles viz., complete devotion and obedience to the Guru, dignity of labour, and love for humanity which, in fact, beautifully sum up the teachings of Guru Nanak. Accordingly, Guru Nanak in token of having nominated him as his successor, placed a coconut and five paisa before him and gave him new name Angad (begot from the self), proclaiming "He, Lehna, had the same light and the same ways. The Guru merely changed his body." This event took place on September 7, 1539.

CONSOLIDATION OF THE SIKHS

Importance of Angad's Nomination to Guruship

The nomination of Angad to the Guruship is a fact of profound importance in Sikh History. When Guru Nanak had stressed the indispensableness of the Guru, he was making no new departure, because this had been recognised by almost all the teachers of the medieval school; but the really vital moment came when he appointed a successor. By doing so, he made it clear that Nanak wanted that his ideals should strike roots among the people. Moreover, by nominating Angad as successor a precedent or tradition was established by virtue of which the Sikhs were integrated into a community under the un-interrupted leadership. In this context Trumpp is right when he says 'the disciples of Nanak would no doubt have soon dispersed and gradually disappeared as well as the disciples of many other Gurus before Nanak, if he had not taken case to appoint a successor before his death. Similary G.C. Narang points out, "Had Nanak died without a successor there would have been no Sikhism today or at best, simply another Kabirism."

The continuing institution of Guruship affected Sikhism in another way also. It helped the Sikhs to integrate themselves as a distinct and self-conscious socio-religious community. Apart from the importance of nomination of a successor as stated above the Guruship acquired an impersonal character. In the coronation ode it is stated:

Guru Nanak, in bowing to Guru Angad,
reversed the order of things.
He put his umbrella over the head of Lehna, who
then was exalted to the skies.
Guru Nanak's light blended with Guru Angad's
and Guru Nanak became absorbed in him.

The personality of the Guru was detached from the Guruship which was to be regarded as one indivisible and continuous. This was entirely a novel feature and it distinguishes Sikhism, from similar institutions in other religions.

The Guruship having been the embodiment of the spirit acquired the character something sacred and infallible with the result that it exacted veneration—the fact which provided cohesion and ensured unity.

Dangers

However, after assuming the pontificate on the advice of Guru Nanak, Guru Angad left Kartarpur for Khadur where his wife and children were living presumably to avoid trouble at the hands of the sons of the Guru Nanak, and addressed himself to the task of consolidating the Sikhs and their faith forthwith. But the task was not an easy one. The Sikh community being infant, had to face a number of dangers. The most potent threat came from Hinduism. It is important to remember that Hinduism has no cut and dried creed and it never prescribed the same code of worship for everybody. Broadly speaking, the adhikara or aptitude has always been regarded as a factor in the prescription or Hindu religious duties and opinions have generally been tolerated almost to any extent provided certain social usages were not want only violated. Under the circumstances it was not at all difficult for Hinduism to accommodate the followers of Nanak within its fold and absorb them totally in course of time, especially when Guru Nanak had concerned himself more or less with the fundamentals and had left the details to take care of themselves. Evidently special care was required to interpret and re-emphasise the message of Nanak in unambiguous terms and in a down-to-earth manner. Besides this the Guru had pointed out the uselessness of mere formalities and observances when they were divorced from the spirit but this was not enough. The supreme need of the moment was to clothe the message with distinctive emblems which might give it an individuality of its own.

The most serious challenge was posed by Siri Chand, the eldest son of Guru Nanak. Though he was not an ambitious man yet he was the elder son of the Guru and a man of pious habits and there were many who believed that Nanak's place should go to him and thus they refused to accept Angad's succession. Besides this, Siri Chand founded a separate seet, known as Udasis, a community indifferent to the concerns of the world. Because of his being the son of Nanak, personal merits and the closeness of his thesis with the marrow-deep ascetic tradition of the country, he was making great impact on the masses, much more on the Sikhs, thereby causing a schism among the ranks of the followers of Nanak. Under such circumstances constant vigil and a peculiar promptitude was needed to safeguard the interests on the Sikhs.

Not only this, priestly classes of the Hindus who had found in the teachings of Guru Nanak a threat to their vested interests and even to their existence as a class started opposing to the nascent Sikh movement. The activities of Vaishnavites, the worshippers of Durga and the jogies had not yet abated. They were still active in the propagation of their creeds.

The only silver lining in the cloudy atmosphere was the indifference of the Muslims and the state who were yet unconcerned with the affairs of the Guru whom they regarded as one of the many pious faqirs.

Personal Example

Notwithstanding the aforesaid handicaps, the Guru started his work of consolidation in right earnest which was obviously the preservation and propagation of the Sikh faith as propounded and preached by Guru Nanak. While doing so, the Guru was acting as a leaven so as to enable the people to grasp fully the implications of Guru Nanak's teachings and to mould their lives in their light—the step which was necessary before any tangible result could be achieved. This was the reason that the Guru spared no pains to preach Sikh ideology. He did so by setting up his own example and by taking various organisational steps. He lived Guru Nanak's tenets. He got up in the ambroisal hours and having taken a bath attended the Sangat (holy congregation) and listened to the recitation of Gurubani by the rebeck players.

After this, he removed the doubts of his disciples. Then he performed service in the Langar (free kitchen). Having taken meals he took rest. In the afternoon, he would chat and play with the children and encouraged the people to take physical exercise to build their body to preserve their health. In fact the keynote of the Guru's life was discipline, simran (meditation) and sewa (service). All these qualities shone with redoubled brightness because of the humility, characteristic of his demeanour and his love for the poor. Hagiographical literature furnishes us many examples.

Advice to Preaches and Followers

The Guru advised his followers to imbibe all the qualities and lead a disciplined life. One Mahna, who refused to serve the low-caste people was advised not to entertain such feelings because the house of the Guru is, in fact, the house of the poor. Similarly he was asked to serve the poor and the weak, instead of bullying them. Any delinquency on the part of a preacher was rarely tolerated.

Re-emphasising what Guru Nanak Said

Guru Nanak's Gospel was preached vigorously and in order it might be embedded in the hearts of the people, Guru Nanak's words were often quoted. The Guru wrote only 62 sloks; but these represented neither the amplification of nor the deviation from the Nanak's teachings—rather a continuation of the tradition to lay still more emphasis. Yet the impression emerges that the Guru purposely avoided using images and examples which were not intelligible to the common stock of the people. Furthermore, he put forth his thoughts in a direct and straight manner without indulging in abstractness and speculative philosophy, obviously to keep them within the range of comprehension of the common people. As for instance, when Guru Angad expressed his views regarding the world, he does not say 'True are the regions true are the universes' as Guru Nanak did, but puts it as 'the world is the dwelling place of God; He dwells in it.' But it should not be, in any case, lost sight of that Guru Angad never attempted to alter the programme as laid down by the first Guru. He, in fact, re-emphasised when Guru Nanak had said. He exhorted his disciples to have faith in the one-ness of the timeless, formless and Deathless God, the Guru, word; name or nam, the futility of the caste-system, the absurdity of the hyprocritical postures on the part of the jogies and votaries of other sects, the significance of the honest creative labour, and so on. Admittedly, certain important topics such as Sikh-point of view regarding islam, Sufi, Sacred thread (Janeu) Sutak, death ceremonies, etc. have not been discussed by Guru Angad in his compositions but it does not signify that he repudiated or did not have faith in the views expressed by Guru Nanak with regard to them.

In fact, Guru Nanak, in his compositions had expressed his views on almost all the essential topics in such an elaborate manner, that Guru Angad presumably, did not feel the necessity of writing again on all the topics. Whichever topics, he touched upon, it appears, he did so either to give vent to his poetic feelings or to re-emphasise whatever his mentor (Guru Nanak) had taught.

It was because of this that Bhai Gurdas describes the succession of Guru Angad as the lighting the lamp from another lamp.

Collection of the Hymns of Guru Nanak

Clear in his mind, regarding his objective, the Guru collected the hymns of Guru Nanak and committed them to writing. Several of these were said to have been handed over by him to Guru Angad, while the rest of them lay in possession of different persons. This step contributed a lot towards the consolidation of Sikhism. It saved the compositions of Guru Nanak from mis-interpretation and also laid the foundation of the Sikh scripture which the fifth Guru compiled and edited. It gave definiteness and distinction to the general ideas laid down by Guru Nanak as also a definite direction to the faith of the disciples. Moreover, it provided a living proof of the Sikh doctrine that there was no essential difference between the Guru and his word (Shabd or Bani).

Thus there is no wonder that Guru Angad Dev assigned a very high place to Shabd—Word—so much so that he made practice of Shabd as the path way to salvation. In fact, Shabd was being given the rank of the Guru and certainly one can discern in these things the shape which Guruship was to have in the years to come.

Biography of Nanak

Besides this, it has been asserted by many eminent scholars that the Guru committed to writing the biography of Guru Nanak which is called Bhai Bala's Janamsakhi. Recent researches have shown beyond doubt that the above-referred Janamsakhi was written round about mid-seventeenth century and not during the period of Guru Angad's pontificate. But it is possible that the Janamsakhi alluded to by deep rooted tradition might have been lost. Had this Janamsakhi been available to us, the step would have been monumental for two reasons viz the Sikhs could have got a sacred book of their own to serve as fount of inspiration for them and secondly it would have formed the first prose work in the Punjabi language.

Gurmukhi Script

The Guru, however, recorded everything in the script which was neither Urdu nor Devnagri but Punjabi, known as Gurmukhi. The script is generally supposed to have been invented by Guru Angad, but the fact that the time of his accession, Bhai Paira Mokha of Sultanpur was asked to transcribe the horoscope of Guru Nanak from Devnagri letters into Gurmukhi shows that these letters existed before Guru Angad. The recent researches have proved beyond doubt that the script was in vogue in some part of the Punjabi. The Guru, however, modified the script.

We agree with Grierson that 'Landa' or clipped true alphabet of the Punjab existed in the time of Guru Nanak, but Guru Angad, finding it imperfect in vowel sounds, which were frequently omitted improved it by borrowing signs from the Devnagri alphabet and after polishing it named it Gurmukhi. Since the Guru adopted modified alphabets, the people began to call it Gurmukhi—spoken through the mouth of the Guru.

Macauliffe also agrees with this view. According to him, Guru Angad deeming that the compositions of Guru Nanak were worthy of a special written character of their own, adopted and modified a Punjabi alphabet called Gurmukhi to give expression to what fell from Guru's lips. Having developed a suitable script, the Guru like Prof. Huxley did not consider it beneath his dignity to write primers for children and he accordingly composed a number of mottos and moral maxims which accompany the letters of Alphabets.

The significance of the adoption of the script by Guru Angad lies in this that he rejected the foreign Persian script. He realised that unless the people adopted a script which was their own and which suited to their language, their culture could not grow. He condemned the adoption of foreign script by the Indians in the strongest term. Guru Nanak had condemned this practice before him in the following verse:

> "And men have changed their tongue and the Muslim way of greetings prevail" (Basant Handol M.I. Page 1191 of Adi Granth)

Furthermore, Gokal Chand Narang writes 'that the name of the script reminded those who employed it of their duty towards their Guru and constantly kept alive in their minds the consciousness that they were something distinct from the common mass of Hinduism.' Moreover, the popularisation of the script was 'well-calculated to make its readers part with Hindu compositions written in Sanskrit. There is a lot of difference between the Devnagri script and Gurmukhi script and a special effort is needed to read sanskrit. The result has been that in most cases Gurmukhi scholars have parted company with Sanskrit works.'

Apart from the results referred to above, this step gave a severe blow to the prestige of the Brahmins and their mystic superiority who, through their monopoly of the knowledge of Sanskrit, had given currency to the belief that their superiority or prestige was ordained by God or Gods above.

Free Kitchen

The institution of Langar (free-kitchen) which was established by Guru Nanak was strengthened and popularised by Guru Angad Dev ji. He organised it more fully, personally seeing to the needs of the poor who came there and with great kindness served them meals, which were taken along with devotees and other visitors, caste being thus fully broken by all in the Ashram. The persons attached with the institution were advised to be polite, sweet and accommodating. Any one acting contrary to the instructions was clearly asked to mend his ways. Lest the dignity of labour and spirit of self-dependence loose their candour, the Guru's wife Mata Khivi worked day and night in the kitchen like an ordinary worker. The institution ran with the contributions made by the Guru's admirers and disciples. The Guru characterised the offerings for the Langar as a poison to himself and lived by twisting coarse turn made of 'munj.' As per rule, the food was served to the people sitting in a line (pangat).

This institution was a great significance. It went a long way towards erasing social and economic inequality; for every one, irrespective of caste and creed, social status, sex and birth was to sit and eat, along with others, the same food. Hence it served as a medium of social integration between the monarch and the commoner on one hand; and as a continuous reminder of the social equality on the other, thereby levelling a mighty blow to the caste-system and untouchability.

Thus, since it was to be run with the help of the contributions made by the Guru admirers, it had its effect on the method and modality of his followers so far as the charity was concerned. Henceforward, they began to think of stopping it to the corrupt and undeserving priestly class. Furthermore, it taught the sikhs the first lesson of contributing money towards a common fund for the common cause.

Moreover, it provided a powerful aid in the publicity work. The poor and helpless, simply appreciated the institution. To the Guru, the architect of it and the persons, intellectually awake and endowed with progressive outlook, it protended something new, beautiful and a right step to build egalitarian-spiritual society.

Sangat

Wherever Guru Nanak went he asked the people to establish Sangat. According to Teja Singh as many as 131 sangats were organised at his behest. Guru Angad continued the tradition initiated by his predecessor. Wherever he went he asked the people to coalesce themselves in Sangat. In his sermons also he eulogised the function of sangat in evolving the Sikh pattern.

He realised that one of the serious banes of Indian society was its individualistic character. He wanted the people to meet regularly on religious platform so that there might be greater understanding and fellow feeling among the various sections of the people.

This institution gave a sense of unity to the people which encouraged them to work for their own spiritual ascent in the context of society.

Udasism — An Anathema

The Guru, by his humility, tact and promptitude tackled the problem which sprang from the challenge of the Udasis. Baba Siri Chand, the elder son of Guru Nanak held strong belief in asceticism and renunciation (Udas) of the world as the correct pathway to Bliss and quoted Guru Nanak as the progenitor and upholder of this view. The view of Siri Chand was obviously a mis-statement of the Guru's Gospel. But Siri Chand's impact on the masses was quite deep. The reasons were not far to seek. Firstly, being the son of Guru Nanak and himself a pious man, he commanded the respect of the people. Secondly, except celibacy and asceticism, the other tenets of the udasis were the same as those of Sikhism and they regarded Nanak with the same veneration as the Sikhs did. Thirdly, asceticism or Udas was in accordance with the temper of the Indian people, who put a premium on asceticism and even to this day the life of a recluse is regarded as the most honourable of all human existences. All these facts made the challenge of Udasis formidable.

Any omission or indulgence on the Guru's part was bound to affect Sikhism adversely, because in case the philosophy of asceticism (Udas) had succeeded, the great aims of Sikhism to set in motion the process of rejuvenating and regenerating the people would have been defeated. Moreover, the division in the ranks of the followers of Sikhism would have assumed a ghastly form and, in course of time, this infant faith might have disappeared as one of the many sects serving no useful social or religious purpose.

Accordingly, Guru Angad took prompt steps and made it clear in unequivocal terms to the disciples that Sikhism was essentially a religion of householders. It was also declared that the Udasis the followers of Siri Chand, even if they held faith in most of the Nanak's tenets, were not true Sikhs. Thus Guru Angad, by doing so, barred the door to asceticism and made the influences of Guru Nanak available not only for religious uplift but also for social regeneration.

This action of the Guru brought rich dividends. Udasism could not become the mass movement much less the part of Sikh movement. The little influence which still they had was eliminated by the constant endeavour of the later Gurus till Siri Chand wound up his order and merged it in the Sikh movement. Apart from it, the status awarded by the Guru to the life of a householder sounded new to the people who were accustomed to listening to Brahmins eulogising the life of an ascetic or recluse. No wonder, the Sikh masses began to drift away, in ideological sphere, from Hinduism.

Vigorous Preaching

The injunctions against Udasis was not the only thing the Guru did for the preservation of Sikh community. In fact, he took many other important steps to this purpose. He spared no pains to bring home to the people the importance of the teachings of Guru Nanak. He composed hymns in the language and style, intellegible to the masses, his compositions indulging very rarely in speculation and abstraction. He exhorted his Sikhs to follow the programme as followed by Guru Nanak at Kartarpur in their day-to-day life. He advised the preachers also to lead a disciplined life. Whenever there was a breach of discipline by anyone, the Guru took serious note of it. In this manner, a set discipline came to be introduced in Sikhism which saved Sikhism from possible disintegration.

The Guru was much particular not to allow any preacher or reciter of the words of the Guru to assume the character of the priestly class such as Brahmins etc. The indicent of *Satta* and *Balwand,* the bards of the court of the Guru is a case in point. According to Macauliffle, two minstrels Satta and Balwand began to boast that it was on account of their skill in music that the Guru had grown popular. And to substantiate their boast, they began to absent themselves from reciting the hymns at regular hours. They were requested to attend sangat but they persisted in their attitude of defiance and at last Angad finished with them and made his own arrangements. The two minstrels soon realised the folly of their action and made repeated attempts to get reconciled with the Guru. The latter refused to relent because they had spoken arrogantly about Guru Nanak also. They had suggested that even the latters' court would not have been known without the music of Mardana. Guru Angad refused to entertain any further representation on behalf of minstrels by saying, "He would have the beard and moustaches of any man, who again spoke in their favour out off and his face blackened and he would have him mounted on a donkey and led in disgrace through the city." In their extremity, Satta and Balwand approached Bhai Ladha of Lahore, who had a great influence with the Guru. Bhai Ladha took up their cause and having shaved his head, blackened his face, and mounted a donkey with his face turned to the tail, went around the city of Khadur, and finally arrived in Guru's presence. The Guru could not resist the entreaties of his devotee and forgave the minstrels. They fell down at the feet of the Guru. They are said to have composed and sung the well-known Ode which with subsequent additions by the bards themselves was incorporated in the Guru Granth Sahib by Guru Arjan Dev.

This incident highlights the fact that the Guru maintained perfect discipline at his court and was determined never to let the bards of the court assume the characteristic defiance and arrogance of the priestly class.

Guru Angad is said to have taken steps to start building a new town, Goindwal near Khadur. Amar Das, a devoted disciple, was appointed to supervise its construction. According to G.C. Narang, the construction of the city started in A.D. 1546. The step was in the right direction. It provided work to the unemployed and a city to the followers, who having gathered at one place, would be a great factor in the dissemination of the Guru's Gospel.

Physical Culture

Side by side the organisational steps as detailed above, the Guru paid full attention towards the physical culture of the Sikhs. He enjoined upon them to take full care of their bodies. To evince their interest in physical exercise, he got prepared a wrestling ground at Khadur. If the words of Confucious, that 'a journey of a thousand miles is started only with a step' are true, the Guru laid the foundation of the martial spirit which in the times of the Sixth and the tenth Gurus blossomed into the Khalsa.

Suraj Prakash, on the basis of Sikh tradition gives the details of the meeting of Humayun with Guru Angad. Emperor Humayun, after his final defeat at Kanauj came to Khadur, enroute to Lahore, to seek the blessings of the Guru. When the Emperor reached therè, the Guru was intrance and consequently the Emperor had to keep standing for some time. The haughty emperor took it as an insult that the Guru had not shown him due respect. Out of a fit of anger, he put his hand on the hilt of his sword. When the Guru's eyes opened, he saw the emperor trying to draw out his sword. The Guru said "when Thou aughtest to have used sword against Sher Shah, thou didst not do so. Now when thou comest among priests, instead of saluting them respectfully desirest to draw the sword on them."

Humayun tendered apology and entreated for the blessings. The Guru prophesied that he would recover the throne but before that, he would suffer for some time because of his un-called for attempt to make an attack on him. There is no historical evidence to vouchsafe the truth of the above story; but at the same time it would be wrong to regard it baseless in the absence of any evidence contrary to this well-established belief. The event of course, enhanced the prestige of the Guru and the popularity of his Gospel.

Estimate of the Guru's Work

From the aforesaid account, it emerges that the Guru was a fine character, of sterling piety and unflinching devotion. It also appears that he was a vigorous preacher and strict disciplinarian who had a keen sensitivity to perceive the psycho-social valuations of the people; and a peculiar sense of practicability to take immediate corresponding actions to keep the Sikh movement on the track.

Admittedly, Guru Angad's period was the most crucial one, for the movement was in its infancy and the dangers were serious and manifold. The credit certainly goes to the Guru for not only overcoming the dangers, but also succeeding in giving the movement a distinctness and definiteness, apart from effecting its consolidation. By popularising Gurmukhi script and closing the doors of Sikhism to the Udasis,he saved Sikhism from merging into Hinduism and his disciples from being absorbed into the Hindu masses. Not only this, the Sikhs began to assume something of a social character in addition to the religious ties that held them together. Thus we can henceforward trace two parallel developments in Sikhism. On the one hand the work began by Guru Nanak was earnestly continued and new religious ties were added one after the other; on the other hand there was manifest signs of drifting away from the orthodox Hindu society and attempts were made through innovations to bring into existence a new brotherhood, social as well as religious, self-sufficient and independent. Nevertheless, during the pontificate of the Guru, it was still doubtful whether the Sikhs had realised their separate entity, although there is no gainsaying the fact that it had started drifting away from Hinduism and any observer with a little common sense, could visualise the shape of things to come.

Guru Angad, finding his end approaching fast, nominated Amar Das as his successor. Herein also, he followed the example of Guru Nanak. He did not give Guruship to any of his sons; his choice fell on Amar Das who had shown on more than one occasions, utmost devotion to him, piety and spirit of unselfish service to both the Guru and the people. The step like that of Guru Nanak was of great significance. Guru Angad passed away on March 29, 1552 at the age of forty-eight.

When the luminous figure of Guru Nanak became invisible, Angad saw the Guru's spirit entering his own soul. He felt elated with joy and wonder. He quietly sought the lowly house of a humble disciple and confined himself to a room. He was unwilling to open his eyes to look at anything else. Angad, lost in himself, sat in a trance of 'Dhyanam,' his soul fast asleep in the Master's soul. Months passed by and no one knew where Guru Angad was. They yearned to see him and to touch his lotus feet. Crowds surged everywhere in the country searching for him and longing to see him.

At last Bhai Budha intruded on the love-smadhi of the Master and implored him to come out and give 'darshan' to his people.

When Guru Angad came out of his seclusion, the disciples saw in him the same aura, the same face and the same speech, as of his Master, Nanak. Guru Angad—Nanak the second, was in reality from the self-same Flame; but the Divine Hand had kept him concealed in the garb of Bhai Lehna till Nanak lifted the veil off him and in the mirror of his heart saw his own image and bowed down to him and announced him as Guru Angad—Nanak's own-self.

From the nectar-laved glance of Guru Angad, a million eyes drew inspiration. By his blissful smile he destroyed sorrows and sufferings of the people and filled their hearts with felicity and joy. His transmuting touch turned the baser metal of the men's mind into pure gold. A mass of people came to the new Master, some to be fed, some to be healed and blessed and others to be initiated in the Gospel of Nam. But whosoever came hovered round the magic personality of Guru Angad in love and wonder, as moths round a lamp in the darkness.

From Angad, the Master, spontaneously flew 'Sparks of Life,' and the soul of the people caught fire from them. His creative power was observed in the raising of the dead by his presence. From him, the life of the spirit flowed in a thousand shining rivers to the soul of the people. He worked in the Unseen.

Guru Angad loved little children. They were also delighted to be round him. The Master took great interest in their education. He opened schools for their instruction and he simplified the old Punjabi Characters (that had come down from the time of the Greeks) into a new alphabet; since then this script has come to be called Gurmukhi. Thus in addition to the Temple of Bread and Temple of Song built by Guru Nanak, Angad the Master gave a third, the Temple of Teaching.

Daya Nath Yogi meets Guru Angad: At Achal Batala, a group of Yogis under the leadership of Yogi Bhangar Nath, came into a violent ideological clash with Guru Nanak. Guru Nanak gave a convincing revelation of his 'Shabad' philosophy and won over the Sidhas to his ideology.

Now when Guru Angad came on the spiritual throne of Nanak, some of those yogis came to Khadur Sahib to test the spiritual greatness of Guru Angad. They had been defeated by Guru Nanak and so some of them perhaps wanted to pay off old scores. But on encounter with him, they found Guru Angad spiritually as formidable as Guru Nanak was. The yogis got peace and cooling solace from him and after paying their homage and humble salutations, they went away fully satisfied.

Now Daya Nath was another Yogi of great renown and acquirements. He was not in the Punjab at the time of discussions that were held at Achal Batala between Guru Nanak and the Yogis. So he was curious to know, how Guru Nanak gave an ideological defeat to such a prominent Sidha, as Bhangar Nath, the Yogi Superior of Achal Batala Centre.

Daya Nath had learnt that Guru Nanak was no more in the world, and that he was succeeded by his disciple Angad, who was with him when Guru Nanak held his doctrinal discourse with the Sidhas at Achal Batala. So Daya Nath came to Guru Angad at Khadur in order to know directly from him what the Sikh view of life was, which had challenged and over powered the leaders of all the Six system of philosophy at Achal Batala.

Daya Nath came to Khadur with about a hundred followers. Guru Angad was sitting in a garden outside the village and there was about 200 people sitting around him and listening to him.

Daya Nath came and sat near the Guru and after exchange of greetings he said that he had come with a definite purpose. So saying he asked the Guru to explain how 'Yoga' (union with God) can be attained. Guru Angad: "Listen please, Yoga cannot be attained by dialectics and wrangling controversies. When a man's mind lives and moves in the Divine Spirit—Pure and Spotless Being (Niranjan) and remains detached from the worldliness, only then he gets union and can be deemed a real yogi."

Daya Nath: "Guruji! But to me it appears only those people can attain Yoga, who join and take up the cult of yoga and wear the garb of yogis—ear-rings, begging bowl, staff and smear their bodies with ashes and carry a conch of horn, and live in forests away from cities, and sit in deep concentration, suspending their breath. What do you think of such practices of Yoga?"

Guru Angad: "Please listen, no Yoga (union with God) can be attained by merely wearing the garb of a Yogi. If an actor puts on the uniform of a king, can anyone consider him to be a real king? He is a mere actor who acts as a king but can never be deemed a real king.

By abandoning one's home and going to forests, one does not became a yogi. Nor can yoga be attained by suspending breath and sitting for long in yogic postures, nor by bathing in places of pilgrimages and wandering from country to country. Nothing spiritual can be acquired through such practices."

Daya Nath: "If yoga cannot be attained through such penance and ascetic practices, then tell me, sire, by what code of restraint and self control can real yoga be attained?"

Guru Angad: Guru Nanak points out:

If one meets the true Guru,

The mind stops wandering,
A stream of bliss flows in the being;
Spontaneous Divine Music pours forth,
And fearless spiritual state is attained.
One remains detached from worldliness
And in one's ownself is God realized.

Daya Nath Yogi; "Revered Guru! I have practised all the severe disciplines and austerities prescribed for sanyasa and yoga. I have met Yogis absorbed in the most difficult practices of austerities and penances. But I have not found the peace of mind. Nor have I met a God-realized man. Please gracious Master, bless me with this gift of peace and enlightenment."

So saying Yogi Daya Nath bowed in reverence and humble salutation and touched the feet of the Guru with his forehead. The touch of the holy feet of the Guru gave him peace and cooling solace. And Daya Nath was transmuted.

Guru Angad receives Amardas: Amardas was an old man of 70 and had been forty times on pilgrimages to the sacred Ganges at Hardwar and had met many saints. Although he was charitable, good and pure, but the Lamp in him had not been lighted. He always felt some void and emptiness in soul. It seemed to him that he lacked something vital in him, but he knew it not what.

Early one dawn, a sweet voice, surcharged with life-aroma fell into his ears. It was the angelic voice of Bibi Amro from the neighbouring house. She was his nephew's wife and daughter of Guru Angad. She was singing the Guru's hymns while she churned to make butter for the family. Amardas was so charmed by the lovely melody and thrilling words that he stood spell bound listening to her song. The hymn she sang ended thus:

"The sear and scarred soul, dry as dust becomes whole again, when the Guru is met."

(Translated)

Do they, the dead ones rise? Do old rickety bones swing back into life? Where did this joy-laden news come from?

The old man ran to the hidden nightingale in the neighbouring house and said. "O daughter, dear, whose song it is that gives good news?"

"Our Father's," said the girl.

"My dear daughter! I am burnt from top to toe. I need the Living-Touch of the Master to burst forth again into life. Pray, take me, take me to the Fountain of Light."

Bibi Amro took this elderly man to her father, Guru Angad. He received him with great respect that was befitting of his age and position in society.

As soon as Amardas beheld the love-lit, glowing face of the Guru, his mind melted like snow in the golden sunshine.

Enraptured by his holy-darshan (sight) he could not bear leaving his presence. So deep and intense was his love for the Master that he would find pleasure in serving him in every way. He would bring him a pitcher of fresh water from the river Beas every morning before dawn for his path, he would wash his clothes and would serve in his Temple of Bread—taking keen delight in the utter effacement of self in his labour of love.

Guru Angad had imparted the hidden Spark of Life to Amardas. This had flushed his soul, body and mind. The Holy Spring him. Having ignited him with the Fire of Truth, the Master left the disciple alone to his ecstasies, to his labour of love, to his Smadhi, making response to him only in the unseen, as the Master chose to conceal his fine work of art beneath a thick veil, away from the vulgar gaze.

Amardas for ever abided by Nam and lived in the charming music of His sweet presence. Found like a child, he would remain gazing at the Guru in a continual trance of wonder, joy and love.

While going every day with a brass vessel to the river to fetch water and returning with it, Amardas never turned his back to the Guru. To him it seemed he would die if he had turned his back on the Master, even in the physical sense.

At the early ambrosial hour of fragrant dawn every day, Amardas brought the water from the Beas, for his Master's bath, irrespective of rain, lightning and thunder. The Master must bathe and the disciple must bring the Beas water and carry the love-load.

On a frightfully cold winter night, Amardas was carrying the vessel full of water through the dark streets. He struck against a wooden peg, which a weaver had driven into the ground, and he fell into the loom-pit.

The weaver's wife, still snugly sleeping in her comfortable bed, was disturbed by the thud of his fall. And she said to her husband beside her, "Ah, who could it be at this hour? It must be that homeless Amru, who sleeps not, who knows no rest and tires never."

The Master sitting at Khadur felt the twitch and he was deeply moved. He took the old Baba to his bosom. The two souls met, as never before, and in that meeting arose another Moon in our sky. A great veil had been lifted somewhere in the depth of his heart and the Fountain of Eternal Joy burst forth in Amardas.

"My Amardas! My Amardas! said the Master," "He is the home of the homeless, the refuge of the refugeless, the honour of the honourless, the strength of the strengthless, the Light of the world. My Amardas! My Amardas is the Divine Master, Nanak himself. He then bowed to Amardas and seated him on the spiritual throne of Guru Nanak.

Guru Angad's hymns: We have 62 hymns of Guru Angad in Guru Granth Sahib (the Holy Book).

They are as brief as they are intense:

I

Were a hundred moons to appear,
Were a thousand suns to arise.
With so many lights.
There would still be utter darkness
If there were no Guru.

II

For those, O Nanak, it is perpetual spring
Who have their Beloved in their homes,
But those whose Beloved is far off—
Day and night they remain burning.

III

My sisters, it is the rainy month of 'Sawan'
Clouds are gathering in the sky,
Think of the Beloved and enjoy,
If I think of another, I die !
My sisters! it is the month of 'Sawan'
It is raining love, it is raining joy !
To awake now is sin;
O let me lie in the embrace of my Beloved.
Wake me not, take me not from here,
It is the sleep of peace !
O sisters! It is the month of 'Sawan.'

IV

He is not to be called a lover
Who attaches himself to a person other than the Beloved.
Nanak, only he can be called God's lover
Who remains in constant communion with Him

If he takes favourable things as good
And unfavourable as bad
He is no lover who deals with Him
In this calculating manner.

V

The Nectar of which we hear is the love of God.
Immortality for which we long is the song of Nam.
The secret of life is hidden in us,
But it opens in the kind glance of the Guru.

2

Guru Amar Das

(b. A.D. 1479; d. A.D. 1574)

Born in April 1479 at the village Basarke, Amar Das was the eldest son of Tej Bhan, who was a Terain Khatri by caste. At the age of 24, he married Mansa Devi and adopted his father's profession—viz agriculture-cum-trade. Amar Das was Vashnavite by faith and he used to pay annual visit to the Ganges. He also practised severe austerities to subdue his mind. While returning from his twentieth visit he was told by a monk that he could have no hope of spiritual ascent unless he had a Guru. This kindled a new desire in his reflective mind which found satisfaction in his brother's house. One morning, during ambrosial hours of the morning, his ears caught sweet strains of music coming from there. Sacred hymns of Nanak were being sung by Bibi Amro, the daughter of Guru Angad Dev ji, who was married to his brother's son. He requested her to take him to her father. She did accordingly. He was so much impressed by Guru Angad Dev that he was converted to be a staunch devotee of the Guru. Under the impact of the teachings of Guru Angad, Amar Das shed off his Vaishnavite prejudices for the use of meat and wrong notions of austerities. The best austerity, he was told, was to exert himself in the service of the people. He followed the instruction of the Guru in letter and spirit. He felt much pleased to fetch water and fuel for the common kitchen. Inspite of his old age and the superior social relation with the Guru, he took upon himself to do any odd job for the Guru and his Sikhs. According to Teja Singh and Ganda Singh, "he would daily bring water from the Beas, over three miles distant for the morning bath of the Guru." He went on doing so for about eleven years (1541 to 1552). Once, in the month of January, 1552, when it was raining in torrents and it was biting cold outside, Amar Das set out as usual to bring water from the river. On his way back, he struck against a peg of Karir wood and fell down before the house of a weaver. The Sound Produced by the fall disturbed the family of the weaver and weaver's wife cried, "Ah, it must be that foot and homeless Amru who revolves round the feet of the so-called Guru." The news reached the Guru who decided that Amar Das would no longer be homeless rather he would be a refuge to the homeless ones. He appointed him as his successor, in preference to his sons because he saw so great a contrast between his own sons' indifference and this aged disciple's tireless zeal. In March 1552, the succession ceremony was performed and the Guru placed five paisa and a coconut before Amar Das as a symbol expressive of passing of Guruship to Guru Amar Das and hence-forward Amar Das would act as the Guru. As a matter of fact "His devotion, service and ability fitted him for the important duties of leading the Sikh church."

Now Guru Angad asked Amar Das to repair to Goindwal. He himself had sufficient experience of the jealously in which his successor would be held by his sons. To avoid direct clash he asked Amar Das to remain out of Khadur. Gonda the founder and owner of the village 'Goindwal' was a disciple of the Guru. The Guru had even helped him to found that village. He thought that Amar Das would be secure there. Besides, Goindwal was situated on the road from Lahore to Delhi and near a ford of the river Beas. By keeping a preacher there, many travellers would become acquainted with the teachings of Guru Nanak and thus an easy opportunity would be offered for the dissemination of the Sikh gospel. Amar Das, therefore, took his abode at Goindwal.

Guru Angad left this world on the 4th day of the bright half of the lunar month of Chet, in the year 1609 of Bikrami era. Just before the event was to happen. Amar Das summoned to the holy presence of the second Guru and was formally installed on the Gaddi with due ceremony. The second Guru made a present of five paisa to him, put a coconut in his lap and bowed to his feet in the presence of the whole congregation. Thus in the seventy-second year of his age, Amar Das was proclaimed the third Guru of the Sikhs.

At the investiture of Amar Das, Dasu and Datu the two sons of Guru Angad felt much upset and claimed that it was their hereditary right to assume the pontificate. On the advice of their mother, Mata Khivi, Dasu withdrew his claim; but Datu remained adament and declared himself as the Guru. Guru Amar Das, with a view to avoiding any trouble, retired to Goindwal. Much enraged at this, Datu went to Goindwal and committed insane act of kicking him in the chest while he was giving instructions to the congregation. Guru Amar Das displayed extraordinary patience and said, "O! Honoured Sir, pardon me; my old bones must have hurt your tender feet", and left Goindwal for his native village, Basarke.

Datu, however, could not convince the Sikhs of the legitimacy of his claim and in despair, left for Khadur. In the meantime, prominent Sikhs such as Bhai Budha etc. prevailed upon Guru Amar Das to return to Goindwal and resume his work.

Like Datu, Siri Chand, the eldest son of Guru Nanak, also lay his claim to the Guru Gaddi on the plea that Guru Angad had got no right to appoint his successor and Guruship must revert to him automatically since it belonged to his father, who passed it on to Guru Angad without conferring on him the powers to pass it on to others. Siri Chand, partly because of his own piety and partly because of the general tendency on the part of the people to put a premium on celibacy and asceticism was attracting people towards him. According to Gokal Chand Narang, "the tide was turning in his favour and it required all the power and statesmanship of Amar Das to save the infant church from an early death." Happily for Sikhism, the old Guru rose to the occasion. The Guru appealed to the people by pointing out the example set by Guru Nanak himself to learn, "how one could live in the world and still not be of the world." According to Macauliffe circular letters were sent to the people enjoining upon them that asceticism was foreign to the creed of Guru Nanak.

In this connection, the author of Mehma Parkash relates that once a man named Gangu, enquired from the Guru as to which was the correct path to salvation. The Guru told him that he should start business at Delhi, earn his livelihood through honest means and give a part of it to the needy.

In this way, the Guru achieved a remarkable success in overcoming the danger from Udasis and their leader Siri Chand. This success was primarily due to the definite and firm stand taken by the Guru himself.

The step was, however, pregnant with far-reaching consequences. The Sikhs were separated from Udasis and thus raised above asceticism were free and fit to follow the course of national progress which depends alike on spiritual attainments and material uplift.

Guru Amar Das, being a tireless and effective preacher, won over many converts. The city of Goindwal progressed, both as a secular and a religious centre. Many Muslims also settled there. They were snobbish and arrogant in their behaviour, because of their being members of ruling community. The Guru's soul-elevating teachings made no impress on them; on the other hand the increasing popularity of the Guru evoked jealousy among them. This being so, they were insolent to the Guru and his followers. In order to over-awe the Sikhs, they often broke the vessels, which carried water for the Guru from the Beas. When the Guru was told the story, he, out of his characteristic forbearance, advised his followers to use leather-vessels instead of earthen pitchers for the purpose. The Muslims, instead of realising their mistake, began to perforate the leather vessels with their sharp arrows. At this, the Guru asked his followers to use brass vessels. But even then, the mischief did not end. The Guru then calmed the Sikhs by uttering "the Sikhs turn a good deed even to those who do no good and God observes everything."

It is said that, after some time, a band of armed men reached there. The Muslims picked up a quarrel with them. In the fight the Muslims lost quite a few persons, including those who entertained animosity towards the Guru. According to Macauliffe, another event took place a few days after. The cash of Government treasury laden on mules was being taken to Delhi. Near Goindwal,a strong gale blew and the mules ran hither and thither. The escort accompanying the mules succeeded in finding all the mules except one. After a great deal of search, the missing one was also found with a Muslim of Goindwal who was reluctant to part with. Accordingly,the matter was reported to the Emperor, who issued orders that the culprit should be punished duly for their attempt to grab the Government money and causing a lot of inconvenience to the Government officials.

The aforesaid event worked upon the minds of the Sikhs in such a way that their faith in God and the Guru re-doubled which was of great benefit for the Sikh Movement.

The mounting popularity of the Sikh Movement with its emphasis on social equality and emancipation of the people from priest-craft and un-meaning ceremonies was ill-looked by the Hindus who instead of taking advantage of the social liberal religious policy of Akbar were once again engrossed in restoring the society based on caste system and stricken from various superstitious totems and many useless practices. Tulsi's Ram Charit Manas, which was the product of this trend among the Hindus, is a case in point. As a necessary corollary to this attitude, the Hindus found in Sikhism a unique development which was giving to Sikhism a distinct individuality and character for different from those of Hinduism. The Sikhs were enjoined upon by their Gurus to discard caste-system, ascetic view of life, untouchability and a host of gods and have faith in the unity of God-head and socio-spiritual equality among the people. The Hindus did not like, particularly two things viz., Langar and construction of Baoli. They disliked the institution of langar because it demonstrated the equality of man between man on practical plane and thus gave a strong blow to the caste system which was considered to be the 'back bone' of Hinduism. Similarly the construction of Baoli at Goindwal provided water to the high and the low alike, giving scant respect to the untouchability and caste system. Moreover, the Guru advised his followers to consider it a place of pilgrimage for them. The idea was appreciated by the Sikhs, because at this centre they met one another in an atmosphere of spiritual and social equality.

The Brahmins and Khatries, the privileged classes of the Hindus who found Guru's teachings contrary to the interests of their class, began to conspire to denigrate him. They complained to Akbar that the Guru was extorting funds from them to maintain his 'court' but Akbar did not pay heed. They instigated the son of Gainda Marwaha to lodge a complaint against the Guru with the Subedar of Lahore to the effect that he might be helped to get his land vacated from the Guru. Although the claim was unjustifiable because Gainda Marwaha, the father of the complainant being the staunch follower of the Guru, had invited the Guru himself to settle there; yet the case was pursued with temerity. According to Sikh tradition, Jafar Beg conducted enquiry into the case and decided the case in Guru's favour.

Gainda appealed to Akbar against the decision and, to impress upon him, he, accompanied by his servant, went to his court. But to his disappointment he was not given even audience of the Emperor and on the other hand, was given shoe-beating by the courtiers.

Guru has thus recorded the event in *Var Gauri*:

"The ungodly clothed the perverse (complainant) in blue and black rags full of lice and dirt. He was not allowed even to approach, more fifth was heaped upon him and the perverse man returned full of dirt, pure and simple. He was sent to backbite and slander others but there also the faces of both perverse men were blackened. At once the whole world knew that along with his servant, the perverse man got a sound shoe-beating till he was senseless. Now the congregation and his own relatives would not associate with him. He was secretly brought to his home by his wife and niece. He lost everything in this world and the next. He cried daily hungry and thirsty. Praise be to the Lord, the creator who Himself sat in righteous judgement. He who slanders the true Guru is destroyed by God. These words are inspired by Him who has created the whole world."

Shortly after, the enemies once again coalesced together and made a petition to the Emperor to the effect that the Guru was preaching against Hinduism. The Emperor invited the Guru to explain his case personally. The Guru, however, begged to be excused to do so on ground of old age and sent Jetha to deputise on his behalf. Jetha presented the case effectively and the petition of the opponents was dismissed. According to the author of Suraj Prakash. 'The Emperor conveyed his message through Jetha to Guru Amar Das that he should pay a visit to the pilgrimage centres of the Hindus so that they might feel assured, and promised that in honour of his visit the Government would not charge any pilgrimage tax.' Macauliffe writes that, in consonance with the wish of the Emperor the Guru paid visits to Pahowa, Kurukshetra and Hardwar. At Kurukshetra, he met jogies, digambaris, sanyasis and men of the six schools and in course of conversation brougt home to them the central points of his teachings, condemning religious externalia and hypocrisy and upholding unity of God-head and universal brotherhood of man. He was accorded a rousing reception everywhere and people of Hardwar came out in hundreds to have his sacred glimpse. The remission of pilgrimage tax heightened the prestige of the Guru and no wonder, the Guru began to be talked about as one possessing devine power. Dr. I.B. Bannerjee agrees in as much as the visit of the Guru to Pehowa, Kurukshetra and Hardwar is concerned; but he disbelieves that he was accorded a hearty welcome. We feel that the statement of Guru Ram Das that the people bubbled with warmth at his visit to the aforesaid places is sufficient to falsify the stand of Shri Bannerjee.

Santokh Singh and Macauliffe both say that the Guru visited the abovementioned places to fulfil the desire of Akbar and to please the Hindus, but the view is unfounded. Two reasons can be advanced to prove the hollowness of their view; firstly, it was contrary to Guru's teachings to go on pilgrimage and secondly there is sufficient internal evidence in the hymns of Guru Ram Das that Guru Amar Das went with the sole purpose of acquainting the people with his mission. All the same, the visit to Hindu pilgrimage centres yielded high returns. The Guru's relations with the emperor enhanced the prestige of the Guru and we might agree with Panth Parkash that crowds of new followers came to him. The fact that a great number of those who were not Sikhs escaped pilgrims' tax contributed a lot towards the popularisation of the Sikh faith. Moreover, it helped in establishing the fact that the Sikhs occupied a position distinct from that of the Hindus, as the pilgrim's tax realisable from the Hindus was not realised from the Sikhs.

It is, indeed, laudable that the challenge could not wear the Guru down, rather it whipped up this zeal to bring the full weight of his energy and acumen to bear upon the course of development of Sikhism which was on the cross-roads. He not only saved Sikhism from accidents of history; but also did the necessary spade work to enable it to shape history.

Evolution and Consolidation

The process of consolidation of Sikhism reached a definite stage during the Guruship of Amar Das. Guru Nanak had condemned some of the social beliefs prevailing amongst the Hindus, as also among the Budhists and Jains. Guru Amar Das's achievement was that he constructed a fence around the sapling that germinated lest it should be destroyed by the gale of all consuming Hindu social practices. He achieved his object by strengthening the institutions of his predecessors, besides establishing new ones.

The Guru attached great importance to institution of 'Guru.' No amount of meditation and penances and moral restraints could help unless the Divine word is lived. Again he remarks :

> "Sat Guru sees everything, the whole universe. Only his glimpse will not do. Shabad the Divine word will have to be contemplated."

In fact, at places more than one, the Guru finds no difference between 'Guru' and 'word.'

The added emphasis at the role of 'Guru' and 'Word' was not without any purpose. It sanctified the institution of Guru obviously to develop the tendency among the people to look towards him for guidance. The true 'Guru' was Nanak which embodied the Eternal flame or Universal spirit. By presenting that light of the Guru Nanak blended with Angad, the Guru made it explicit that Guruship represented a continuity, a unity. Since Guru Nanak proclaimed that he was a poet or a bard, his words or the words of his successors acquired sanctity and status as great as that of Guru. Thus in the compositions of Guru Amar Das, we find that whereas the Sikhs were being hammered again and again the divine character of 'Guru' and his pivotal position in the process of spirit-social regeneration, Shabad was also being raised to the status as great as that of Guru. By imparting so much importance to the 'word' the Guru was doing the spade work for Guru Gobind Singh to declare Adi Granth as Guru.

A careful study of the different aspects of Guruship as said above, two conclusions emerge. Firstly the Guru was lying redoubled emphasis on the impersonal character of Guruship, side by side its personal one. Secondly, Shabad which came to be regarded as the word of Guru was exalted more explicitly than it was done by his predecessors thereby lending the status of the Guru to the 'word.' Judged in the context of the cultural and educational level as also the growth of Sikhism, the institution of 'Guru' played a remarkable part in the consolidation and the integration of the Sikh Church as well as Sikh community. The Guru, being one of the embodiment of the light became cynosure of the faith of the people and thus their rallying point. Since the sanctity which was attached with the role of Guru Nanak came to be associated also with his successors in all of whom there appeared to shine the light of Nanak, it bestowed upon the office of the Guru a legitimate authority for initiative. No wonder, they were entitled to take vital decisions by virtue of their office and these decisions became the extension of Guru Nanak's mission both logically and historically. The raising of the status of 'Shabd' as high as Guru also had its rule to play. It protected the Sikhs from falling under the influence of the words (shabds) of others.

Furthermore, it helped the multiplicity of sangats in their functioning. The Guru could not attend the affairs of all the sangats. The difficulty must have been faced by Guru Nanak, even by Guru Angad. Guru Amar Das tried to overcome the difficulty by appointing different missionaries to serve as link between the Sangats and the Guru. But still the solution was far from satisfactory under the circumstances, the Guru's shabd helped a lot. Shabd could reach anywhere and since it represented the spirit of the Gurus it served as a remarkable cohesive force among congregations apart from its being valuable instructional means.

During the times of Guru Amar Das, it began to be felt that the Sikhs should have their own seats of religion and pilgrimage so that it might not be necessary for them to go to tirtha (Holy places) of the Hindus.

The Guru constructed 'Baoli' at Goindwal. The work was constructed under the personal supervision and instructions of Guru Amar Das. The work on it started in A.D. 1552 and finished in A.D. 1559. He sanctified it and fixed the first day of Baisakh as the day for the annual gathering of the Sikhs. The 'Baoli' was a monument of the devotion of the people to the Guru and an embodiment of the co-operative effort which the people put to bring this into existence. The Guru took keen interest in its execution. The Baoli had eighty-four descending steps. According to Macauliffe, the Guru had decreed that "whoever should attentively and reverently repeat the 'Japji' on every step should escape from the wanderings in the wombs of the eighty-four lakhs of luring creatures." It is said that before Guru Amar Das started the construction of Baoli, he fell into a trance and saw Guru Nanak appear and order him to make a place of pilgrimage where God alone should be worshipped. Thereupon the Guru purchased land and with due religious ceremony, the work commenced. But after some work, the Guru found that large stones were hindering the progress. The Guru then called his Sikhs that he wanted one of them to drive a peg into its base; but this involved a great danger to life. Shri Manak Chand of Virowal volunteered. The peg was duly driven; but the Baoli was so much over-flowed with water that Manak could not stem the current which issued from the aperture formed by the peg and he was drowned. According to Sikh tradition lamentations of the Manak's mother and wife moved the Guru so much that he went to the Baoli and assured the two ladies that the youngman was not dead. He called him by name and the body rose to the surface. The Guru touched it with his feet and 'Manak Chand' walked forth from the water in the full possession of life and vigour.

Obviously the story that the Guru made use of miraculous power, is a fabrication and contrary to the teachings of the Guru who disclaimed and denounced all miraculous power that was bound to lead to spiritual sterility and hypocrisy.

However, the Baoli marked a very important step in the history of Sikhism. It soon developed into a very important place of Sikh pilgrimage.

The step helped the cause of Sikhism in many ways. The Sikhs started visiting the place in a large number with a view to seeking salvation and this thing afforded opportunity to the Guru to come into contact with the Sikhs. The very fact that so many people gathered at one place generated among them the spirit of common brotherhood. Moreover, they began to feel the futility of going to Hardwar while a place of pilgrimage near their hearths and homes was available, and in this way, they were helped to save themselves from falling under the debasing superstitions of the common mass and that of crafty Brahmins. Moreover, the Baoli, being reservoir of water catered to the needs of the people, and on this account also, the Guru's esteem in the eyes of the people rose very high thereby imparting strength to the body social of the Sikhs.

The institution of free kitchen started by Guru Nanak and developed by Guru Angad Dev was taken care of with assiduity. The standard of food was improved and the ideals of the institution were more clearly defined. In the 7th Pauri of the coronation ode, Satta, and Balwand in Ram Kali di var sang "Ever in thy kitchen O, Amar Das, are clarified butter and refined flour and sugar to eat." The Guru formally ordered that all his disciples should take their meals from the same kitchen and no distinction was made between a Hindu and a Muslim or between the high caste and the low caste. The Guru had declared unequivocally that all visitors were to sit in one line and eat from the kitchen before they were allowed to behold him. All had to sit in rows and eat together. The Guru's langar remained open till three hours after night fall. Whatever remained after the guests were fed was thrown to the beasts and the birds. Nothing was wasted. The Sikhs accounts go so far as to make Dr. Ganda Singh say that `even Akbar and the Raja of Haripur had to take their meals from the Kitchen before they were allowed to see the Guru. The cut and dried declaration as stated above and its steadfast pursuit struck a blow to the caste and creed prejudices. The Guru emphatically puts:

Be not proud of thy caste
For, he alone is Brahmin who knows the Brahma, the only God

O unwise one, be not proud of thy caste
For, a myriad errors flow out of this pride.

Nor did Guru repose any faith in the pollution of food if it is touched by a low caste or a meat-eater. The Guru says to Mai Das, a reputed Pandit from Kanshi (Benaras) that even if he were a great Pandit, he would take care to remember that nothing is polluted in the mess. "All outlined dining squares are false. Only God is pure (Maru ki Var). Such thoughts occur because the mind is impure and separateness from the Almighty exists" (Majh Mah 3). In this way, the people were made to renounce their social prejudices and to look upon one another as brothers. The institution helped in removing untouchability and caste prejudices. It proved a powerful aid in the propaganda work. Besides serving as an asylum for the poor, it also became a great instrument for advertisement and popularity and it gave a definite direction to the charities of the Guru's followers.

Sikhism in its earlier stages was not only liable to relapse into orthodoxy against which Guru Angad Dev had tried his best to guard it, but there was greater danger of its degenerating into a narrow sect of ascetical enthusiasts or fanatics. There is no doubt that Guru Nanak was himself a married man and had not spoken of married life in contemptuous or condemnatory terms; but even then his followers were prone to believe that the world was nothing, that it was all 'maya,' a delusion and a mirage. According to Malcolm, Guru Amar Das told his Sikhs through *Hukamnamas* (fiats) that any one who believed in renunciation and ascetic way of life (udasi) was not a Sikh. He enjoined upon them to reject the path of renunciation and to consider the life of a householder as the only way approved for practising religion. The Guru repeatedly said "This body is beautiful bride with whom her husband constantly lives. He is the giver of life, sustainer of all and He lives in this body. Some fools go to the jungles, rivers or mountains in search of God not knowing that He and all His incarnation are within this body."

He also laid emphasis on the necessity of believing in 'One Guru, One Word, and only one Interpretation (Var Sorath).' "There is no Guru", he said, "except the consecrated Guru; and it is disreputable not to acknowledge him." These opportune steps saved the Sikh church from disintegration and prevented the Sikhs from going the way of the followers of Kabirs and others medieval saints. It was decided once for all that the Udasis had nothing to do with Sikhism. In view of all this Macauliffe is right when he says that Guru Amar Das was responsible for separating the Sikhs from the Udasis. Malcolm and Mohsin Fani also are of Macauliffe's view but there are some modern scholars who state that the aforesaid work was accomplished by Guru Angad Dev. We however, support the former view because the latter view is unwarranted.

To make the teachings more effective and to emphasize still more the superior-most position of the word (Bani) in the process of regeneration. Guru Amar Das had more copies made of the hymns of Guru Nanak and Angad which he got from

Guru Angad, and added to them his own compositions and those of the Hindu Bhaktas whose teachings were in conformity with those of Nanak.

These copies were later on used by Guru Arjan for the compilation of the Holy Granth. Guru Amar Das declared the Guru's Word to be superior to all the scriptures of the world, and the Sikhs were advised to use only the Guru's word in worship. He rejected the six systems of Hindu's philosophy in favour of the Guru's Gospel. He said "This system of God is obtained by the fortunate only and that also through the Guru's word by means of true detachment. The six systems of the Hindus are in vogue now a days, but the Guru's system is profound and unequalled. It provides the way of salvation and makes the true one reside in the heart. "The system, if adopted with love, can save the whole world."

This step of the Guru resulted in the integration of the Sikh doctrine which helped the Sikhs to appreciate the difference between the teachings of their Gurus and Hinduism as it was existing during those times. It also made the Sikhs more and more self-contained in social matters. Since this anthology was in Punjabi, it gained enormous popularity among the masses, who did not understand either the Sanskrit texts of the Hindus or the Arabic texts of the Muslims. It reduced the importance of the Brahmin priests, who had maintained a strict monopoly over the knowledge of the sacred texts, and that of Mullahs who alone could interpret the Koran. Once Guru Amar Das was asked why he had given up Sanskrit which was the language of gods. He replied, "It rains on earth even though the earth has water in the well meaning thereby that Sanskrit was like water in a well and has a limited utility whereas Punjabi was like rain which fell over all the land.

Manji and Piri Systems

During Guru Amar Das's pontificate, the number of the followers of the Guru's increased considerably, and it was felt necessary for the Guru to take requisite steps to organise the scattered Sangats or congregations into a system. With a view to achieving this object, Guru evolved a system known as Manji system. He divided his whole spiritual domain into twenty two provinces called Manjies (bishoprics), so named because the incharge of a Manji sat on a cot to deliver the message of the Guru. The incharge of a Manji was a devoted Sikh and acted as vicegerant of the Guru. His business was to preach the mission of the Guru to make arrangements to keep the sangat in touch with the guru, and to encourage the people to organise the sangats. Besides this, he was responsible for the remittance of the offerings of the Sikhs which they made in token of their veneration for the Guru.

The Guru established another organisation called Piri system. The incharges of piries were ladies whose objective was to lit the flame of Guru's word among women. Bibi Bhani, Bibi Dani and Bibi Pal were some of the most revered incharges of different piries.

Some scholars state that the Guru divided his spiritual domain into twenty-two Manjies or divisions which were no other than the twenty-two provinces of Akbar. But this is absolutely incorrect; firstly because when the Manji system was evolved, Akbar had just occupied the throne and secondly, the number of the provinces organised by the Akbar even upto his end was far less than the number of the Guru's bishoprics. However the Guru trained and sent out 94 men and 52 women as preachers of the 22 Manjies, Kaniya Lal gives the names of five Manjies (1) village Wayan, tehsil Kharar, district Ropar, (2) village Dharmsala, tehsil Ambala, (3) Viarowal in district Amritsar, (4) Lahore, (5) a village gardnoh, in district Patiala.

Kahan Singh in 'Mahan Kosh' gives the following names of the incharges of the twenty-two dioceses: 1. Allah Yar, 2. Sachan Sach, 3. Sadharan, 4. Savan Mal, 5. Sukhan, 6. Handal, 7. Kedari, 8. Kheda, 9. Gangu Shah, 10. Darbari, 11. Paro, 12. Fera, 13. Bua, 14. Beni, 15. Mahesa, 16. Mai Dass, 17. Manak Chand, 18. Murari, 19. Raja Ram, 20. Rang Shah, 21. Rang Dass, 22. Lalo.

The system, however, made tangible contribution to the development and progress of Sikhism. According to G.C. Narang, "It is evident that this measure of the third Guru have gone a long way in strengthening the foundations of the Church and in carrying on the propaganda in all parts of the country."

Indu Bhushan Bannerjee says "A great step was in this manner taken towards giving the Sikhs an organisation of their own but the Guru was not less careful about his duties at the centre. His own person no doubt provided a strong binding force."

Some scholars have attributed political motives to the organisation and have asserted that the Guru aimed at establishing parallel Government. We, however, do not find any substance in the aforesaid assertion because the protagonists of this view do not base their conclusion on any solid evidence. All the same, any organisation that brings the people together and attempts at uplifting them morally and socially can breed a political movement.

Social ethics of Guru Amar Das

Apart from taking the aforesaid steps which went a long way to bring about new social consciousness, the Guru took steps to evolve structure as might suit to his scheme of social regeneration. Guru Nanak did not exclude social affairs pertaining to society out of his scheme for the spiritual regeneration and hence advised the people to keep up certain ethical standards. Guru Amar Das, therefore, addressed himself to the task with vigour and enthusiasm. From the various steps he took, it becomes clear that he made conscious efforts to emancipate the minds of the people from the fetters forged by outmoded customs and social practices as also to create new customs, symbols and practices to build a separate social structure—very much in need at this stage of evolution of the Khalsa for new ideals could only be preserved if there was special structure reflecting them.

Guru Amar Das, true to his objective, launched a frontal attack on the caste system or the Verna Asram that formed the spinal chord of the Hindu society. Once Pirthi Mal and Tulsa who belonged to the stock of Bhalla Khatri said, "Revered Sir, you are Khatri as we are. We have come to you with this confidence that you being one of our caste brotherhood would help us." The Guru replied 'He has no caste and he is no more than a human being.' The Guru regarded the pride born out of caste as narrow-mindedness while to attain eternal bliss, there was need to transcend self and to merge in self.

Condemnation of Untouchability

Untouchability, the offshoot of the caste system also did not escape condemnation on his part. Guru Nanak's heart went out to the lowly and the despised. He vowed to emancipate them. He took with him a Musalman Mirasi a man of low origin, called him *Bhai* (Brother) and laid the foundation of his fellowship. To all and sundry, he carried the joyful tidings "Despise no man, God dwells in every heart." "All are equally the sons of the Father above. Birth in this or that family cannot exalt or degrade a man. It is actions that do so. A good pious man of humble birth is far more dear to God and men of God than a high born rascal. Doors of the Father's mansion are open to all. Live well in the world, love and serve your fellow creatures, your creator and it will win a seat of honour in the darbar (court) of the Almighty Father...All prejudices of birth and family will have to be laid off." Thus it was Guru Nanak who founded the Holy Fellowship where the lowest is equal to the highest in race as in creed.

Guru Amar Das, likewise promoted the cause of the 'Holy Fellowship.' He, in addition to his preachings against customs adopted another technique which sounded novel. He proclaimed that no one, howsoever high he might be, could see him without sitting and taking the meals in Langar. The instructions were followed in letter and spirit so much so that even Akbar had to partake of the food in Guru's kitchen, while sitting in Pangat (line). The Guru advised the people not to indulge in the evil customs of untouchability because "one would take care to remember that nothing is polluted in the mess. All outlying dining squares are false, only God is pure." In this way the people were made to renounce their social prejudices and to look upon one another as brothers.

Inter-caste Marriages

Yet another step he took to bring about social harmony among the people segmented into castes and sub-castes was the encouragement which he gave to inter-caste marriages. Before him inter-caste marriages were not favoured, with the result that caste pride prejudices had taken root. The Guru enjoined upon his followers that there was nothing wrong in contracting inter-caste marriages. He banded his views by marrying his own daughter to one, Jetha (Guru Ram Das) without asking him his caste or sub-caste. The Guru gave special attention to the improvement of the status of women in society. He prohibited the practice of Sati, i.e. to say burning of widow on the funeral pyre of their husbands. In popular opinion the woman who does so was Sati (truthful). In fact the practice implied that women had no independent and separate entity and her salvation lay only in committing herself to fire along with her deceased husband. The Guru exploded the myth and said that woman was sati or true who experienced pangs of separation instead of burning herself on the pyre.

Furthermore, the Guru prohibited the practice of 'Satti' i.e. to say burning of widows on the funeral pyer of their husbands. G.B. Scott acclaims the Guru as 'first reformer who condemned the prevailing Hindu practice of Sati.' The Guru declares that "the Satti is one who lives contented and embellishes herself with good conduct, and cherishes the Lord ever and calls on Him." As the advice of 'cherishing the Lord and calling on him, is the advice to everyone throughout the Adi Granth, the above declaration requires widows to conduct themselves as all others do. In order to be virtuous (Satti), women ought to maintain families knit of love. As a matter of fact, the virtues of the housewife are to be in terms of her role in the family and in terms of self immolation. The Guru says "The women burn themselves on the pyres of their husbands. But if they love their spouses well, they suffer the pangs of separation even otherwise."

Cunningham remarks this was rather a very mild discountenance 'leading the way to amendment by persuasion rather than by positive enactment,' but this is too strong a criticism. As a matter of fact the Guru was the first reformer in the medieval India who condemned the religiously sanctified practice of Satti.

Prohibition of Drinking

The Guru did not like the fast-developing habit of wine drinking. As a matter of fact he, like Guru Nanak, motivated a person to work for God and his people on earth. Says the Guru :-

"One man bringeth the full goblet
another cometh and filleth the cup

The intellect of him who drinketh departeth
and intoxication entereth his brain

He distinguishes not between mine and thine
and is buffeted by his master

If possible, drink not at all the false wine
by which man forgetteth God and receiveth
punishment at his court."

Widow Re-marriage

He initiated the move to bring about self reliant, fearless and upright ladihood in the country. The contemporary society denied them equality to man and regarded them as hewers of word and drawers to water. Guru Nanak in his discussion with jogies remarks "It is sin to regard ladies as 'undesirable' who give birth to the most desirable." Guru Amar Das, true to the spirit of Nanak's teachings, preached in favour of widow-marriage; and obviously he was right in doing so if he was to make an attempt to place woman on equal footing with man. It helped them develop themselves in personality and confidence.

Denunciation of Pardah

The custom of 'Pardah' among the ladies was also disapproved. The reasons were obvious. In the first place, it implied the inferiority of woman as compared with man, and secondly it presumed that the ladies were meant for house only and could not partake of the activities of the world. The Guru, fully aware of the consequence which this custom had led to, regarded it an evil to be got rid of as early as possible. Macauliffe states that when the ruler of Haripur and his queens came to have his sacred glimpse, they were allowed to see him only if they would discard 'pardah.' Tradition says that all queens except one discarded 'pardah.' The Guru cursed the Rani in pardah and so she became mad. The tradition obviously displays the theme that the Guru did not approve of pardah.

New Birth and Death Ceremonies

Many useless and expensive customs which were stalking the Hindu society, no less than Muslim society were also considered undesirable and useless. The Guru wanted to emancipate his followers from the fetters which these customs prevailing among the people had forged.

Accordingly he enjoined upon his followers to dispense with the elaborate ceremonies connected with the birth and death of a person. Thirty years after the death of Guru Amar Das, Guru Arjan Dev requested Sunder, the grandson of Guru Amar Das to write an account of the instruction which Guru Amar Das left regarding the ceremonies to be performed at the time of his death. Sunder compiled with the ordainment of the Guru and composed a long poem, popularly known as 'Sadd' says Sunder:

"Finally, the true Guru spoke
After my death sing God's praises

Call God instead of a Pandit and, for
the Puran, read God's word;

Read God's word hear God's name; The
Guru desireth God's love instead of a
lofty bier.

Barley rolls, bread in leaves, Hindu

obsequies, lamps, and throwing his bones
into the Ganges.

The true Guru spoke as it pleased God,
and he was blended with Omniscient Being."

In this way, the Guru effected a departure from the Hindu social practices. The point may no doubt be raised that Sunder was not an eyewitness of what happened at the time of his great-grand father's death and that the statement might easily have been coloured by subsequent developments but the fact that Sunder wrote not more than thirty years after the death of Amar Das when several of the latter's contemporaries were still alive and that his statement obtained a ready acceptance considerably weakens the above objections. In fact there seems to be little doubt that in the 'Sadd' we get a genuine hint about the views of Guru Amar Das regarding the Hindus' obsequies.

Moreover, the Guru considered neither the customs of Hindu marriage nor those of the Muslims conducive to the growth of the society of his vision. He made the marriage ceremony simple and inexpensive. He enjoined upon the Sikhs to recite 'lawan' (the Sikh Epithalamium) on the occasion of marriage and to reject unnecessary ceremonies connected with it. The recitation of Sikh Epithalamium hardly takes four minutes and needs no priest to recite it. This being so, the Sikh epithalamium robbed the Brahmins of the occasions when they could get the chance to assert supremacy over the people. This hymn, says Dr. I.B. Bannerjee, may or may not have been written on the occasion of the marriage of Guru Ram Das "but that hardly effects its significance. It clearly appears that the Guru was commenting on a custom already in existence and we may as well accept the Sikh tradition that the change had been introduced by his predecessor."

Commenting upon the death and marriage ceremonies Dr. Bannerjee writes: "The change he described to introduce in the very important ceremonies connected with marriage and death struck at the very root of the influence of the priestly class and though in such a matter, where long standing and cherished practices were concerned, success must necessarily have been slow, the ball had been set rolling and Sikhism put on the way of gradual consolidation into a separate sect."

The ethos of Guru Amar Das's preaching was the uplift of the down-trodden, the meek and the neglected. He denounced the hypocrites, and the superstitious. Nor did he spare the capitalists who bereft of any streak of idealism, regarded wealth as the be all and end all of life. The Guru utters:

The wealthy are blind, cares not to listen to
the word and makes different faces.
He is a great hoax and his mind is wicked.

Visit of Akbar to Goindwal

Another important event of the Guru's pontificate was the respect shown by Akbar for the Guru and his teachings. Guru Amar Das could lay claim to many of the hill Chieftains among his followers who contributed thousands to the funds of the Church but the greatest triumph of the church in the eyes of the people was scored when the Guru's fame brought Akbar to his doors. According to Gyan Singh "Akbar sent a trusted official, one Bhagwan Das Khatri of Sirhind, to beseech the Guru to pray for his success." The Guru was then engaged in the constructions of Baoli and is stated to have said that the Chittour would fall as soon as the wheel of the well would settle in position. The siege ended in Akbar's victory and he visited Goindwal. He took his meal at the Temple of Bread (Langar) and met the Guru. The working and the laudable objectives of the institution of the free kitchen impressed him so much that he made an offer of eighty four villages. But the Guru declined the offer and uttered "I wish not that the langar should be run by one man. The institution owes its existense to the people, let them run it." Even then "Akbar got effected the deed of 84 villages in the name of Bibi Bhani where the city of Amritsar was raised."

How far the reason embodied in the tradition is correct it is very difficult to judge because of scanty historical material but Akbar's friendly visit was undoubted. The friendship of Akbar with the Guru operated in two ways for the benefit of church. In the first place, it increased the prestige of the Guru and made their mission more popular with the higher classes of the society. Yatha Raja Tatha Praja (As is the King, so are the subjects). The truth of this proverb is nowhere better illustrated than in India, the land of its birth. The early recruits to all new churches are the caste-aways of established organisations. The early Sikhs too were mostly those who could hardly claim high places in the Hindu society. The attention of the sovereign, however, tolerant and broadminded by nature he may be, are bound to tell in favour of the object of his attention and as Panth Prakash says that the very fact of Akbar's doing homage to the Guru brought crowds of followers to the fold of Sikhism.

The other way in which Akbar's friendship was utilized was that the Guru took advantage of it to relieve oppression or popular sufferings. Two examples of this are recorded in Panth Parkash and other books. In the first instance, Guru Amar Das and his followers were exempted from paying pilgrimage tax while they visited Hardwar. Secondly, when the Guru put the case of the peasantry before the Emperor and asked him to remit the whole land tax for the year, in view of the likely loss to the peasants because of expected sudden fall in the prices of the grains owing to the rich harvest and Emperor's marching off the punjab, Akbar readily consented.

This timely intercession for the sake of peasants immensely increased the popularity of the Guru and made him an idol with the peasantry of Majha and

Malwa who, in course of time, provided almost all the fighting strength of Guru Gobind Singh.

Appraisal of the Guru's Achievements

Guru Amar Das was nominated, as the Guru at the age of seventy, but the works, he did during his ministry clearly indicate that age had no adverse effect on him. He was active both in mind and body. Jogis, Vaishnavites and others came to him to dislodge him from his stand through argumentation, but all were made to submit to him. In enunciating and propounding Sikh doctrine, he was unique; in evolving institutions to ensure the continuous growth of Sikhism, he showed wisdom; in introducing innovations in social and ethical sphere, he exhibited exceptional originality and a keen awareness of the process of regeneration and rejuvenation. He had the rare quality of taking quick and firm decisions. The way he handled the challenge of the Udasis speaks volumes in his favour. No wonder Satta and Balwand in their Var say "in the age of utter darkness he rose like the sun. He sowed the seed of truth and reaped its fruit."

During this period of the Guru's pontificate the fame of the infant church spread far and wide, rudiments of a separate organisation were given to the Sikhs and new forms and practices were introduced to supersede the old and bind the neophytes more closely together. The period was significant for something else also.

The introduction of many innovations such as building of a temple at Goindwal etc. tended to break the close affiliations of the Sikhs with the Hindus who led by Brahmins began to harass the Sikhs. When their own resources failed, they concocted complaints and lodged them with Akbar. When even he did not do anything in the matter, they bribed the local officials to harass the Sikhs. This was the first serious break with the Hindu social polity and the beginning of the oppression of the Sikhs.

Undoubtedly Amar Das's Guruship was a 'land mark' in the process of crystallisation of Sikhism. Dr. I.B. Bannerjee regards the pontificate of Guru Amar Das as a 'turning point.' He says so because he believes that the original object of sikhism was to reform and restate Hinduism. But since we feel that Sikhism was distinct movement even in the beginning we do not subscribe to the view held by the learned scholar. He, however, is clear that the Amar Das's ministry was a definite phase in the building of the Sikhs church and Church nation.

Succession of Guru Ram Das

Amar Das lived to the age of ninety-five. He did not consider any of his sons fit to succeed him and chose instead his son-in-law Ram Das whose conduct was marked by utmost devotion, piety and complete understanding of the various aspects of the Sikh religion. It is said that once when Guru Amar Das, seated on a foot stool was taking a bath, one of the legs of the stool broke; but before Guru

Amar Das should fall down, Bibi Bhani placed her hand under it and did not allow the Guru to feel the loss of the leg of the stool. After some time, when the Guru came to know that the hand of Bibi Bhani was bleeding profusely, he was moved, and overcome by the sense of gratitude asked Bibi Bhani if there was anything in the world that he could do for her. She then begged her father that the Guruship should be made hereditary in her own family. He granted the boon and the office of Guruship became hereditary.

The story has sparked off three important questions. Firstly was it due to emotional outburst which influenced the Guru to take decision ? Secondly was it to lend stability to the institution that the Guruship was made hereditary? Thirdly was the principle of hereditary succession a guarantee for ensuing the requisite Guruship. It was certainly not an emotional step, it was done because Guru Ram Das and Bibi Bhani had won over the Guru by their object surrender to his ordainment, their spirit of service and their keen understanding of the Sikh principles. The decision pertaining to the succession to Guruship seems to have been taken with a view to reducing the chances of disputes over the issue of succession and eliminating the possibility of laying the claim to the Guruship on the part of the persons outside Guru's family.

The decision is full of wisdom because in the case of dispute among the family members it could not have been more than a simple affair, but in case the outsiders lay claim to Guruship, and there is a dispute there was likelihood of it assuming the form of a schismatic move.

So far as the third question was concerned, it is not difficult to understand that there is no incomptibility involved. Guru upto now had been given impersonal character and could be transferred to any one whom the Guru deemed fit. This being so, Guruship could be transferred to any body, fit for the job. It was irrelevant whether that particular person belonged to the same family or to any other family.

A Society on the Anvil. Before the advent of Guru Nanak, the religious teachers in India usually impressed the people that the world was a mere empty dream and advocated renunciation. They did not at all concern themselves about the social, economic, and political conditions of the masses. Guru Nanak realized what they failed to see: that a religion, if it is to be a living force, must be a practical religion, one that teaches mankind not how to escape from the world, but how to live worthily in it, making the best use of life, not how to avoid evil but how to meet and overcome all evil and live a victorious life.

So along with living a godly life as an individual, the Sikh was to form a part of a corporate life—be it a society, community or a nation; so a Sikh must tune himself to several strings. The development of this kind of life is most difficult and the teachers of the world have often ignored it. It is the glory of the Sikh history that the Gurus had in mind the duties of a society or a community or a nation as much as the duties of an individual. This was a task not to be achieved in a life or two. Hence it was that successive Gurus by their precept and example inspired to men, to cultivate human nature both in mundane and spiritual sense, in all its aspects and in all its bearings. So we shall see that while the principles of life remained the same, the Sikh community as a whole underwent transfiguration, assuming a great variety of forms according to the circumstances that arose from time to time.

How the Fragrance Spread. Guru Amardas, out of the abundance of his generosity, gave authority and power to 146 of his apostles to go to various parts of the country and spread the fragrance of Nam. And to preach the truth through the language of action in one uniform spirit of the Master. Out of these 146 persons, 94 were men and 52 women. They were all glowing with Nam and filled with the divine spirit. The Guru also appointed 22 dioceses (Manjian), each under a pious Sikh.

Wherever these itinerant preachers went, they poured out floods of love in utter effacement of self. The women acted as mothers to the orphans and protectors of many poor girls, deserted by their cruel husbands—gamblers, thieves and drunkards. These disciples of the Master brought solace to those in despair, nourished the sick and poor with milk of love. Every one in need and distress called upon them.

These disciples of the Master were akin to a secret river flowing in a thousand channels bringing the water of life to the dead and dying. Every act of the holy brothers was a prayer, every step a song and like full bloomed roses they spread their fragrance far and wide without knowing and without asking. Many would catch the gleam of their souls and following the same would come to the Fountain of Light at Goindwal and join the holy association of the Guru.

Prema, the Leper cured. Prema was a leper and had lost his limbs and had become crippled. He heard about the Guru and came all the way crawling to Goindwal, where Guru Amardas lived. He stayed at a little distance from the Guru's 'Darbar' but where he could listen the hymns sung by the congregation. Some of the disciples fed him and looked after him. One day he was called by the Guru and given a bath. Prema was cured not only of his leprosy, but he got his limbs also restored, as he uttered Sat-Nam Wahguru, as directed by the Master.

The Guru then looked at him gracefully, and Prema was transformed. He was renamed Murari and the Guru also got him married into a good family. He was then sent out as one of the itinerant preachers of the Guru's gospel.

Mystics Scholars visit the Guru. Some mystics and scholars of Uttar Pradesh came to Goindwal seeking the 'Hidden Light' that illumines the mind. They were genuine seekers of truth and had wandered all over India but had not found the peace anywhere. They had at last received this life of the spirit at the feet of the

Guru and were wholly transformed. We have in record what they spoke about the Guru from their personal knowledge and experience of him.

Thus writes Bhikha, who was one of them :
"In vain I wandered about
In search of a true saint.
I met many a recluse.
Many a 'sanyasis' I contacted
Many hermits and adepts I came across
And these scholars
Who were outwardly good and sweet.
For full one year in this search I wandered
But no one could give the glow and solace to my mind.
They talked a lot in high sounding words
But their actions were most disappointing.
Discarding the Name of God,
They indulged in worldly pursuits
No need to talk of them any more.
At last God by His Grace
Brought me in touch with Guru Amardas
The lotus in me, bloomed and my mind was set at rest
I shall ever abide
As be Thy will, O Guru Amardas."

(*Translated*)

Salh, another mystic and a poet, thus speaks of him;
"Wearing the armour of meditation,
Mounting the steed of knowledge
With the bow of righteousness in hand
And arrow of peaceful devotion
You O, Guru Amardas, thus fought the battle of life.
Keeping the fearless Lord in your heart,
Holding the lance of Guru's Word
You have cut to pieces the demons
Of lust, anger, avarice and of ego and attachment
O, thou son of Tejbhan, monarch of a honourable lineage,
You had the blessings of Guru Nanak, the king of kings,
Salh proclaimeth the truth.
Guru Amardas fighting thus
Defeated the satanic forces in the battle of life."

(*Translated*)

Jalap, another mystic of Uttar Pradesh speaks of him:
"Blessed are the feet
Which lead on to Guru Amardas;
Blessed are the hands
That touch the holy feet of the Guru;
Blessed is the tongue
Which sings the glory of Guru Amardas;
Blessed are the eyes
Which have the opportunity to look at him;
Blessed are the ears which listen to his words;
Blessed is the heart
In which dwelleth Guru Amardas,
The Divine Father of the world.
Blessed is the head, says Jalap
That bows at the feet of the Guru."

(*Translated*)

Akbar visits Guru Amardas. Akbar, the then Emperor of India, travelled all the way from Delhi to visit Guru Amardas at Goindwal. But he could not be shown into the presence of the Master unless and until he had dined with others in the common kitchen or the Temple of Bread. The king partook of the simple food in the langar. The more he had it, the more he wanted it. "There must be something mystical in the Guru's food that it is so delicious that I like to eat more and more of it," remarked the Emperor.

The Emperor, having complied with these preliminaries, obtained the audience of the Guru. The Guru rose to receive the Emperor in his arms, but Akbar spontaneously bowed to touch the feet of the Master. The Guru lifted him up and seated him nearby. The monarch, by the holy touch, felt a thrill of joy in him. Peace and comfort came to him. He was deeply moved and impressed by the few words that the Master spoke to him.

Having received the Guru's blessings, when the Emperor took leave, he offered a large estate for the service of the Temple of Bread. But the Master declined the offer saying. "I have already more than enough from my Creator. The people are my lands and estates. We receive our daily bread from God: we do not think of the morrow. We are contend to be of the poor and think of the Beloved."

"But as a token of my love and in keeping with the lessons of unity and universal brotherhood that you have given here, from now on—I regard your daughter as my own—all the same, whether they be your daughters and sons or mine. Therefore, I present this little Jagir to Bibi Bhani (Guru's daughter). It is my sincere wish and promise that I treat all equally." Said the king.

"All right, all right, as thou wishes O King Akbar, the great. I do not want it either for me or for the Guru's kitchen, your contribution would be utilised for the widows and orphans and Bibi Bhani will be the trustee and treasuress," said the Guru.

This was the estate where later on Guru Ram das, Bhani's consort, built Amritsar, the City of Golden Temple. To this day, all the inhabitants of Amritsar approach Guru Ram Das in prayer in all their needs, troubles and distress.

Bibi Bhani. Bibi Bhani was the younger daughter of Guru Amardas. From her very childhood, she used to recite the Guru's hymns and sit alone in meditation. Later on, she used to serve in the Guru's kitchen.

As Bhani came of age, one day her mother spoke to the Guru about her, "We must give away Bibi Bhani in marriage now."

"To whom shall we give her," said the father.

"To a young man like him," she said, pointing at the same time to a youngman passing by.

"Yes give her in marriage to him then; for no one else can be like him." said the father.

The youngman thus chosen was Ram Das. He was from Lahore.

When Ram Das was just a small boy, his father had died. Driven by circumstances, he used to sell boiled grams. Once he chanced to come to Goindwal along with other pilgrims from Lahore. When he saw Guru Amar Das, he was so much fascinated and charmed by his grace that while other pilgrims went back to their homes, he continued to stay at Goindwal and daily used to attend the holy congregation.

He was selfless, meek and sweet like hundred thousands of the Master's other disciples at Goindwal. He also did the service of live, digging the Guru's Baoli (a big wide well with masonry stairs leading down to the surface of the water). Ram Das like others carried baskets full of earth and mud on his head. He surrendered himself to the divine in his love and devotion, renouncing all cares of the past and all anxiety for the future. He lived in continuous remembrance of 'Nam.' He was thus discovered by the Guru's discerning eye and was chosen as the bridegroom and was married to Bibi Bhani.

At the time of marriage of the bridegroom was asked by the Guru to chose a gift for himself, as was customary.

"Sire, Give me the gift of Hari Nam, give me the Song of His praise."

It was here that Ram Das realized the Noontide Influx of Light, the Sun of suns-golden, the Moon of moons! The Source of Illumination! The very life and Soul of the universe! When Nam illumines human vision, all is drenched, enveloped with this Holy-Radiance Divine. It turns the Face—from our little self to the Universal-Self. Ram Das thus came in tune with the Infinite.

Bridegroom Crowned. What Nanak saw in Angad, what Angad saw in Amardas, Amardas saw in Ram Das. And in due course, one day.,

As Guru Amardas sat up
And of his own sweet will,
He sent for his family and disciples.
"I go, I go, O Disciples Dear.
This is the Will of the Lord
Let no one weep after me
That would not please me in the least.

"A friend who desires that his friend be esteemed
Must be pleased when his friend
Goes to the Lord to receive the robe of honour.
Reflect then my children and brothers
Is it good to weep and wail
when God adorns the Guru
With a robe of honour ?

"No more barley rolls, nor bread on leaves
No more Puranas, no more dead obsequice of the dead.
—I live, I live, the Living Flame leaps,
Leaps up into the Flame Hidden,
The only obsequice that I order is holy, all holy song."

As said the Master, so did they comply
And patiently surrendered to the Will Divine.
The Guru then made all his disciples, relations, sons and brothers
Bow to the feet of Ram Das.

(Sunder Sadd: Ramkali) *Translated*.

Amardas then asked his younger son Mohri, how he would look upon Ram Das, "sire, to me, he is Nanak, Angad and thyself in One." replied Mohri.

Song of Bliss. Guru Amardas contributed 907 hymns to Guru Granth Sahib, all of which were written between the age of 73 and 95. Translation of a few stanzas from his Song of Bliss is given below:

I

"Bliss, Bliss, O Mother, Transcendent Bliss!

The Eternal Master's lotus feet have I kissed!
The True Guru I have found with all ease,
And my mind is filled with felicitations indeed.
The heavenly muses, the be-jewelled ones,
All hover around to sing
In response to Celestial Music from above.
Sing ye the hymns of praise to Him
Who dwells in my heart.
Saith Nanak verily, this ecstatic joy dawned on me
When I discovered the True Hidden Lord in me."

II

"O my mind, abide thou ever with God,
If thou dost abide in His presence evermore,
No more sin, no more sorrow.
If He accepts thee
All thy affairs will be set right.
The Lord is Perfect and All Powerful in every way.
Why shouldst thou forget the Lord ?
Saith Nanak, O my mind,
Abide thou ever with God."

III

"O my True Lord!
What is there that is not in Thy house?
Everything is in Thy house
But he alone getteth whom Thou givest.
He sings Thy glories forever,
And enshrines Thy Name in his heart.
Heavenly Music resoundeth
In the heart where the Lord dwelleth.
Saith Nanak, O my True Lord,
What is there that is not in Thy house?"

IV

"Thy Name, O Lord is my only sustenance;
It hath appeased all my hunger;
It hath quenched all the fires.
The True Name abiding in my heart
Hath given me peace and joy

And fulfilled all my desires.
I am ever a sacrifice unto the Guru,
Whose gifts these are,
Saith Nanak, Listen O saints, Love the Word,
Thy, Name, O lord, is my sustenance."

V

"Celestial Music is heard in that blessed house,
The heart, where God dwelleth,
Yea, It dwelleth in that happy house
In whom God puts forth his spiritual power
Therein the Lord subdueth the five evil passions
And destroys the fear of death.
They on whom descendeth Thy Grace from above,
Only they discover Thy Nam hidden
Saith Nanak, they obtain happiness,
And in their heart Divine Music is heard."

XVII

"The consummation state is not reached
Through rituals and outward religious observances
And without this state of Supreme Equilibrium being attained
Doubt and illusion will not depart,
No amount of outward observances
Will remove doubt and illusions;
The mind is filthy with falsehood
How can it be made clean?
Wash thy mind in the light of the Word
And fix it upon the Lord,
Saith Nanak, It is by the Grace of the Guru
That knowledge of Transcendent dawns
This way, this way alone the doubts and illusion depart."

XL

"Listen, O fortunate ones, this song of Bliss!
No more, no more, earthly yearning
Peace! Beatitude! Fullest Fruition!

I have found, yea, I have realised
The Lord in His uttermost supremacy

No more sorrow, no more suffering,
My grief, my sickness and all torments departed
When the True Word was heard.

The saints and all holy men
By this, from good to better become and are filled with joy
When they hear the Word from the Perfect Master;
The listeners of the Word become pure,
The speaker is sanctified.
The Master True pervadeth everywhere;
Nanak humbly humbly proclaimeth,
For him the Divine Music resoundeth—
He who falleth at the feet of the Guru."

Equality

But Obedience, though extremely useful in the early stages of spiritual training, is not always helpful in bringing a man forward towards the goal of responsibility. When indulged in too indiscrimiately, it might do positive harm by making men slavish. Guru Angad himself had realised this danger, when he set down the following ideal of obedience:

Nanak, obey him who is worthy to be obeyed.

He, who acts according to the will of the Lord, receives His reward, Nanak, *he* is worthy of homage.

Obedience is, therefore, dangerous to the spirit of truth, unless it is allied with Discrimination and Fixity of Purpose.

Guru Amar Das, the third Guru, followed up with an opportune teaching. A bard sang of him:

Firm as the mountain of Meru, thou art swayed not by the gusts of wind.

Such stories as those of Prema of Talwandi and paro of Dalla, who would seek the company of the Guru in the face of all difficulties, show that constancy to the fixed ideal had become a common feature of the Sikh character by that time. But more needful was it for the Guru to see that too much was not made of worldly position or religious differences. He, therefore, developed into a regular institution the custom of inter-dining started by Guru Nanak. He would oblige all his visitors, Hindus and Mohammedans alike, to partake of his free kitchen before he would consent to see them. Even Akbar and the Raja of Haripur, when they came to see him, had to do the same. All had to sit in a line and eat together. There was no superstition of the *chauka*. The third Guru says that, even if he were a most learned Pundit of world-wide renown, "he would take care to remember that nothing is polluted in the kitchen. All outlined kitchens are false. Only He is pure."

In this way, the people were made to renounce their social prejudices and look upon each other as brothers.

This feeling was further strengthened in men by their being made to practise virtues that spring out of the sense of brotherliness. The greatest virtue of the third Guru was his self-restraint in dealing with others. He says:

He, in whose heart there is love, has already obtained salvation.

He controls his senses and finds the way of truth and self-restraint.

when Datu, the son of Guru Angad, attacked Guru Amar Das and kicked him off his seat, the latter's only reply was, "O honoured Sir, pardon me. My old bones must have hurt your tender foot." The same humility and self-restraint he taught others: "O Sheikh, restrain thy mind which now Wanders towards the four cardinal points, the sport of the four winds." He succeeded Guru Amar Das, and was called Guru Ram Das. He married bibi Bhani, the daughter of the third Guru. He occupied the privileged position of the Guru's son-in-law, but he was daily seen carrying baskets of mud out of the Bawali which the Guru was constructing. His wife worked with him. One morning, while her old father was bathing, she noticed that one leg of the wooden seat on which he sat was broken off. Fearing lest he should fall and hurt himself, she put her hand under the broken leg so as to keep the seat level. When the Guru arose after bathing and saw that a nail had pierced her hand, he asked her why she had endured such a torture. She replied, "If my wretched body could in any way serve the Guru, I should be fortunate." Bhai Jetha's and Bibi Bhani's patient service clearly shows how the Sikhs had fully imbibed this spirit. The Mohammedans in those days often annoyed the Sikhs. When they went to take water for the kitchen from a well, the Mohammedans would set upon them and break their earthen pitchers with stones. When the Sikhs complained to the Guru, he told them to use goat-skins instead. When these, too, were pierced with arrows, the Guru asked them to use vessels of brass. But these, too, were not safe against the pellets of the mischief-makers. The Sikhs were driven almost to desperation; but the Guru insisted on patience, and only prayed for the softening of the enemie's hearts. He would not allow his Sikhs to retaliate, because the wrong came from the people, and not from the Government; because the Emperor could still be appealed to, and often with much success. At this time patience was the rule. Guru Amar Das once said to a village headman, "God is patient, and patiently He rewardeth. If any one ill-treat you, bear it. If you bear it three times, God Himself will fight for you the fourth time, and extirpate your enemies."

But the qualities of forbearance and patience, so needful for acquiring self-control, have often led people, especially in India, to be very careless about the higher duty of self-preservation. In the time of the Gurus, many persons would willingly immolate themselves at the altar of Shiva, get themselves sawn alive at Banaras or be crushed under the car of Jagannath. The nation as a whole had acquired the spirit of servility and abject contenment. It was most necessary for the regeration of the higher self of India that the Guru should teach the true value and sanctity of human life. Man, who was considered to be a mere wretched vermin crawling on the face of the earth, was declared to be a great manifestation of God's divinity. For this purpose, the belief in particular incarnations of God had to be rejected. All avatars were shown up to be simply human beings :-

The thirty-three crores of divinities are Thy slaves.

The kings created by Thee in different ages are sung of as Thine avatars.

The pandits and astrologers do not understand the matter; Brahma, Vishnu and Shiva were created to obey His will.

Man rose in the estimation of man. His body, which had been considered as the source of sin, was now to be considered as the holy shrine of God :-

"We may take human body as the temple, nay, the fort of God."

Again :

"All mankind that you see created is the image of God; God's image appears in it" See also his lines inserted by way of contradiction after the 51st slok of Farid, which says that the bodies of the lovers of God are to be ever pale and bloodless. Guru Amar Das, when questioned once by his Sikhs as to why he had hastily ridden past a crumbling wall, had replied that he wanted to teach his disciples that it was their sacred duty to preserve the human body. It was a precious trust of God, to be kept pure and strong by Temperance:

If possible, drink not the false wine at all.

Simplicity goes along with temperance. The Guru lived such a simple life that he did not keep more than one suit of clothes for himself and not more than one day's provisions for his kitchen.

Woman also became sacred in the sight of man. It was the third Guru who forbade Sati:

They are not Satis, who burn themselves with their husbands' corpses.

Nanak, rather are they Satis who die by the mere shock of separation from their husbands.

And they, too, ought to be considered as Satis, who abide in modesty and contentment;

Who wait upon their Lord, and, rising in the morn, ever remember him.

Women are burnt in the fire with their husbands;

If they appreciate their husbands, they undergo sufficient pain by their death.

And if they appreciate not their husbands, Nanak, why should they be burnt at all ?

He held women equal with men. Perhaps he remembered what he owed to a woman, Bibi Amro, who had brought him to his saviour. This is his ideal of married life :

They are not wife and husband who sit together;

Rather are they wife and husband who have one spirit in two bodies.

This ideal was amply realized in the time of the next Guru. Read the beautiful story of the conscientious daughter of Patti's magistrate. She did her duty by her leper husband even under most trying circumstances. Truly has Bhai Gurdas (155-1629), the missionary Sikh of the time, said, "From temporal as well as from spiritual point of view, woman is man's other half and assists him to salvation. She assuredly brings happiness to the virtuous." Guru Amar Das was also against the custom of pardah, as may be seen from his exhortation to the Rani of Haripur.

The effect of all this was that the men, with whom it was usual in troubled times to leave their females to the mercy of the invader, now came forward as defenders of the honour of their homes, Women woo came to realize their position; and after this we often hear of their making a bold stand for their own defence.

Hymns of Guru Amar Das

Amar Das's conversion to Sikh faith is said to have occurred after his hearing a recitation of Nanak's Japji. He remained with Guru Angad for the last six years of the latter's life and succeeded him in 1552 when he was himself an old man of seventy-three.

Amar Das organized the scattered Sikh congregations into twenty-two dioceses and appointed spiritual mentors for each, some of whom were women. He was a great reformer. He made communal dining compulsory amongst Sikhs converted from different castes of Hindus and Muslims and forbade the practice of Sati amongst his followers.

Amar Das contributed 907 verses to the Adi Granth, all of which were written between the age of seventy-three when he became a Guru, and ninety-five when he died.

I

THE ANAND SAHIB

(i)

anand bhea meri mae

Rejoice with me, O mother,

That I have found the True Guru,
The True Guru have I found without penance,
And songs of rejoicings are in my heart.
The excellent Ragas and the race of the heavenly Muses
Have come to sing hymns to the Lord;
Those in whose hearts the Lord indwelleth,
Sing the Song of praise to Him.
Saith Nanak: My heart is full of joy
That I have found the True Guru.

(ii)

eh man meria tu sada rauh hari nale

O my mind, abide thou ever with God,
Abide with God, O my soul,
Who will make three to forget all thy sorrow,
Thou shalt be acceptable unto the Lord.
He will manage all thine affairs for thee;
The Lord is Perfect and in all things all-powerful;
Why shouldst thou ever forget the Lord ?
Saint Nanak: O my mind,
abide thou ever with God.

(iii)

sace sahiba kia nahi ghar tere

O my True Lord, what is there
That is not to be found in Thy House?
In Thy House are all riches;
He to whom Thou givest receiveth;
He will sing Thy Glories for ever,
And house Thy Name in his heart.
Heavenly Music resoundeth,
In the hearts where the Lord indwelleth;
Saith Nanak: O my true Lord,
What is there, that is not to be found in Thy House.

(iv)

saca nam mera adharo

Thy Name, O Lord, is my sustenance,

only on the True Name, which quieteth all my hungers do I live;
The true Name, abiding in my heart,
Hath granted me peace and joy,
And fulfilled all my desires.
I am ever a sacrifice unto the Guru,
Whose gifts these are.
Saith Nanak: Listen, O Saints, love the Word.
Thy Name, O Lord, is my sustenance.

(v)

vaje panc sabad tit ghar subhage

Celestial Music is heard in the blessed house,
The heart, where God indwelleth;
In that happy house,
In which God hath put forth His strength;
Heavenly Music is heard.
Therein the Lord has subdued the five evil passions,
And destroyed the fear of death.
Saith Nanak: They obtain happiness
And in their hearts the heavenly Music is heard.

(vi)

saci livai bin deh nimani

Without true love there is no honour for this mortal body
This mortal body is without honour if without love;
Besides Thee, Lord, there is none other all-powerful;
What can the wretched creature do? Have mercy on us, Lord.
For mortal man there is no other refuge but Thy Name.
By love of the Name the soul can be made beautiful;
Saith Nanak: What can the wretched creature do,
Without the love of the Lord.

(vii)

anand anand sabh ko kahe

All men talk of bliss, but true bliss,
Can only be got by keeping the company of the Guru;
It is through the grace of the Guru,
That eternal bliss can be known.

In his mercy the Guru destroyeth all sins,
And he putteth on the eyes the salve of divine knowledge,
Those who in their inner hearts have achieved detachment from the world
The True One hath made holy with the Word.
Saith Nanak: That is the true bliss,
That can be got by keeping the company of the Guru.

(viii)

bhagtan ki cal nirali

The path of the saint is a strange path;
The path of the saint is strange indeed,
He walketh by a hard road;
He renounces avarice, greed, self-will,
And attachment to the goods of the world;
And he maketh but little use of speech;
He walketh by a way sharper than a sword's edge,
By a way narrower than a hair's breadth.
By the grace of the Guru,
The desires of those who renounce self-will
Are set upon the Lord.
Saith Nanak: In every age, the path of the Saint
Is a strange path.

(ix)

karami sahaj na upjai

Knowledge of the Transcendent is not to be obtained,
Through outward religious observances, without knowledge,
Doubt and delusion will not depart;
No amount of outward observances
Will remove doubt and delusion.
The mind is filthy with ignorance,
How can it be made clean?
Wash thy mind, O man, in the light of the Word,
And fix thy heart and thy soul upon the Lord.
Saith Nanak: It is by the grace of the Guru
That knowledge of the Transcendent is obtained.
In this way only will doubt and delusion depart.

(x)

jion maile bharon nirmal

Those who, impure within, seem pure outwardly,
Fair without and foul within, have gambled their lives away,
They have contracted the vile disease of desire;
They have forgotten they are mortal.
Though the Name of the Lord
Is the most precious thing in the scriptures,
To that they attend not,
And they wander wildly like demons.
Saith Nanak: That man who hath discarded truth
And attached himself to falsehood hath gambled his life away.

(xi)

jion nirmal bahron nirmal

Those who, pure within, are also pure without,
Who are fair without and fair within, act virtuously,
Through the grace of the True Guru,
They have not heard even the name of falsehood;
All their hopes are set upon the Truth;
Blessed are such traders in virtue,
Who have earned the jewel of life.
Saith Nanak: Those who are pure within
Abide ever with the True Guru.

(xii)

eh sarira meria is jag mai ae ke

O my body, what hast thou brought to pass,
In thy sojourn on this earth? What hast thou done, O body,
Since thy coming into the world?
To the Lord who shaped thee,
Thou hast given no place in thine heart.
It is through the Guru's grace
That the Name in the heart indwelleth.
The Lords Name in the heart
Is the gift of past good deeds.
Saith Nanak: That mortal human body is acceptable
That hath set its heart upon the True Guru.

(xiii)

eh netro merio har tum mai jot dhari

O mine eyes, it was the Lord who gave ye Light,
Look on none but Him,
Look on none but the Lord;
By His grace will you see him,
The world which appeareth so poisonous to you,
Is the manifestation of God.
when by the grace of the Guru I was granted understanding
I saw that there is One God.
And I saw that there is no other beside Him.
Saith Nanak: These eyes of mine were blind,
But when I met the True Guru,
They were graced with divine Light.

(xiv)

anand suno vadhbhagio

Listen, O fortunate ones, to my joyful Song,
And all the desires of your hearts shall be fulfilled;
When we grasp the Lord in His uttermost supremacy,
All griefs must then go from us;
Through listening to the True Word
My griefs, my sicknesses, my torments have departed;
The saints and the holy are filled with joy
When they hear the word from the True Teacher;
He who heareth the Word is made pure;
He who speaketh the Word is made holy,
The True Guru filleth all their beings.
Nanak proclaimeth: For those who prostrate themselves
At the True Teacher's feet, the heavenly Music soundeth.

Rag Ramkali, pages 917-22: 3,5,7,10,14,18,19,20,35,36,40.

2

man tu jot sarup hai

Mind, thou art a Spark of Divine Light, so grasp the True Source of thy being.
The Lord is ever with thee; through the Guru's teachings rejoice in His Presence.

By grasping thine own true nature, thou graspest God's,
And the meaning of birth and death.
When through the Guru's grace thou hast grasped the Supreme One
Thou shalt lose the illusion of otherness.
Thou shalt abide in peace, honoured, and acceptable.
Nanak saith: O my mind, thou art an image of God,
Grasp the True Source of thy being.

3

ram ram sabh ko kahai

All men cry 'Lord, Lord.'
But by vain repetition man is not made one with the Lord.
It is only when, by the grace of the Guru, God in the heart indwelleth,
That human effort bears fruit.
He who loveth the Lord from his heart's core
Shall never forget him, but from his heart and soul
Shall ever repeat the Lord's Name.
They who are deceivers in their hearts but outwardly ape holiness
Shall not lose their lusts, and shall grieve at the time of departure.
However strenuously a man may wash himself
At the many holy places,
It is not thus that self-will is cleansed from him!
The King of Death, Dharmraj, shall chastise him
Who hath not cast down his self-will.
Only by the Guru's grace shall man meet God and understand Him!
Nanak saith; The man who destroyeth his own self-will
Shall certainly meet God! *Rag Gujri*, 491

4

nanak giani jag jita

Nanak, the man of divine knowledge hath conquered the world,
Which itself hath conquered all other men:
Through the Name, his affairs prosper.
And all his actions are as the Lord willeth.
Through the Guru's teaching his mind is steadfast and none can shake it.
God Himself standeth by him, and all that he doth is beautiful.
The perverse have been led astray from the Lord
By greed, by avarice, by proud self-will.

Day and night, they wrangle; they contemplate not the True Word.
The Lord hath taken away from them their good understanding;
So all their conversation is sinful.
In their hearts are avarice and the pitch black of ignorance;
However much they are given, their desires are insatiable.
Nanak saith: It is wise to break with the perverse
Who are attached to the illusory goods of the world.

Rag Bihagra, Var, 548

5

man maile sabh kich maila

If the mind is unclean, all else is unclean;
And ceremonial washings cannot wash the mind.
This world is the realm of illusion:
There are few who grasp the Real.
O my mind, remember the Holy Name!
That is the precious gift of the Guru of men.
Were a man to learn all the postures of the most austere Yogis,
And mortify all his senses,
Not so would he cleanse the mind, or discard self-will.
There is no cure for the mind's sickness
But taking shelter at the Guru's feet.
To meet the Guru is to experience
A change of outlook that cannot be described.
Saith Nanak: From the mind of him who dies to self
Through meeting the Guru, and is reborn through the Guru's Word,
All uncleanness is removed.

Vadhans, page 558

6

haumain navain nal virodh hai

Self-will is opposed to the Holy Name. The two cannot dwell in one house.
None can serve in a state of self-will, and the self-willed mind is worthless.
O my mind, fix thyself upon God's Name, and practise the Guru's Word.
By obeying God's Will, thou graspest Him, and sheddest thy self-will.
Self-will is the cause of all shapes and their coming into being:

It is the source of illusion, and veils the Reality from us.
The self-willed man cannot love God or understand His Will;
The soul is imprisoned in self-will and the Name cannot dwell in the heart.
But when a man meets the True Guru his self-will is destroyed,
And then the Truth alighteth in his heart to abide there
So, practising truth, a man lives in Truth
And, serving God who is Truth, is absorbed in Him.

Rag Vadhans, page 560

7

satgur no sabh ko vekhda

All men have access to the Guru
But a mere glimpse of the Guru does not save them;
Without understanding of the Guru's word
The self is not made clean nor the love of the Name implanted;
Some through God's Grace give up all self—will and sinfulness
And are made one with God:
Others, saith Nanak, at the sight of the Guru
Die to self, through the Guru's live,
And are at once made one with the Divine Spirit.

Rag Vadhans, page 594

8

janam janam ki is man ko mal lagi

Soiled by its former births the soul is as black as jet:
Like an oily rag that could not be clean, were it washed a hundred times!
But if through the Guru's Grace a man dies to self
And be born to new understanding,
Then the soul is free from its soiling, and is not born again.

Rag Sorath, Var, page 651

9

satian eh na akhian

It is not they who burn themselves alive
With their husband's dead bodies, who are *Satis,*
Nanak, they rather are Satis,
Whom the shock of separation from their husbands kill;

They also are known as Satis,
Who abide in modesty and contentment;
Who wait upon the Lord
And ever rising in the morning remember Him.

Rag Subi, Var, page 787

10

dhan pir eh na akhian

They are not truly husband and wife,
Whose bodies merely come together;
Only they are truly wedded
When two bodies have one soul.

Var Subi, page 788

11

jagat jalanda rakh lai apni kirpa dhar

Save this world consumed in fire,
O Lord, with Thy gracious Mercy!
Save it in any way it can be saved!
The Satguru hath shown the path of peace
In the contemplation of the True Word.
Nanak knoweth none besides God
Who is the only Saviour.

Var Bilawal, page 853

12

murakh hovai so sunai murakh ka kehna

Only a fool listens to an ignorant fool.
But what, may one ask, is the sign of a fool ?
And how does he conduct himself ?
A fool is a stupid creature
Whose soul is sick with self-love.
Leading such a life he suffers,
And his life is continual suffering.
If the poor thing is about to fall in a well
Who, really, can save him?
But the man who seeks truth takes life seriously,
He lives in detachment, Nanak,

He does what pleases God, the saint
Accepts whatever happens to him
As being God's Will.
Var Ramkali, page 953

13

jat ka garb na kerio koi

Let no man be proud because of his caste.
For the man who graspeth God in his heart
He, no other, is the true Brahmin:
So, O fool, about thy caste be not vainglorious!
From vainglory emerge too many of the mind's evils!
Though they say there are four castes
One God created all men:
All men were moulded out of the same clay,
The Great Potter hath merely varied the shapes of them.
All men are mixed of the same five elements,
No one can make any element less in one, more in another.
Man is born in chains:
Without meeting the True Guru,
He cannot attain liberation.

Rag Bhairon, page 1128

14

basant cadia phuli banrae

With the coming of spring,
There is blossom on every spray;
In the same fashion,
With the coming of inner devotion to God,
All sentient creatures have an inner blossoming,
And in this way the mind becometh fresh and green.
Day and night repeating the Name of the Lord,
Those who have seen God wash away all self-will!
The True Guru hath given to mankind
The Holy word and the hymns:
The whole world blossometh with love through the True Guru.
Life beareth flowers and fruits when the Lord willeth it:
It is by the devotion to the Lord, the source of life,
That the True Guru is attained.

The Lord Himself is the springtime

And the world is His Garden.
Only through His gracious gift to us
Can we attain the blessing of devotion to Him solely.
Rag Basant, page 1177

15

babiha na billae na tarsae

O babiha, wail not and cry not for water:
Let thy mind abide by His Will!
Only by abiding by His Will, saith Nanak,
Will all thirsts be slaked
And love and joy fourfold attained.

Rag Malar, Var, page 1282

16

satgur purkh nirvair hai

The True Guru, the divine one, is without enmity.
He fixeth his heart ever on God.
If a man should hate the Guru who is without hatred,
Such a man setteth fire to his own house;
Wrath and self-will are within him,
Day by day he burneth in their flames,
Living ever in agony and grief.
The wicked bark like dogs, telling lies;
Pursuing worldly gains, they swallow poison;
Shamelessly they go begging from door to door,
Asking for what will make them ill;
They are like the sons of a whore
Who cannot name their father.
They remember not the Name of God.
God Himself has confounded them;
When He takes mercy upon those gone astray,
He will unite them to Himself through the Guru.
The humble Nanak is a sacrifice to any man
Who taketh refuge at the feet of the Guru.

Slok Vadhik, 23, page 1415

17

asi khate bahut kamanvde

Our transgressions are past counting,
There is no end to our sins,
Be merciful, Forgive us, O Lord:
We are great sinners are wrongdoers.
There is no hope of our redemption.
O Lord, dear Lord, our deeds weighed in the balance
Would get us no place in Thy Court!
Forgive us and make us one with Thyself
Through the grace of the Guru.
If the Lord God can be attained to,
Then all evil is destroyed.
Victory, O Nanak, be unto them
Who meditate on His Name!

Slok Vadhik, 29, page 1416

18

sabd marai soi jan sijhai

He who dies in the Word
Attains to success.
Without the Word
None can be saved.
Man lives like a hypocrite,
The victim of his own acts:
Man is destroyed
By worldly attachments.
O Nanak, without the Guru
The Name cannot be known,
The Word's spirit cannot be known
However a man may crave for it.

Slok Vadhik, 32, page 1416

19

lobhi ka visah na kijai

Trust not the avaricious man.
He will deceive you, drive you into a corner
Where you are helpless.

A man only shames himself
By keeping company with the self-willed;
The avaricious are shamed,
They will depart from here
Having wasted their lives.
They have wrecked their lives.
Lord, give us the company
Of Thy holy saints
So that our hearts may become
Receptive of Thy Name.
The dross of life and death
Can be washed away, saith Nanak,
By singing the Lord's Praises!

Slok Vadhik, 40, page 1417

20

gurmukh budhe kade-na hovai

The souls whom the Guru has enlightened
Do not fall into decay.
They are absorbed in the praises of God.
And their understanding hath been shaped
By the Divine Knowledge.
With their minds fixed on the Transcendent one
For they live ever in blissful comprehension
For them joy and sorrow are one,
Since they see the One everywhere
Whose spirit pervades all things.

Slok Vadhik, 44, page 1418

Great honour from serving the holy Lord comes:
Through devotion the Lord of His own accord takes abode in the devotee's self.
The Lord is the fruit-yielding tree—
Whoever quaffs of this Amrita, his thirst is slaked. (1)

May I be a sacrifice time and again to the Master who brings together the holy company—
The Lord Himself brings together the holy company chanting His laudation. (1-Pause)

On one serving the holy Master glory by the holy Word is conferred—

Such glory comes from the Lord's Name in the self lodging,
The Lord imaculate removes impurity *of mind—*
One so cleansed finds acclaim at the Portal Divine. (2)

None found the Name except through the holy Preceptor.
Yogis and practitioners of austerities yearn for this attainment fruitlessly.
None found joy except through devotion to the Master:
Only by supreme good luck comes union with the Master. (3)

The mind is as the hand mirror only one devoted to God looks into it;
As egoism is dried up, this mirror from rust grows immune.
The true devotee makes mystic music with the immaculate Word,
And through the Master's Word is merged into *holy* Truth. (4)

None ever had the *Lord's* Vision except through the Preceptor's Guidance:
By the Master's grace the Lord revealed Himself to the devotee.
He Himself made union for the devotee in his state of perfect serenity and poise. (5)
Only the truth devotee in the one Supreme Being is absorbed.
His illusion of Duality by the Master's Word is consumed.
In his self he carries on the commerce *of truth:*
His gain the treasure of the holy Name. (6)

The true devotee's endeavour is the Lord's holy laudation;
Such devotee reaches the Door of Liberation;
Dyed in devotion, ever does he chant the Lord's laudation.
By the Lord is he summoned into the holy Mansion. (7)

The holy Preceptor, found of bounty, if found as the Lord ordains:
Through supreme good fortune is the holy Word in the self lodged.
Saith Nanak: Through the Name and chanting laudation of the holy Lord,
Is true greatness found. (8) (9.10)

All boons by sacrificing the ego shall come,
And entering on true devotion through the Master's Word.
One carrying on commerce of Truth deals in Truth—
Truth too his hoard of gain. (1)
May I be a sacrifice time and again to those chanting the Lord's praise:
Lord : I am Thine, Thou the Master—
Dispenser of Merit through gift of the Word. (I-Pause)

Auspicious are all times and occasions,

In which love for the holy Lord enters the heart.
From service to the Holy Master comes greatness of the life of truth:
This *path of Truth* is found through the Preceptor's grace. (2)

The fare of devotion is found through the holy Master's grace;
Then with false pleasures discarded,
Pleasure in God is lodged in the mind.
The blessings of truth, holy content, the ineffable joy of peace
All given by the holy Word, come from the holy Master. (3)

The purblind fool devotees himself not to the Lord—
How may such find the Door of Liberation ?
Involved in the cycle of death and birth,
They enter bodily life again and again,
And stand abjectly at Yama's portal.
One knowing joy of the Word may alone know his self:
By contemplating the immaculate Word does such knowledge come.
These serving the holy Lord are in everlasting joy—
The Name, Supreme Value, in their hearts is lodged. (5)

Blessed is the spot approved by the Lord—
Such is where the Lord's praises are chanted in holy company,
Where everlastingly are chanted the Lord's praises,
And the holy immaculate mystic Note is uttered. (6)

The man ego-centred carries false capital,
False too all his concerns.
Those with tainted actions must grievously suffer.
Such wander about in delusion day and night—
Their human incarnation a waste,
The cycle of birth and death their lot. (7)

Most beloved of me is the holy Lord—
This love resting on the holy Master's teaching.
Saith Nanak : From the holy Name comes true greatness
In holding joy and sorrow alike. (8)

Thine are all species and all tongues—
Without the Name all in delusion are lost;
Devotion to the Lord's Name comes from obeying the Preceptor—
None without the Preceptor's guidance found it. (1)

May I be a sacrifice time and again to those immersed in devotion to the Lord.

Through devotion to the Preceptor is found the way to the holy Lord.
By those seeking Him with heart in poise.
Through devotion to the Master are all boons attained—
All rewards the heart desires.
The Lord is bestower of all gifts—
Union with Him from supreme good luck comes. (2)

The impure mind meditates not on the sole Supreme Being—
From Duality impurity gathers on the mind.
One wandering over holy water-edges, bathing spots and various places held holy—
His pride increased, the impurity of egoism further on him accumulates. (3)

Such impurity goes through devotion to the holy Preceptor,
Through dying to God while alive,
And absorption of heart in the Lord.
The Lord pure, immaculate, holy,
Is beyond impurity, and annuller of impurity of mind. (4)

Without the Preceptor's *teaching* all is pitch-dark;
The man of unenlightened mind is blind, in the dark grouping,
Like worms crawling in offal.
Filth they gather, and in filth are again absorbed. (5)

One serving the liberated is liberated himself;
His egoism, accquisitiveness through the holy Word annulled.
One serving the holy Lord each day of his life,
Through supreme good fortune finds the true Preceptor. (6)

The Lord shows grace Himself and to the devotee grants union:
From the holy Master is attained the wealth of the holy Name.
Through devotion to the holy Name the mind abides pure—
Through devotion to the holy Lord all sorrows vanish.
The Lord is ever by—think not He is far:
Through the holy Word behold Him within ye.
Saith Nanak: Greatness comes through the Name—
Devotion to the Name from the holy Master comes. (11.12)

Those that in the world are holy are adjudged holy in the hereafter;
Their minds pure, in the holy Word are they absorbed.
One serving the holy Lord, acting purely,
In pure actions is absorbed. (1)

May I be a sacrifice time and again to those lodging the holy Name in their mind.
Those serving the holy Lord, chanting His praise,
Are in Him absorbed. (I-Pause)

Learned Brahmins study sacred texts, but taste not their joy;
In Duality are their minds deluded by Maya;
Of true wisdom are they deprived by stupor,
And repent after of their evil deeds. (2)

From the Preceptor's touch alone comes knowledge of the Essence,
And the Lord's Name in the self lodged.
One dying in the Word disciplines His lower self,
And finds thus the Door of Liberation. (3)

One lodging in his self the Master's Word
His sins removes and eliminates wrath from his heart.
Those dyed in Truth are everlastingly the true anchorites—
Their ego suppressed, they find union with the Supreme. (4)
The jewel Name in the mind through the Preceptor's guidance is found;
Threefold are man's desires; three are Maya's attributes.
Brahmin scholars and devotees of silence despite their study to exhaustion
Fail of access to the secret of the Fourth State. (5)
The Lord himself dyes the self in the fast dye of devotion;
Those alone are truly dyed that in the Master's Word are dyed:
Soaked in the dye of God unlimited,
Does the self chant His laudation in ecstasy. (6)
For the true devotee discipline of truth is the real miraculous powers;
From him true liberation in enlightenment and devotion to the Name lies.
The Lord's devotee acts truth,
And in truth is absorbed. (7)
The devotee beholds the vision of God making and unmaking the universe;
For him devotion to God alone is pride of caste and honour.
Saith Nanak: The true devotee ever meditates on the Name,
And in it is endlessly absorbed. (12.13)
From the divine command occurs creation and dissolution of the universe.
By the Command in the universe manifested again.
To the God-enlightened all happens as God wills,
And all creation and dissolution is seen to be by Him. (1)
May I be a sacrifice time and again to those lodging in their hearts the holy Master.

By divine prompting comes poise of mind and unending devotion,
And through utterance of God's attributes,
Absorption into these. (I-Pause)
By divine command exist earth and water,
By divine command occurs the wonderful play of air and fire.
One without the Maker's instruction is born again and again and dies—
One uninstructed by the Master is in transmigration involved. (2)
The creator has fashioned His play;
In the human frame is included the universe

By penetating to the secret of the holy Word alone may one reach the divine Mansion,
And be called to enter therein. (3)
Holy is the Divine Merchant,
Holy those holding commence with Him—
Through unending devotion to the Lord in Truth they deal.
Truth they buy and Truth they gain-
Truth alone their earning. (4)
Without capital, no gain may be made;
The whole world by egoism is deluded;
All without the capital of Truth depart this life,
And in the hereafter suffer. (5)
Those loving the Divine Word deal in Truth;
Swimming across themselves, they take across all related to them
Their coming into the world approved of God;
Through union with Him they get bliss. (6)
The fool seeks outside the Lord lodged within;
The egoist purblind wanders about like a ghost perturbed;
They seek not what they are after in the proper place—
In delusion of egoism involved. (7)
He Himself beckons the seeker through His word,
And on him the boon confers;
Entering the Divine Mansion he attains poise and bliss.
Saith Nanak: Greatness comes from devotion to the Name,
Through listening to it and meditation. (8)
(13.14)

The holy Master has imparted the true teaching:
Meditate on the Lord—
Such meditation shall be your succourer at the end.
The Lord inaccessible, unknowable, sole master of Himself

You shall meet through devotion to the holy preceptor. (1)
May I be a sacrifice time and again to those discarding egoism.
One shedding one's ego finds the Lord
Through merging in Him in poise of mind. (I-Pause)
Man acts as primally ordained.
Devotion to the holy preceptor gives everlasting joy.
Without good fortune is not found the holy preceptor,
Who brings about union through the Word. (2)
God's devotee lives in the world untouched by its impurity—
Leaning on the Lord and support of the Name.
God's devotees remain unconcerned at those committing aggression against them—
Such fall into suffering through exhaustion by their own evil. (3)
The egoist purblind is of all thought bereft—
Turning a suicide and general murderer;
He carries the burden of slandering others—
Bearing loads gratuitously on his head. (4)
This world is a garden plot—
The Lord its gardener,
Cherishing all, none neglected.
From each comes the flavour that is put into him—
By such flavour is each known. (5)
The world by the malady of egoism is gripped,
And has forgotten the Giver of all joy, inaccessible, endless.
Those gripped by egoism wander about the world, wailing in pain—
Without the Master no peace they find. (6)
The Lord who created all, alone knows the way to joy and peace:
He alone confers knowledge of His own Ordinance.
Man acts as destined:
From such bonds God alone extricates. (7)
None is my prop but God All-Truth:
Purity comes to whoever He prompts towards it.
Saith Nanak: Devotion lies hidden in the heart,
On whomsoever He confers it, is alone truly blessed. (8)
(14.15)

As the immortal Name is lodged in the heart,
Maladies such as egoism and possessiveness are annulled:
Who so forever lauds the immortal Word,
Shall find Amrita to quaff. (1)

May I be a sacrifice time and again to those who lodge the immortal Word
in the heart—
To those lodging in the heart the immortal Word
And meditating on the Name Eternal. (I-Pause)

The God-enlightened ever in their speech utter Amrita;
Their eyes view in loving admiration nothing but Amrita;
Day and night they speak to others Amrita: (2)
Through love of Amrita its dye settles on *the devotee;*
Such Amrita by divine grace comes.
One dyed in Amrita utters day and night Amrita with his tongue,
And with mind and body offers to all the feast of Amrita. (3)

God wills what man never may expect—
His ordinance none may alter.
The immortal Word divine is made manifest by Divine Ordinance:
By Divine Ordinance is the draught of Amrita attained. (4)
Strange is the way of the Divine will.
Man's deluded mind wanders in various directions.
Let man in his heart the immortal Word love,
That plays the immortal Harmony. (5)
Lord! Thou hast made the good and the worthless.
Thine the *touchstone* to judge the whole world.
The genuine ones dost Thou put in Thy treasury;
The spurious remain in delusion caught. (6)
How may I view Thee? How laud ?
By divine grace may Thou be lauded through the holy Word.
In Thy will abides Amrita—
Those submitting to it are on this Amrita feasted. (7)
God's Word is Amrita; Amrita His utterance:
This through devotion to the holy Preceptor in the heart is lodged.
Saith Nanak: The Name immortal brings everlasting joy—
A draught of it banishes all hunger for ever. (8)
(15.16)

In the self rains Amrita spontaneously—

This bliss only to the rare God-enlightened ones comes.
One quaffing this Amrita is for evermore filled—
By divine grace is life's thirst quenched. (1)
May I be a sacrifice time and again to the Master offering the draught

of Amrita.
The palate tasting it abides in everlasting ecstasy,
And the tongue spontaneously utters divine laudation. (I-Pause)
Such spontaneous love a rare one gets through divine grace—
One subduing Duality and fixed in love of the Sole Supreme Being.
Through divine grace may one chant divine laudation,
And his eyes be filled with the union of the Eternal Truth. (2)
Lord! On all Creation is Thy glance of grace—
Some have it in full measure,
Over others is it cast partially.
Nothing happens except by Thy will—
This awareness too by divine grace comes. (3)
The God-enlightened have learnt of the Essence:
With Amrita are Thy treasures overflowing.
This Amrita none may get except by devotion to the holy Master—
By the Master's grace is it acquired. (4)
One devoted to the holy Master acquires *true* beauty—
One in whose inner mind is love for the immortal Name:
His mind, body, speech are in Amrita dyed. (5)
The egoist, deluded in Duality is ruined;
Devoid of devotion he dies of swallowing poison,
Ever does he abide in filth—
His life a waste without serving the Lord. (6)
Only one offered Amrita by the Divine Hand may quaff it,
And through the Master's grace spontaneous devotion lodge in him.
The Lord's vision, whose presence fills all Creation,
By God-given enlightenment is got. (7)
Nothing is real but the Immaculate Lord—
His the Creation and His the dissolution.
Saith Nanak: Meditate ever on the Name—
Thou shalt then spontaneously in holy truth be absorbed. (8)
(16.17)

Those pleasing Thee are in Truth absorbed;
Ever serve they Truth spontaneously;
Through the holy Word ever they laud Truth,
And unite others to Truth. (1)
May I be a sacrifice time and again to those lauding Truth:
Those meditating on Truth are in Truth dyed,
And therein are absorbed. (I-Pause)

Wheresoever I look, Truth pervades all places;
Through divine grace is it in the mind lodged.
Those listening to Truth and to others relating it—
Holy their limbs, in holiness their tongue dyed. (2)
By overcoming desire comes absorption in Truth:

By the mind of such the whole world is viewed as evanescent.
Through devotion to the holy Master the mind gets poise,
And in its own home is settled. (3)
From the Master's Word has come the vision of God abiding in the self
And Maya-delusion is by the holy Word burnt away.
As is holy Eternal Truth visioned, the self lauds it:
Through the Master's teaching is Truth realized. (4)
Those dyed in truth are with it in love:
Truly fortunate are those meditating on the Lord's Name.
The Lord through the holy Word has united them to Himself:
In holy company chant they God's laudation. (5)
One may reflect on God should reflection compute Him.
Inaccessible, unknowable-through the holy Word alone may He be realised.
Laudation unceasing through the holy Word,
May alone bring realisation of Him. (6)
Endless study and learning bring not Peace of minds;
Desire burns inside, Smothering all realization.
Poison they buy, of poison are they enamoured—
Through their false utterance poison they consume. (7)
By divine grace have I realized the sole Supreme Being;
Suppressing Duality, has the self in Truth been absorbed.
Saith Nanak: God's Name alone fills the self—
Such state by divine grace is attained. (8)
(17.18)

All hues, forms are Thy manifestation;
These die, are born again—
Many cycles in which they wander—
Thou alone immutable, inaccessible, immeasurable.
By divine wisdom alone mayst Thou be realized. (1)
May I be a sacrifice time and again to any
In whose mind God's Name is lodged,
Who is without form, feature, hue—
By the Master's guidance alone realized. (I-Pause)

Should the seeker know all existence to be a manifestation of One Effulgence,
Through devotion to the holy preceptor will it become manifest to him.
God's presence, secret and manifest, is everywhere—
The seeker's light merges into His light, (2)
In the fire of desire is the world burning—
Of greed, pride and egoism :
Those cherishing such evils die and are reborn,
Dishonoured at the Court Divine are reborn,
Wasting their human incarnation. (3)
Rare is the person who the Divine Word realizes,
One suppressing one's ego learns the Mystery of all the three worlds.
Never does he die or is reborn.
By meditating on God in holy Truth is he merged. (4)
Let not man attach himself ever to Maya,
And in the Master's Word forever remain absorbed.
The holy Truth should be lauded.
That in each vessel shines forth. (5)
One lauding holy Truth is ever in the Divine Presence.
Through the holy Master's Word fulfilled.
By divine grace does truth on the vision flash—
Only those by it inspired get *true* joy. (6)
As Truth the self pervades—
Truth immutable, everlasting—
Those devoted to it have minds purified,
And through God-given wisdom into it are merged. (7)
Laud the Eternal, no other:
Such devotion eternal joy brings.
Saith Nanak: Those in the Name dyed are the truly wise—
Holy all their endeavour. (8)
(18.19)

Pure is the holy Word, pure the *Master's* speech:
Pure is the Light that pervades all Creation.
Pure is the speech of divine laudation—
Those meditating on the Lord Immaculate are rendered pure. (1)
May I be a sacrifice time and again to those lodging the Bestower of Joy in the self.
The Lord Immaculate through the Master's Word is lauded—
By listening to his Word is all desire annulled. (I-Pause)

As the Name Immaculate in the self is lodged,
Mind and body are rendered pure,
And stupor of Maya is removed.
Such chant ever the holy laudation of the Eternal—
Holy the sound they raise.
The Amrita purifying, from the Guru is obtained—
Vouchsafed to one with ego dead,
Relieved of attachment to Maya.
Pure is his knowledge, doubly pure his meditation;
Pure the speech in his self lodged. (3)
One devoted to the Immaculate *Lord* is rendered Pure;
His impurity of ego is washed through the Master's Word.
In his self is heard the pure music of the mystic Melody and the holy Word. (4)
At the Eternal Portal is he honoured.
The Immaculate renders all else pure;
The mind purified is strung on the Divine Word.
The immensely fortunate alone to the holy Name are devoted—
Through the holy Name in splendour they shine forth. (5)
He alone is pure to whom the Word imparts beauty,
And whose mind and body to the holy Name are devoted.
One holding the holy Name never is defiled—
The Name imparts a glow to his face. (6)
From feelings of Duality comes impurity of mind:
The cooking-spot and the site of such, all are impure.
One consuming the food of impurity only multiplies filth.
The egoist through his impurity gets immense suffering. (7)
The pure and impure all to Divine Ordinance are subject,
Those pleasing the Lord, pure and holy, alone are pure.
Saith Nanak: as the holy Name in the self is lodged
Through Divine enlightenment is impurity removed. (8)
(19.20)

Pure is the Divine *Pool,* pure the Swan selves disporting on it—
In such company, my mind, speech and thoughts have been rendered pure.
The face reflecting a pure self,
Of those meditating on God, is ever radiant. (1)
May I be a sacrifice time and again to those chanting the Lord's laudation—
To those repeating God's Name day and night
And uttering the sacred Word redolent of God's attributes. (I-Pause)

Such devotees spontaneously laud God
Rendered pure by fear of God, relieved of the impurity of egoism.
Ever abide they in bliss, engaging in devotion night and day,
And learning the Lord's attributes, chant them. (2)
As dances the mind, *its rhythm* strengthens devotion:
And through the Master's Word is self united to Self.
The devotee beating holy time, of Maya-stupor divests himself. (3)
One yelling aloud with vibrations violent,
At last falls into the grip of Yama, the agent of death.
Such mind dancing to the Maya-Stupor tune
In false show, in the end meets with suffering. (4)
True devotion is alone God-prompted,
When body and mind in spontaneous devotion are dyed;
The Divine Word brings the rhythm:
True devotion verily He rewards. (5)
One assiduously keeping time in music and playing a concert—
His mind attends not to the Divine Word,
Nor holds it:
For lucre he in the theatre dances
And, caught in Duality, into suffering falls. (6)
One in devotion engaged is truly liberated;
One controlling one's senses is Master of true discipline.
One meditating on the Lord through the Master's Word—
Such devotion alone pleases Him.
In *submission* to the Master's teaching alone,
In all ages lies devotion:
In no other way may one find it.
Saith Nanak: Realization comes alone through devotion to the Master—
To those bound in devotion to his feet. (8)
(20.21)

While performing devotion to the holy Eternal,
While lauding Him,
While meditating on the holy Name,
No suffering may ever come to man.
In devotion to the Bestower of Joy lies joy,
For those in the self lodging His teaching. (1)
May I be a sacrifice time and again to those absorbed in the state of unbroken joy.
Those devoted to the Lord are eternally radiant,

And with fame and beauty of inspiration endowed. (I-Pause)
Many Thy devotees claim to be—
The true devotee is one pleasing Thee alone.
Lauding thee through the holy Word
And immersed in joy in devotion. (2)
Holy Lord! All are Thy *creatures*.
By guidance by the master is transmigration annulled.
By Thy grace is devotion to the Name formed !
By Thy inspiration comes meditation on the Name. (3)
By God-give wisdom is the Lord in the self lodged;
Gone is pain, the lure of pleasure and Maya-delusion.
In devotion to the Sole Supreme Being,
Eternally is the Divine Name in the self lodged. (4)
Thy devotees are ever in passion for Thee dyed—
The Name, Source of the Nine Treasures, in the self is lodged,
By supreme good fortune is the holy Preceptor found,
Who through the Word grants union with Him. (5)
Thou art ever gracious, bestower of joy.
Thou makest Thyself the union,
And by the enlightened art realized.
Thou dost Thyself bestow the greatness of devotion—
Those dyed in Thy Name find true joy. (6)
Lord Eternal! May I ever unceasingly laud Thee;
Those inspired by Thee have realization and know no other—
Their hearts absorbed in the sole Supreme Being alone;
Through faith dost Thou to the seeker's self grant union. (7)
One God-inspired alone lauds Him,
The Lord eternal, transcending all want.
Saith Nanak: With the Name lodged in the self,
Is He realized through the holy Word. (8)
(21.22)

Thy devotees shine in beauty at the Court Eternal,
By the holy Master's Word exalted.
Day and night abide they in bliss,
Absorbed in divine attributes through their utterance. (1)
May I be a sacrifice time and again
To those lodging in their selves the Name
By constant remembrance of it.
Higher than the highest is the holy Lord,

By annulling egoism to Himself uniting the seeker. (I-Pause)
Holy is the Lord,
Holy His greatness.
Rare are the devotees winning His grace, united to Him.
Those by grace united to Him get alienated never—
Through spontaneous devotion in the holy Eternal absorbed. (2)
Outside of Thy will nothing occurs.
All that occurs is Thy doing,
And all is in Thy mind.
The Creator is the sole Doer—
Through God-given enlightenment to Himself uniting the seeker. (3)
The woman endowed with noble qualities with the Lord is united,
One with fear and love of the Lord decked.
One serving the holy Master is of abiding bliss in matrimony,
And through holy teaching in Him is absorbed. (4)
Those neglecting the holy Word shall no shelter or anchor find—
Lost in delusion like raven in ruined cottage.
Such have forfeited this world and the next—
Life passed in suffering evermore their lot. (5)
Let one record thoughts of Duality, exhausting stores of paper and ink—
None found joy through indulging in such;
Those recording what is false,
Falsehood their recompense.
Cursed be those fixing their hearts on false vanities. (6)
The God-inspired record thoughts of what is true and holy:
These holy ones the door of liberation shall find.
Holy the paper, pen and ink of such—
Through recording truth, in the holy Eternal absorbed. (7)
The Lord seated within each
Has the whole universe under His gaze.
One by the Master's grace united to Him,
Alone counts with Him.
Saith Nanak: In devotion to the Name lies true greatness:
Such gift by the holy Master is bestowed, (8)
(22.23)

Through the Preceptor's guidance does the self get illumination of the Supreme Self;
The impurity of egoism is removed through absorbing the holy Word.

The self, thus purified, engages unceasingly in devotion.
And through devotion to the Lord attains. (1)
May I be a sacrifice time and again to those engaging in devotion and inspiring others to it.
Ever bow to these devotees who endlessly chant the Lord's laudation. (I-Pause)
The Lord Himself is the supreme cause of *all devotion* He inspires,
And sets, to such task whoever wins His pleasure:
Only by perfect good fortune may one do service to the Lord,
That brings bliss.
Who dies to the world again and again
May make some attainment.
By divine grace is the Lord in the self lodged.
Eternally liberated is one who lodges the Lord in his self,
And thus through spontaneous devotion in Him is merged. (3)
Excess of ritual brings not liberation;
One wandering from land to land is in Duality deluded.
Wasted is the hypocrite's human incarnation.
Without inspiration of the holy Word is he condemned to suffering. (4)
One who restrains the restless mind
And holds it from wandering,
Attains by divine grace the supreme state:
Such union is made through the holy Preceptor's teaching—
One to the Beloved united attains bliss. (5)
Some are engaged in falsehood—
Their reward too is worthless:
Involved in Duality, their human incarnation is a waste.
Drowned themselves, all related to them are drowned too.
Involved in the lie, poison is their food. (6)
Only the rare God-instructed one may view the conscious self in the flesh concealed;
Love and devotion to God come when egoism is dried up.
Yogis, practitioners of austerities, observers of vows of silence,
Those engaging in long concentration—
All such too fail to view the conscious self in the flesh. (7)
Such blessing comes as the Creator ordains:
None else may accomplish anything.
Saith Nanak: Only such get inspired to devotion as by God are inspired—

He alone may lodge the Name in the self. (8)

(23.24)

In this cave *of the human frame* lie inexhaustible treasures;
In it abides the Lord unknowable, beyond limit,
Invisible as well as manifest,
Revealed to those lost to the ego through the holy Master's Word. (1)
May I be a sacrifice time and again to those lodging the Name Amrita in their selves:
Amrita of the Name is the delectable supreme juice—
Through God-given enlightenment quaffed. (I-Pause)
The Lord, annulling man's ego, throws open the adamantine door;
By divine grace is the Name invaluable attained.
Without absorbing the holy Word none the Name has attained—
Only by divine grace is it in the self lodged. (2)
As was the collyrium of divine enlightenment drawn in the eyes of truth-seeking
The inner self got illuminated and the darkness of ignorance lifted,
Light merged into Light.
Faith was struck in the mind—
Thus may the seeker get honour at the Portal Divine. (3)
One looking for the Divine Light beyond this frame,
Neglecting devotion—
Much suffering would he see in such travail of slavery.
The egoist purblind sees not
That ultimately must he return to the self.
By the Master's guidance
The valued objective to attain. (4)
By divine grace is the Lord, holy eternal, found:
As is the self viewed, the impurity of egoism is removed.
Then must the seeker enter a hallowed spot.
Chant ever divine laudation
And merge into the Lord through the holy Word. (5)
Let him bar the Nine doors and restrain the restless mind,
And lodge in his own abode in the Tenth State,
Wherein day and night would he hear the mystic harmony played.
And by the Master's guidance listen to the holy Word. (6)
Without the Word is the self enveloped in pitch darkness—
In such state neither is the supreme objective attained nor transmigration annulled.

The key to this attainment in the hand of the holy master lies—
None else may force open this door:
Only by perfect good fortune may union with the Supreme Being come about. (7)
Invisible and manifest, everywhere art Thou:
Such wisdom is attained through divine grace.
Saith Nanak: Laud ever the Name,
That through the Master's guidance may in the self be lodged. (8)
(24.25)

The Lord, through the Preceptor's guidance, Himself grants union to the seeker:
One so united falls not into the grip of death, nor is oppressed by suffering.
Subduing his egoism he breaks asunder all bonds,
And by absorbing the holy Word shines in true beauty. (1)
May I be a sacrifice time and again to those by the holy Name imparted splendour,
By the Master's guidance they sing and in ecstasy dance,
Their minds in the Lord fixed. (I-Pause)
The God-enlightened are approved in life and in death:
One realizing the holy Word knows not the dissolution of life.
One God-enlightened dies not, becomes not death's morsel—
In holy Truth absorbed. (2)
The God-enlightened are at the Divine Portal accorded honour,
Their egoism subdued.
Swimming across themselves, all of their tribe are saved,
By God-given wisdom their incarnation made fruitful. (3)
The God-enlightened are not afflicted with suffering of body,
Their pain of egoism annulled.
The God-enlightened are pure in mind,
Never after subjected to impurity—
In spontaneous devotion absorbed. (4)
The God-enlightened find true greatness through devotion to the Name
And by chanting the Lord's laudation are exalted.
The God-enlightened living the holy Word,
Are ever in bliss day and night. (5)
The God-enlightened are dyed perpetually in the holy Word,
And in all the Four Ages venerated.
The God-enlightened by chanting laudation of the Lord are made everlastingly pure,
And through the holy Word practise devotion. (6)

Without the preceptor all is utter darkness;
Those without the Preceptor fall in the grip of Yama, the Destroyer
And wail—
For ever turned into filth-worms,
Fallen, suffering therein. (7)
By grace the Lord Himself accomplishes all;
Lodged in the heart, Himself He unites with the devotee.
Saith Nanak: True greatness comes from meditation on the Name,
That by grace of the Perfect Master is acquired. (8)
(25.26)

One sole light pervades all beings,
This the holy Master through the holy Word reveals,
Himself has he made them distinct, apparent to the mind—
This mode of creation has He made as He willed it. (1)
May I be a sacrifice time and again to those chanting laudation of the holy
Lord.
None without the Preceptor's teaching can follow the way of enlightened
devotion—
By divine grace may one be absorbed in devotion to Him. (I-Pause)
By Thy beauty dost Thou fascinate all Creation,
By Thy looks dost Thou the creation penetrate;
In Thy will lies suffering and bliss,
Lord Creator!
By the Preceptor's grace art Thou visioned. (2)
The Creator in His will is solely supreme;
Himself He lodges in the heart by the Master's Word
From the Word rises Amrita of the Preceptor's teaching—
That the God-enlightened *to others* relate. (3)
Himself He the Creator and Enjoyer,
Breaker of bonds, eternally liberated Himself.
Eternally liberated is the Lord,
Himself leading the seeker to encompass the unencompassable.
(4)

Himself is He Maya and Maya-shadow,
Himself is has He created the delusion world-enveloping:
Himself Bestower of merit, singing His Own laudation;
Himself making the narration. (5)
Himself the sole Doer,
Creator and Destroyer:

Nothing can happen except as He wills—
The world He sets to is tasks. (6)
Himself lord of death and restorer to life;
Himself bringing about union:
Service to Him brings joy perpetual—
Those inspired by Him attain perfection of inner peace, poise. (7)
Himself high, higher than *all existence;*
This vision comes to one He is pleased to give;
Saith Nanak: One with the Name lodged in Him
Has this vision and to others impart it. (8)
(26.27)

The Lord fills all space;
By the Preceptor's grace may He be viewed in the self.
May I ever serve Him with meditation unbroken;
By divine inspiration can one be absorbed in His Truth. (I)
May I be a sacrifice time and again to those lodging the life of the Universe in their selves.
The Lord, Life of the universe, fearless, bountiful—
By the Master's guidance may He be lodged in thee. (I-Pause)
In the self are located the earth, the Bull and the nether world,
In the self abides ever the Beloved, eternally youthful.
Ever does He abide in bliss, the Bestower of joy—
By divine inspiration may one in perfect peace *be absorbed.* (2)
In the human body is lodged egoism and acquisition's urge;
Because of these the birth-and-death cycle comes not to end.
One divinely inspired alone may annul his egoism
By unceasingly meditating on the Truth. (3)
The pair evil and good lie side by side in the self;
Both jointly have shaped Creation.
One transcending both and entering the House of Supreme Unity,
By the Master's guidance in perfect peace is absorbed. (4)
In the self lies too the darkness of Duality;
As appears the light, egoism and possessiveness are discarded;
The Word manifest, bestowed on those ever meditating on the Name,
Of perennial joy is the source. (5)
Within the self is effulgence manifest and spread;
By the Master's teaching is darkness lifted.
As blooms the lotus of the heart, comes everlasting joy,
And light into light merges. (6)

With the self are mansion with stores overflowing with jewels;
These jewels of the Name immortal by the Master's guidance are attained.
The devoted seeker trades solely in these,
His profit the Name everlasting. (7)
Himself the keeper of stores, Himself the Bestower;
Rare are the God-inspired merchants, dealing in these.
Saith Nanak: This bliss by His glance of grace is attained.
By who so through His gracious inspiration lodges Him in the self. (8)
(27.28)

The Lord Himself grants union and sets man to devotion;
Through the Master's holy word is Duality lifted.
The Lord Immaculate is bestower of merit everlasting—
Thereby may the self in the divine attributes be absorbed. (1)
May I be a sacrifice time and again to those absorbing in the self holy Truth.
The holy Name is ever immaculate—
By the Master's holy Word is it in the self lodged. (I-Pause)
The Bountiful Lord is Himself Ordainer of Retribution.
His devotees serving Him,
By divine inspiration have realization.
Those contemplating the Name-Amrita in eternal glory shine;
The juice of divine joy is by the mind God-directed attained.
In this cave of the self is a lovely spot- (2)
Reached as the illusion by the Perfect Master is lifted.
Those rid of it laud ever the Name, drenched in ecstasy,
Attained by the Master's grace. (3)
Through the Master's teaching may this cave be explored—
Within is the Name Immaculate of the Lord.
Those exalted by the holy Word chant laudation of the Lord;
And finding union with the Beloved,
Abide in joy everlasting. (4)
Those in the grip of Duality are taxed by the harsh tax-gatherer Yama;
He chastises those forgetful of the Name.
Accounting for each minute of life,
Is he unsparing of the least deviation. (5)
The self-female, sojourning in the parent's home,
Has forgotten the husband by whose side she must be;
Deluded by Duality, she weeps tears of bitterness.
Such self is a low-born woman, ungainly, ill-mannered,
Who gets not even in dream her lord's love. (6)

One who even in her parent's home cherishes the husband in her heart,
Is blessed with his sight manifest through the holy Master's grace,
The woman who keeps her lord close to her bosom,
Through the holy Word has union with him in a blessed couch. (7)
The Lord bestows devotion Himself, beckoning to Himself the seeker,
And lodges in him His Name.
Saith Nanak : True honour comes to one chanting God's laudation for ever each day. (8)
(28.29)

Those resorting to holy congregation are of blessed birth;
One devoted to the holy Master is in truth an anchorite while keeping a household:
Such live dyed in the ecstasy of God's love,
Their hearts satiated with joy in the Lord. (1)
May I be a sacrifice time and again to those who after their learning lodge the lord in their selves.
The God-enlightened study scriptures and laud the Lord's Name.
And are honoured at the Portal Divine. (I-Pause)
The Lord beyond understanding, inscrutable, is pervasive everywhere,
And by no device may be attained:
Only through grace may the holy Preceptor provide union with Him,
By his glance of blessing. (2)
The study of one caught in Duality leads not to enlightenment,
And provoked by Maya of the Three Qualities enters into disputation:
Those bonds of the Three Qualities are scrapped through knowledge of Master's Word—
Through the Word is liberation attained. (3)
The mind restless is hard to restrain;
Caught in Duality, over the entire world it runs:
Such a mind is a filth-worm, involved with filth,
And in the end in filth is absorbed. (4)
One asserting his ego only exposes his low nature;
By excess of ritual no place may be found in the Court Divine.
Lord! Nothing occurs but with Thy will—
Only those ennobled by the holy Word find liberation. (5)
Not even the Vision of God's process of Creation and Dissolution brings to man realization:
Day after day he goes about involved in Duality.
The egoist's human incarnation is gone waste,
Leaving him in the end full of regret. (6)

The egoist is like the woman, doing make-up, with husband gone to strange lands—
Such is the doing of the egoist purblind:
Neither in this world not in the next finds he honour and succour—
His human incarnation a waste. (7)
Rare are those realizing the Lord's Name:
Through guidance of the holy Master comes such realization.
One engaged in devotion everlastingly day and night
Finds joy descending on him. (8)
The sole Lord supreme pervades all creation:
Rare is the God-inspired person to realize Him.
Saith Nanak : Truly noble are those dyed in the Name—
By grace does God Himself make union for them. (9)
(29.30)

The ego-centred man studies scriptures and is known as a Pandit:
But involved in Duality he only gets suffering.
Overwhelmed with such poison all discrimination he lacks,
And keeps circling in transmigration. (1)
May I be a sacrifice time and again to those uniting with the Supreme through suppression of egoism:
Their hearts attuned to God's service—
Joy in God they quaff evermore. (I-Pause)
Study of scriptures brings not joy in God—
Such only brings disputation, deluded by Maya.
The unenlightened are ever in darkness—
The God-inspired, realizing God, laud Him. (2)
Expressing the inexpressible makes language beautiful;
Through enlightenment the mind loves Truth.
The enlightened contemplate day and night on Truth alone—
Their hearts in Truth dyed. (3)
Those dyed in Truth are in love with it.
Those thus endowed experience no sorrow in their lives.
Through the Master's Word is realized Truth Immortal, whose realization brings joy. (4)
Those in love with Truth remain unsoiled by falsehood and evil;
Day and night are their selves awake by divine grace.
The Name immaculate in their selves is lodged,
In the Divine Light is their light merged. (5)
One with learning involved in the Three Qualities knows not the Essence.
Deluded away from Truth, he realizes not the Master's Word;

Delusion grips him, rendering him blind—
Through the Master's Word alone is the Lord realized. (6)
The scriptures proclaim, the Three Qualities attach to Maya.
This the ego-centred man realizes not, gripped by Duality.
Those with learning involved in the Three Qualities realize not the sole Supreme Being—
Their ignorance bringing on suffering. (7)
God makes union as it may please Him:
Through the Master's Word are annulled doubt and suffering.
Saith Nanak: True greatness inheres in devotion to the Name—
One with faith in the Name gets bliss. (8)
(30.31)

He is Himself the Unattributed and the Attributed—
Only one who realizes His Essence is a true scholar,
Such a one, lodging the Lord's Name in the self,
Shall swim across Himself and his tribe. (1)
May I be a sacrifice time and again to those tasting joy in God,
And finding in it fulfilment.
Those testing joy in God are rendered immaculate,
Through contemplating the immaculate Name. (I-Pause)
One contemplating the holy Word is freed of the consequences of deeds;
Such a one realizing the Essence in his self
Suppresses his egoism:
He shall obtain the blessing of the Name and the Nine Treasures,
And effacing the Three Qualities, in the Supreme shall be absorbed. (2)
One in the grip of egoism shall not be rid of his deeds;
Only by divine grace is egoism discarded.
With a discriminating mind should one contemplate the self,
And through the Master's word chant divine laudation. (3)
The Lord is a sacred Pool and Lake—
His devotees pick up pearls from inside these, thus obtaining realization:
Day and night bathing in its waters, shedding the impurity of egoism. (4)
Through love and devotion is the self rendered pure,
And, suppressing the ego, is immersed in the Divine Lake.
Day and night to the Word are they devoted, (5)
And in the Divine Lake find lodgement,
The egoism is everlastingly the impure crane—

Despite all his bathing, his impurity is not shed.
The impurity of egoism is removed through dying to the world,
And the Master's Word contemplating. (6)
The wealth of the jewel devotion is obtained from within the self,
By listening to the holy Master's Word,
By the Master's grace was the derkness lifted,
And by the illumination within was the true self visioned. (7)
The Lord Himself creates and cherishes all;
One serving the Lord alone is entered into the blessed reckoning.
Saith Nanak : As the Name enters the self,
By divine grace is the Lord realized. (8)
(31.32)

The whole world is in the grip of Maya-delusion:
All Creation coloured by the Three Qualities is by Maya deluded.
Rare is the person who realizes Truth by Divine grace
And in the Fourth State is absorbed. (1)
May I be a sacrifice time and again to those burning away Maya delusion in the holy Word.
One burning Maya-delusion can alone be devoted to the Lord
And at the Portal of the Divine Mansion be exalted. (I-Pause)
Maya is the origin too of gods and godesses
As also of Smritis and Shastras;
Lust and violence are pervasive over the earth;
The whole world in the cycle of birth and death is in grip of suffering. (2)
In the world is lodged too the sole jewel of Realization,
That may find lodgement in the self by divine grace.
One observing chastity, purity and restraint alone can meditate on the Lord's Name. (3)
The self-female is by delusion gripped in her parents' home,
And caught in delusion, lives to be full of regrets after.
Such a one forfeits blessing in this world and the next,
And even in dream comes not to her joy. (4)
In her father's home let the Woman bear in her thoughts her lord,
Whom by divine grace will she ever find by her side.
Let her keep dyed in joy of her lord,
Wearing the holy Word as her true decoration. (5)
Blessed is the human birth of those realizing the holy Lord,
And burning Duality in the Masters' Word.

The sole Lord pervades their whole being,
And in holy company His laudation they chant. (6)
One without devotion to the holy Lord, worthless is his sojourn on earth,
A shame on his life that is a waste.
The egoist forgetful of the Name—
Without the Name is subject to endless suffering. (7)
He Who Created the universe alone,
Himself makes union for the devotee through realization of the holy Word.
Saith Nanak: Only such have been blessed with devotion to the Name,
As bear on their forehead the holy Writ from the primal hour. (8)
(32.33)

(The Ashtpadis (Octets) of
Guru Amar Das's compositions close here.)

Next follows an Octet of the Composition of Guru Ram Das

The Primal Purusha is beyond and reach;
Himself He creates and after Creation, dissolves.
He alone pervades all existence—
One turning towards Him gets true glory. (1)
May I be a sacrifice time and again to those meditating on the
Name of the Formless:
Neither has He form nor feature,
Yet is seen pervading all Creation—
By devotion is the Inaccessible approached. (I-Pause)
Thou art the Lord merciful and gracious—
None other than Thou has such power.
Through the Preceptor's grace is devotion acquired.
And by meditation is the seeker into his reality merged. (2)
Thou alone art verily the Creator;
Thy treasures with devotion are full.
As through devotion meditation on the Name is acquired,
The self is ever in the state of absorption. (3)
May I Lord! Ever chant Thy laudation.
Beloved! Ever may my tongue praise Thee!
Nothing do I crave but devotion to Thee,
That by the Master's grace is acquired. (4)
Inaccessible, unknowable Thou,
Beyond computation;
By grace dost Thou unite to Thyself the devotee.

Through the Word given by the holy Master may one meditate on Thee—
Such meditation as brings bliss. (5)
The praiseworthy tongue alone utters Thy praises;
Such laudation as pleases the holy Eternal,
Through devotion is such tongue ever dyed in ecstasy,
And by union with the eternal acquires glory. (6)
The ego-centred man acts from egoism;
His whole life lost as on a gambler's throw:
In his mind are centred greed and utter darkness.
And in transmigration he whirls about. (7)
The Creator alone confers greatness,
On those bearing His primal Writ.
Saith Nanak : One acquring the Name, annuller of fear,
Through devotion to the Master's word acquires bless. (8)
(1.34)

(Next follow four Octets of the composition of Guru Arjan Dev. The pattern of rhyming and the scheme of the preceding stanzas are followed in two of these- Nos. 35 and 37.)

Pervading all Creation is the Lord, inaccessible, unknowable;
The jewel-Name has been placed in a secret place within the self;
The Lord, inaccessible, unknowable, highest of all—
Through the holy Preceptor's Word alone may be approached.
(1)

May I be a sacrifice time and again to the Master,
Revealing the holy Name in the Dark Kali Age.
The cherished devotees of God, whose sole prop is the Eternal—
By supreme good fortune is their sight granted. (I-Pause)
The Lord, for a sight of whom yoga-practitioners and accomplished yogis wander about,
And on whom Brahmas and Indras meditate in their souls,
Thirty-three crores of deities seek Him—
Yet those listening to the Master's teaching laud Him in their hearts.
(2)

Day and night the wind the Names utters;
The earth is Thy handmaiden;
In all species and their speech art Thou pervasive,
And of all beloved.
The holy Lord through the Master alone is known;
Through the holy Preceptor's Word realized.

Those quaffing this joy are filled,
Satiated with the fare of holy Truth. (4)
Those fixed in God's abode alone are happy,
Disporting themselves in joys manifold.
One with mind fixed on God's feet alone
Is rich, master of true wealth. (5)
Thou hast first apportioned to each creature its wherewithal,
Then brought it into being.
None, Lord! is bountiful as Thou art—
None Thy equal. (6)
Only one pleasing Thee in meditation on Thee engages,
And in living the teaching of the holy.
Such a one getting liberated himself,
Liberates also all his tribe—
None to bar his way at the divine Portal. (7)
Thou art great, higher than the highest,
Infinite, immeasurable Thy greatness
May Nanak, servant of thy servants.
Be a sacrifice to Thee!
(8)
(1.35)

Who is truly liberated? Who truly with God united ?
Who is the illuminated one ?
Who the true exponent of scriptures ?
Who is the householder? Who the world-renouncer?
Who has realized God's greatness ? (1)
How is one bound, how liberated ?
How are birth and rebirth annulled ?
Who in Karma engaged? Who has broken free of it ?
Who in divine laudation engaged ? (2)
Who is joyful? Who sorrowful ?
On whom shines God's presence? Who from it far ?
How with God be united? How be thrown apart ?
Who to make this manifest ? (3)
What the Word to still the restless mind ?
What the teaching whereby joy and sorrow it bears alike ?
What the path leading to meditation on God ?
To chanting His praise ? (4)
Those God-instructed are liberated;
Those God-instructed with Him united.

Those God-instructed are illuminated;
Of scriptures the true exponents.
Blessed are the God-instructed—
Be they householders or anchorites;
To them has realization of His greatness came, (5)
Those by egoism gripped are bound,
The God-instructed liberated.
On the God-instructed is the birth-cycle annulled.
Of the God-instructed the Karma is liberated—
The God-instructed is of Karma liberated—
His Karma from divine will arising. (6)
The-instructed are truly joyful, egoists miserable.
The Divine Vision to the God-instructed is manifest,
From the egoist turned away.
The God-instructed are truly united;
To the God-instructed is known the path of renunciation. (7)
To the God instructed is revealed the Word that the restless mind stills,
To the God-instructed is granted the teaching enabling them to bear joy and sorrow alike.
To the God-instructed is revealed the way to meditation on the Supreme;
To chanting God's praise. (8)
Himself has He fashioned all;
By His will he created everything :
Himself He turned into innumerable forms;
Into Him shall all these be merged. (9)
(2.36)

What anxiety for one by the Eternal Master befriended ?
With help from the Lord, Master of all Bliss, for man is joy abounding.
Bestower of life, breath, honour joy;
Our happiness in Thy will lies. (1)
May I be a sacrifice time and again to those offering devotion to God with heart and soul.
Thou my firm mountain-prop, my shelter—
None like unto Thee! (I-Pause)
One to whom in Thy doings lies joy,
Has truly visioned the transcendent Absolute in all Creation.
All places are filled by Thee and Thee alone—
All manifestation is Thine alone. (2)
Thou the Bestower of all boons;

Of those devoted to Thee are the treasures overflowing.
In Thy grace hast Thou saved such:
Through supreme good fortune are they merged in Thee. (3)
Thy devotees dost Thou pull out of the dark Maya-cavern,
By Thy grace hast Thou cast Thy glance of favour on those that serve Thee.
Those that laud the eternal Lord, perfect,
Inexhaustible is their bliss in devotion. (4)
Thou the protector Here and Hereafter
In the mother's womb too art Thou cherisher;
The Maya-flame touches not those
That dyed in joy of Thee laud Thee.
What power in me to contemplate and state Thy qualities?
In the self Thee alone do I view.
Thou art friend, cherisher, Lord:
Except Thee, none else do I know. (6)
One under Thy wing
Untouched by suffering remains.
Thou the true prop and bestower of joy—
Through meditation in holy company revealed. (7)
Thou art all-Highest, unencompassable, immeasurable, of value inestimable;
Thou the holy Lord, I Thy slave;
Thou the Master, holy Thy suzerainty—
Nanak is repeatedly a sacrifice to Thee. (8)
(3.37)

Meditate unceasingly on God,
From the mind never putting Him away.
Seek company of those to God devoted,
Thus avoid treading the way to Yama.
Take with you God's Name as provision for your life's journey—
Thus shall your family escape the stigma of blame. (1)
Those contemplating the Lord,
Shall escape being cast into hell.
Those lodging God in their selves shall not feel on them the blast of host air. (2)
They alone have true beauty,
Who frequent holy company,
Those garnering the wealth of God's Name,
Alone are truly and profoundly wise. (3)
Quaff the Amrita and miracle-juice of God's Name,

And live by the sight of God's devotees;
Worship at the feet of the holy Preceptor—
Thus shall you obtain all boons. (4)
Only such meditate on the Lord
As are owned by the Lord.
He alone is the hero and of the elect,
On whose forehead is recorded good fortune. (5)
I have found on contemplating the Lord in my mind:
Such joy in God only the true kings among men may enjoy,
They from whom evil never proceeded,
The river of existence have crossed through their good deeds. (6)
One lodging in his self the Creator,
Has truly plucked the reward of his human birth,
The Lord-spouse is truly the Beloved,
With whom thy marital blessing eternal shall be. (7)
Under shelter of the Annuller of fear
Have I found the eternal Bliss.
Saith Nanak : He saves those clinging to His scarf.
Such have verily salvaged their invaluable human birth. (8)
(4.38)

ELUCIDATORY NOTE ON *ASHTPADIYAN MAHALLA III* IN RAGA MAJH

Ashtpadi (of eight stanzas) is a form of composition in which groups of eight stanzas, built on a certain set pattern, are included. The nearest English equivalent for Ashtpadi would be octet, which is the term used in discussing the units of this composition. Ashtpadis in the *Adi Granth* are placed in each Raga, according to the order observed in the Scripture, towards the close, after other forms of composition falling within that Raga have been recorded. The sequence, according to the precedence of the Gurus whose composition these are, is observed, beginning, of course, with Guru Nanak.

Guru Amar Das has left a comparatively large body of hymns and pieces, which were found recorded in the Pothis or manuscripts got prepared by him, containing a great deal of the matter that was incorporated later into the *Adi Granth*. Appearing at a period in the history of the Sikh faith, when its doctrines and spiritual bases were taking shape, he evidently composed fairly voluminous holy texts, to supplement what had been left by Guru Nanak. Guru Angad, the second Apostle, has left behind a very slender volume of hymnology. Guru Amar Das, whose compositions breathe fervent and unparalleled reverence for his Preceptor, Guru Angad, in this composition followed the stylistic pattern set in an

Ashtpadi of Guru Nanak's composition, which stands at the head of this work. In that Ashtpadi, as in all the others following, there is an opening verse, announcing the particular facet of the spiritual experience adumbrated in the verses to follow. Next is an expression of self-dedicatory fervour, in a two-line verse, yearning to sacrifice oneself to those devotees who have lived up to the ideal enumerated in the opening verse. This second verse ends in a rhyme which is adopted throughout the work to echo in this particular verse in each respective Ashtpadi. Then follow seven verse-pieces, each of three or four lines, amplifying the theme indicated in the opening verse. This is some aspect of the practice of devotion, falling within the spiritual path called *Sahj,* which is the path of prayer and meditation, devotion and supplication for divine grace, in contradistinction to ritual, yoga-practice or any other path involving what may be called Sadhana or 'praxis.' Sahj is explained in its etymology as 'that which is born with the individual, in other words, the method or way that is not 'forced' or artificially formulated as in so many creeds. In the Sikh religion Sahj is one of the cardinal doctrines and its amplification and elucidation directly or indirectly forms one of the principal themes of *Gurubani*. After its elucidation in Guru Nanak, who uses the term itself sparingly, Guru Amar Das in his compositions has taken up the elucidation of the term on an ample scale, and in the work under discussion along with others of his compositions, it may be met with repeatedly. Since there is perhaps no particularly felicitous English equivalent for this term, it has to be interpreted as 'poise,' 'devotion,' 'spontaneous meditation,' 'absorption' and in such other terms according to the context— a clear evidence of the vastness of connotations attaching to this term. And to repeat, Sahj forms one of the principal themes in Guru Amar Das's *Bani.*

This work gives evidence of being structured after a 'guided' and conscious inspiration. Unlike numerous other portions of the *Gurubani,* where the inspiration has a free flow, not regulated by the demands of the poetic structuring, in this work each Ashtpadi is built round a particular vision which finds ample expression in the course of its eight verses. There is a gradual transition of vision from Ashtpadi to Ashtpadi. This will be evident to the attentive reader on careful study.

The themes on which these Octets are built are the same as form the basis of the Sikh faith in the rest of the corpus of its sacred literature. Only here they find a somewhat greater reiteration, as in point of historical time, after Guru Nanak, Guru Amar Das must have taken it upon himself to elucidate further what in Guru Nanak's *Bani* finds a highly compact expression, often elliptic, not achieving full grammatical form of lucid prose statement. This highly compact and symbolical structure in Guru Nanak makes the study of his compositions a task for minds highly inspired to interpret the mystic word. Guru Amar das is usually lucid, though in him too the inner relationships of sentence to sentence have very often to be established after careful thought. This is the usual way that inspired expression takes, as not being bound to take the form that plan statement does.

While like his two holy predecessors, Guru Amar Das emphasizes the barrenness of ritual and the processes of the praxis, particularly of Hatha yoga, and inculcates the pursuit of the path of Sahj to which reference has been made earlier, the themes that find particularly forceful emphasis in him are as follows: The most prominent and repeatedly iterated of these is grace. Grace is conceived of not only as indispensable for 'liberation,' but its mystic nature is further emphasized by a process of divine 'election' of the individual self to be visited by grace. Such election is stated to be from the primal hour, and while some are fortunate in being recipients of grace, others are, so to say, primally deluded. But the doctrine of Karma, on which in the Guru's teaching emphasis is laid everywhere, makes out grace to be 'earned merit,' the result of the devotion and good actions of previous births, whose memory is nowise retained by the individual self, and whose process is hidden by the mists which engulf all that is created; but from whose operation the Creator is exempt, being *Akal* (beyond time). Grace does not operate in the way of a sudden descent of liberation, but its manifestation is in the union of the self with the holy Preceptor, the Guru, whose Word liberates. The Guru, truly so called, is integral to the process of working out liberation. The Guru, however, is not an intercessor as in certain other creeds, but is what his name indicates, the guide to devotion and the way of Sahj which should lead to liberation. So, the twofold emphasis on grace and the Guru must in no way be missed. These two terms must, however, be understood as clarified briefly just above.

Other themes are the joy and bliss that come in life through devotion and the agony and suffering that involvement with Maya or Duality brings, despite apparent worldly success. There is mention of the agent of retribution, Yama, whose image, however, remains symbolic as embodying the principle of the fruits of Karma which nowise may be ignored. The figure of Yama is not concretized or dramatised as in Puranic Hinduism. There is mention of the human tendency of neglect of devotion, the sliding again and again into evil and of the final goal in life to be achieved--spiritual poise wherein man transcends the worldly conditions of pleasure and pain, and stays in a state of equable calm. All these experiences are expressed in an idiom with which the ardent student of the Guru's teaching must familiarise himself. In the footnotes aids are provided for translating the original imagery into forms of expressing that the modern reader may find more familiar. The difference between the expression achieved in the rendering of the *Bani* and the literal translation should be noted in all cases. That will help deeper understanding and make for greater clarity.

There is in the text a twofold scheme of numbering : There is the total of the Ashtpadis recorded at the end of each, preceeded by another number pointing out the total of the authorship of Guru Amar Das. Thus 19.20, for example, would emphasize that until that point, the total number of Ashtpadis recorded is twenty with nineteen of Guru Amar Das's authorship—one at the opening being of Guru Nanak's composition. The numbering in the *Adi Granth* is highly systematized and meticulous and helps to locate each verse with precision. This would help the seeker to realize the careful devotion with which the Scripture has been composed.

From Var Majh Mahalla I
Slokas of Guru Amar Das's Composition

One born in fear of *God* and dying in such fear;
Bearing in his heart fear of God—
Saith Nanak, one dying with fear of God in him,
His human birth is fruitful.
One living without fear of *God* with abundance of pleasure to his share—
Saith Nanak, one dying without fear of *God*.
In shame will die. (XXV. P. 149)

Note : These Slokas occur towards the close in a longer composition-The *Var* in the measure Majh.

In Raga Gauri—Composition of Guru Amar Das— Chaupade ((Quartets) by Grace of Sole Supreme Being; Realized by the Preceptor's Grace

The Preceptor's touch brings about union with the Lord:
Such company too is found as God wills.
The Lord Himself knows how best to bring about Union—
By Divine Ordinance does Union come.
And through the Word is He realized. (1)
Through fear of God is lifted fear of the *world* and illusion:
One immersed in fear of God in joy in Truth is absorbed. (1-Pause)
Through the Preceptor's company, the Lord takes abode spontaneously in the heart.
Of immense worth is the Lord,
Immeasurable His greatness.
His immensity may through the holy Word be lauded—
Thus may the gracious Lord grant liberation. (2)
Through the holy Rreceptor's company is wisdom aroused,
And in the purified mind is lodged God's truth.
Through truth lodged in the mind are all actions rendered pure:
Noble actions joined to contemplation of the *holy word* are joined. (3)
Through the Preceptor's inspiration, holy service is rendered to *God:*
Rare are those realizing God's truth through divine inspiration.
Long live the bestower of this blessing:
Saith Nanak : *Through his grace* love for God's Name be inspired:
(1.21)

In the Raga Gauri Guarari-Composition of Guru Amar Das

Rare are those that from the Preceptor get realization—
Only those acquiring such realization are of truly fruitful *lives*.
From the preceptor come spiritual poise and truthful thinking;
Through supreme good fortune is the Preceptor met,
From whom comes illumination and absorption it truth. (I-Pause)
Union with the Preceptor assuages the fire of desire,
Through the Preceptor is peace lodged in the mind.
Through the Preceptor is acquired purity, holiness sanctity.
Through the Preceptor is does union with the holy Word come about.
One without the Preceptor in doubt and delusion is involved; (2)
Without devotion to the Name comes immense suffering.
One devoted to the Preceptor alone is absorbed in meditation.
Has vision of the Lord eternal,
And acquires true glory. (3)
Whom to supplicate? God alone is the real Bestower.
By His grace alone does union through the holy Word come about.
May I laud the Eternal in the loved Master's company!
This is Nanak's prayer: May I get absorbed in holy Truth. (2.22)
(In the measure Gauri Guarari—Composition of Guru Amar Das)
Holy is the spot where the mind is purified;
Truthful is the mind that in truth lodges.
The holy Word through the Four Ages lasts.
The holy Eternal is almighty, absolute. (1)
Through good fortune comes union with holy company,
Where one may settle to laud the Lord (I-Pause)
May the tongue burn that utters thoughts of Duality,
That tastes not joy in God and speaks worthless words.
Without realization mind and body are of no worth.
One without devotion to the Name in sorrow and tears leaves this life. (2)
Spontaneously, the tongue tastes of joy in God,
And by the Preceptor's grace in truth is absorbed.
Through meditation on the holy Preceptor's Word is the tongue dyed in devotion to God,
And tastes of the stream of Amrita. (3)
Only in a fit vessel will pour the Name,
Nothing will stay in a utensil turned upside down.
Through the Preceptor's teaching is God's Name in the mind lodged.
Saith Nanak: Holy is the vessel that thirsts for the holy Word. (3.23)

Gauri Guarari-Composition of Guru Amar Das

Some chant God's laudation,
Yet their heart *therein* finds no joy.
Those chanting with hearts full of egoism,
Their labour is of no avail.
True chanting is of those bearing devotion to the holy Name:
Theirs is the holy text and true contemplation. (1)
Laudation comes to those with whom the Preceptor is pleased;
Their mind and body dyed in devotion, by the holy Name glorified.
(I Pause)

Some sing, while others do miming-
None without devotion realization finds.
True performance through love of the Master's Word comes,
With the Lord ever in the heart lodged. (2)
The ignorant performing mines only expose their folly
Their dancing and capering only bring them suffering abounding.
In dancing and capering lies not devotion:
One dying in the holy Word alone to devotion attains. (3)
The Lord, Beloved of His devotees, Himself prompts devotion,
True devotion in shedding egoism lies.
To the holy Lord all ways are known—
Liberation from realizing holy Truth comes. (4)
(4.4.24)

In the Measure Gauri Guarari—Composition of Guru Amar Das

Suppression of desires ends wandering of mind:
Without such death no realization comes.
Few know of the medicine obtained through suppression of desire.
Only as desire in the holy Word dies, does realization come (1)
He confers greatness on whoso wins His grace:
Through the Preceptor's grace does the Lord find lodgement in the self.
(I Pause)

Only when through holy instruction man performs *good actions,*
Does he have true understanding of his self.
The self is self-opinionated, like a mad tusker:
The Preceptor by his pike-stroke grants him true life. (2)
The self unteachable is hard to control.
Only by treading the untrodden way is it rendered pure.
By Godward-turning is the self ennobled,
And sheds off egoism and evil inclinations. (3)

Those united to God from Primal Time,
Never are alienated,
And in the holy Word remain absorbed.
The Lord alone knows His mystery.
Saith Nanak: Only by listening to the Preceptor's teaching,
Does one get realization. (4.5.25)
The whole word in egoism's grip is mad,
And caught in Duality in illusion is lost.
Man involved in anxiety knows not himself—
Engaged in lust for lucre are his days passed. (1)
Brother! Meditate on God with your whole self,
By Godward turning the tongue tastes of joy in God. (I - Pause)
One who turning Godward sees the Lord in his self,
By his devotion to the Lord, life of the Universe,
His fame in all Four Ages in spread:
Suppressing his ego, the Preceptor's Word has he realized.
This Lord, Dispenser of Rewards, on him showers grace. (2)
Those alone are pure and holy as through the holy Word, with God are united.
Their restless minds restrained and composed.
From the Master have they acquired the holy Name, repository of Nine Treasures:
By divine grace is the Lord in their selves lodged. (3)
By meditating on God come joy and peace in life.
With the Lord's Name in the self lodged,
Yama's tortures are kept away.
The Lord is Himself King and counsellor.
Nanak! Serve thou ever the Lord,
Repository of noble qualities, (4.6.26)

(Gauri Guarari, M.III)

Why neglect Him who is Lord of self and life ?
Why neglect Him who pervades all-
By serving whom comes from the Divine Portal the Instrument of Honour? (1)
May I be a sacrifice to the Lord's Name!
Forgetting Thee is to me death. (I Pause)
Those forget Thee whom Thou has in Duality Thou hast involved.
The egoist ignorant of God in transmigration is involved. (2)
Those with whom He is mighty pleased are assigned the Preceptor's service-
By Godward turning in the holy Name are they absorbed. (3)
Those with merit garnered turn towards Godrealization;

Those with merit garnered suppress the ego.
Saith Nanak: May I be a sacrifice to those dyed in devotion to the Name.
(7.27)

(Gauri Guareri, M. III)

Inexpressible art Thou: How to express Thee ?
By the chemical of the holy Name lodged in the self.
Innumerable Thy attributes, beyond valuation. (1)
The holy Word in God is absorbed-
Through the Preceptor's Word is Thy inexpressible greatness expressed.
(I-Pause)
Wherever is the Lord, there are set up the holy congregations.
Wherever is the holy Preceptor, spontaneously is He lauded;
Wherever is the holy Master, there lie burnt all thought of egoism. (2)
One turning Godward in devotion to the Divine Mansion finds admittance;
By Divine prompting is God's Name lodged in the self.
By Divine prompting is the devotee in the holy Name absorbed. (3)
He is the sole Bestower of *boons*
As devotion to the perfect Master is inspired.
Saith Nanak: True victors are those dyed in the Name. (4)
(8.28)

(Gauri Guareri, M. III)

All forms and figures from the One Sole Supreme have emanated.
From union of air, water, fire, has *the world been* manifested.
The varied Creation under the Lord's eye lies. (1)
The one inscrutable Being, One and Sole—
Only one by the Master's guidance may contemplate Him. (1-Pause)
The Lord has eternally moved in all space;
All is His wonderful plan,
Manifest and unmanifest.
He Himself awakens the self asleep. (2)
None His Worth may know,
Though all may seek to express it in words.
Only one absorbed in the Divine Word may realize Him. (3)
One listening to His greatness may have a sight of Him—
United by the holy Word.
From service to the holy Preceptor comes exaltation.

Saith Nanak: Those dyed in the Name,
Are in His contemplation absorbed (4)

(9.29)

(Gauri Guareri, M. III)

The egoist in stupor of *Maya* illusion and attachment is asleep:
Awake are thé God-directed, contemplating
His qualities and seeking enlightenment.
Such alone awake as to the holy Name are attached. (1)
One awakened in enlightenment never again falls into sleep.
Rare is the man who takes instruction from the holy Preceptor,
And realization finds. (I-Pause)
The impious and raw in mind acquire realization never:
One on combating *Maya* lives the Word.
Never do the purblind unenlightened attain *nearness* to God. (2)
In this Age devotion to God is the way to liberate.
Rare is the man who the Master's Word contemplates.
Liberated himself, his associates too he carries to liberation. (3)
In this Kali Age little practice of piety is there—
Kali is born of low unclean ancestry.
Saith Nanak: None ever without *devotion* to the Name attained liberation. (4)

(10.30)

(Gauri Guareri, M. III)

Holy is His ordinance and holy His rule.
With the mind sincerely dyed in the Lord, Who is above want,
Man would be absorbed in the holy Mansion and holy Name. (1)
Listen, my self! to the holy Word and contemplate it:
Repeat the holy Name, thus crossing the ocean of worldliness. (I-Pause)

In illusion is man born and in illusion dies;
In Duality is the manifestation of this world.
The egoist forgetful of God, remains involved in transmigration. (2)
Has man deluded himself or is he by the Lord deluded?
The egoist's self-serves alien *Gods;*
This brings him immense suffering and waste of human life. (3)
The holy Preceptor through grace unites man with God;

Enjoining on him meditation on the Sole Name of God, thus lifting illusion.
Saith Nanak: To one contemplating the Name come the Nine Treasures. (4)
(11.31)

(Gauri Guareri, M. III)

Ask about the bliss enjoyed by those who by the Master's guidance on God have meditated.
Devotion to the Lord gives poise to the mind.
Such alone are truly rich as have laboured in meditation on the Name:
From the Master perfectly endowed comes enlightenment to them. (1)
Brother! meditate on the Name Divine.
Service of God brings unfailingly its reward. (I-Pause)
By realizing the self is the mind purified :
Such a one attains to liberation in life and to the Lord.
Through Divine laudation is understanding exalted,
And the seeker spontaneously into God is merged. (2)
With duality service of God cannot be:
Such a one gripped in egoism and Maya feeds on virulent poison.
Maya deludes man in the shape of progeny, family, home.
The egoist purblind in transmigration remains involved. (3)
Truly noble is one to whom is given the Name Divine :
And who day after day performs devotion through the Master's Word.
Rare is the God-inspired man to whom realization comes. (4)
(12.32)

(Gauri Guareri, M. III)

In all Four Ages has devotion to the Master been performed—
Only the noble spirits in devotion have been engaged.
Wealth of the Name is inexhaustible, unending—
Those garnering it have found perpetual bliss here and glory at the Portal Divine. (1)
My self! enter not into doubt-
Through Divinely inspired devotion quaff the Juice of Immortality. (1-Pause)

Those serving the holy Master are reckoned great in the world;
Liberated themselves, have they brought liberation to the relations.
Those bearing the Lord's Name in their hearts,
And dyed in the Name, cross the ocean of worldliness. (2)

God's servants ever serve Him with their hearts,
Their egoism suppressed,their heart's lotus is a-bloom :
The Divine minstrelsy they listen and abide in their true self—
Dyed in the Name, are they true recluses even with home and family.
Those serving the Lord, holy is their utterance, (3)
That in all ages is spoken by God's devotees.
Day after day on the Lord of the Universe they meditate.
Saith Nanak: Those dyed in the Name are immaculate, liberated. (4)
(13.33)

(Gauri Guareri, M. III)

By Supreme good fortune and auspicious conjuction of stars in the holy Master met;
By union with him in the Name in the heart lodged,
And the Divine nectar quaffed. (1)
By the Master's guidance is man given to meditation on the Name Divine,
Whereby fulfilling himself in life may he win devotion for reward.
(I-Pause)

All illumination, meditation lies in absorption in the delectable holy Word Divine:
This by the Master's grace a rare one alone tastes. (2)
One performing multiple ritual practice
Divorced from devotion these strengthen egoism, bringing ignominy. (3)
Such a one, bound in Maya's noose-
Saith Nanak, finds liberation through illumination by the Master given. (4)
(14.34)

(Gauri Guareri, M. III)

Behold rain-clouds in showers falling on the earth—
There is water too in the soil,
Water appears in the soil in wells:
From the sky it rains, without feet hovering over. (1)
Brother! Remove all thy doubt;
All that happens is by His Will:
In the end all in Him are absorbed (I-Pause)

Beings male and female created by Thee engage in all manner of *Karma*—
Yet all diverse forms are Thine, and in the end in Thee are absorbed.
(2)

For countless births had they forgotten Him.
As illumination came, never after was darkness.
Only those absorbed in the Master's Word find enlightenment,
Should they in the Master's Word be absorbed. (3)
In Thy Word lies Thy essence,
Let there be no doubt thereafter.
Saith Nanak: Essence in Essence is absorbed-
Whereafter closes the cycle of rebirth (4)

(1.se 15.35)

(Gauri Bairagani, M. III)

The whole world to death is subject,
And in thoughts of Duality is bound.
Those indifferent to God, acting from egoism at the Divine Portal bear chastisement. (1)
My self! Fix thy heart in devotion to God's feet:
By the Master's guidance acquire treasure of the Name,
Which in the Hereafter shall liberate.
The eighty-four lakh species, deluded by stubbornness of egoism,
Are born and reborn:
Contemplating near the Preceptor's Word, their transmigration is ceaseless. (2)
When by the Master's guidance is the self-visioned,
God's Name a place in the heart finds.
Immersed ever in devotion bliss comes from attachment to the Lord (3)
As desires in the holy Word die, comes honour;
Egoism is shed and evil courses discarded.
Saith Nanak: by good fortune alone are found attachment to God,
And the treasure of devotion. (4)

(2.6.36)

(Gauri Bairagani, M. III)

Brief is one's sojourn in this life—
Such is each creature's destiny recorded by the hand of God.
The noble woman by the Master's guidance lauds the Lord.
One remembering the Lord's qualities in the father's home shall find happy stay in the husband's.
Spontaneous shall be their absorption in God,
And love for the Lord in their hearts shall abide. (1)
In this world and the next abides the Lord.

By what device may He be found ?
He is immaculate, inaccessible-
Himself shall He grant union (I-Pause)

Himself the Lord prompts devotion to His Name.
By supreme good fortune is the holy Preceptor met,
Offering the cup of Amrita,
Whereby are egoism and dualism shattered
And the mind in poise is absorbed in bliss.
He the sole cause-of all,
Himself He inspires devotion. (2)
The egoist ignorant, of small understanding, finds not union because of his pride:
He serves not the holy Master—
His life a continuing regret.
Such take birth again and again, and in this cycle are destroyed.
Such is the Creator's Will that the egoists must Whirl about in transmigration. (3)
The Lord has recorded in the primal hour each creature's full destiny:
Those engaging in contemplation of God's Name shall find the holy Preceptor.
God's Name is my father, mother, friend, brother.
May the Lord in His grace grant union with Nanak, a humble worm. (4)
(3.17.37)

(Gauri Bairagani, M. III)

As enlightenment from the Preceptor was obtained.
Was the Divine Essence contemplated;
Then was the foulness of understanding exposed through meditation on God's Name.
The Divine Principle effaced traces of Maya, and all darkness was lifted.
Those on whose forehead the writ is inscribed from the Source,
Alone of God's Name are devoted. (1)
My devotee friends! by what device may God be found whose light is my life?
Without *sight* of the Lord I live not for one instant.
Grant me union with the holy preceptor,
That I may quaff the nectar divine. (I-Pause)

Ever do I laud the Lord, listen to His Name:
The Lord alone have I made my objective,
From the Preceptor have I found joy in God,
In which my whole self is absorbed.

Blessed by the Preceptor, holiest among men,
Who *to me* has granted the gift of devotion.
That Preceptor have I adopted from whom I found the way to the Lord
(2)

The Lord God is bestower of merit-
We are full to the brim with sin.
The Lord by Divine inspiration has made sinners stone-heavy to swim across.
Thou Bestower of merit, immaculate, we are full to the brim with sin.
Lord! redeem us, come to Thee for succour—
Thou that hast saved those ignorant,
Of sleepy minds. (3)
Through the Master's guidance
And contemplation of the Lord,
Comes joy everlasting.
With the Lord God, my true friend,
Paeans of joy have I chanted.
Lord ? This is my supplication :
Show Thy mercy to me who have ever borne Thee in my mind.
Nanak, servant of God, seeks dust of the feet of those,
Who to the holy Lord have attained (4)
(4.18.38)
(Pages 157-163)

In the Measure Gauri Guareri Mahalla-III (Composition of Guru Amar Das)—Ashtpadian (Octets)

Duality is the mind's impurity :
Those lost in delusion in transmigration remain involved. (1)
Never is the egoist's impurity removed,
Till through devotion he engage not in the holy Word and God's Name.
(1-Pause)

All existence delusion-gripped impure,
Ever and again involved in the birth and death cycle. (2)
Fire, air, water all bear impurity;
All food consumed is impure. (3)
In the impure state no ritual worship may be performed—
Only when dyed in the Name is the mind purified. (4)
Impurity through devotion to the holy Preceptor is removed—
Through such devotion transmigration and death are annulled. (5)

The study of Scripture reveals :
Liberation only through devotion to the Name comes (6)
In all Four Ages the noblest path is devotion to the Name,
And contemplation of the holy Word.
Through Godward-turning alone may one find liberation in the Kali Yuga. (7)
The Lord holy, eternal dies not, nor undergoes birth and death.
Saith Nanak: By the Master's guidance is one in the Eternal absorbed. (8.1)

Devotion divinely inspired is life's true prop :
Keep lodged in the heart the holy Lord.
The God-inspired at the Eternal Portal find glory. (1)
Thou learned Brahmin! study devotion to God, Discard foul thinking,
By the Master's guidance given across the ocean of worldliness, (I-Pause)

By The Master's guidance is egoism from the mind removed;
To those Godward-turned no impurity attaches;
By Godward-turning is the holy Name lodged in the mind. (2)
By the Master's guidance are acquired holy action, *dharma* and truth;
By the Master's guidance are burnt away egoism and Duality.
By the Master's guidance is the *heart* dyed in the Name,
And bliss found. (3)
Instruct your mind, learn the truth about God;
None listens to what one *without enlightenment* may preach.
Learning God's truth brings imperishable joy. (4)
One ego-prompted makes show of piety and is full of cleverness—
His doings to the Lord are unacceptable.
Involved in transmigration, no rest he finds. (5)
One ego-prompted from pride acts;
His meditation false like the heron's—
His end regrets at Yama's chastisement. (6)
Liberation comes not without devotion to the holy master:
The Lord through grace of the Preceptor is found.
The Preceptor is eternally the bestower of *grace.* (7)
By the Master's guidance all honour and greatness, in devotion to the Name
is found.
Such destroy and cast off Maya, Ocean's daughter.
Saith Nanak: Without devotion, all intellectual feats are worthless. (8.2)

In the Measure Gauri—Composition of Guru Amar Das

Brother! Contemplate the religious practice appropriate to this age-
From the perfect Master does such awareness come :
In the Hear and Hereafter God's Name is our *true* friend. (1)
Repeat God's Name and contemplate on it.
By Divine grace will thus your impurity be removed. (I-Pause)
Not through disputation and opposition is He realized :
In Duality mind and body become joyless.
Only through the Master's Word does absorption in truth come. (2)
This world by egoism is fouled :
By constant bathing at holy spot egoism is not shed :
Without the Master's touch is one chastised by Yama. (3)
He alone is holy who suppresses egoism,
And guided by the Master's Word destroys the five evils.
Such a one is liberated himself and liberated are his family. (4)
Through Maya—delusion—is this magic show enacted :
In this are purblind egoists involved.
Those by the Master guided and contemplating Him by this are untouched. (5)
The hyprocrite like a showman assumes many guises.
Inside him is egoism and desire—
Not contemplating his self, has he lost the game of life. (6)
In assumed guises, he tries to play tricks,
Yet is he lost in *Maya*— delusion—and doubt :
Without devotion to the holy Preceptor comes to him much suffering. (7)
Those dyed in devotion are the real recluses
Who even when householders, are to holy truth devoted :
One devoted to the holy Master is truly fortunate. (8.3)
From Brahma has originated the study of Vedas:
From him too originated the Gods, imbued with attachment and desire:
Involved in Three Qualities they wander, not finding poise in their true selves. (1)
The Lord saved us through the holy Master's touch,
Who confirmed in us ceaseless devotion contemplation of the holy Name. (I-Pause)
Brahma's Word involved in Three Qualities is Yama's snare :
Those studying it are in disputation involved,
And are by Yama chastised.
Not contemplating the Essence, are they gathering bundles of straw. (2)
The egoist in ignorance traverses the false way;

Practising much ritual has he neglected the Name Divine,
And involved in Duality does he sink in the ocean of worldliness. (3)
One hankering after the world is styled *Pandit;*
Dyed in poison much suffering he gets:
Caught in yama's noose, death ever torments him. (4)
Death approaches not those *blessed* with divine guidance,
That burns away egoism and thoughts of Duality.
Dyed in the Name, such ever laud the Lord. (5)
Maya is handmaid to God's devotees and serves them;
Those touching their feet find liberation;
Ever pure, they find serenity and poise. (6)
Those listening to divine discourses are in the world truly rich--
All to them bow and *at their feet* worship :
In their mind, they ever laud the holy Lord. (7)
Through the teaching of the holy Master,
The Three Qualities got effaced and the self in the Fourth State was fixed.
Saith Nanak: Thus was egoism removed and union with the Absolute found. (8.4)

In the Measure Gauri — Composition of Guru Amar Das

Brahma from his study of Vedas only makes controversies:
His mind darkened, no self-realization has he.
Only through study of the holy preceptor's Word does one find the Lord (1)
Through devotion to the holy Preceptor one escapes death:
Egoists through Duality are destroyed. (I-Pause)
By the Master's guidance even sinners are purified;
Through the Preceptor's teaching their selves in poise are fixed.
The Lord through absorption of the Preceptor's Word is realized. (2)
The Lord himself brings about the seeker's union with the Preceptor:
Such blessing comes to those that please the holy Lord.
In spontaneous absorption the Lord they laud. (3)
Without guidance of the Preceptor is man lost in illusions:
The egoists purblind ever consume poison,
Bear Yama's chastisement and undergo suffering. (4)
One under the Lord's protection escapes yama:
Eliminating egoism, such in holy truth are absorbed.
Ever are their minds absorbed in the Lord's Name. (5)
Those serving the holy Lord are pure, immaculate.
One uniting his self with the Universal Self is man victor over the world.

Friend! Thus shalt thou be happy and blessed. (6)
One serving the holy Master shall find the true reward—
Bearing the Name in his heart, his ego shall be eliminated,
And the mystic melody shall from him rise. (7)
Brother ! On none has the holy Preceptor's teaching failed.
Purified through devotion, have they got glory at the Divine Portal.
Saith Nanak: Only through the Lord's holy Name does true glory come. (8.5)

Gauri Guareri* (contd.) *Ashtapadiyan

One expounding *tests based on* the Three Qualities is of illusion not divested;
His bonds not loosened, he finds not liberation;
In *this* Age the holy Preceptor alone is bestower of liberation. (1)
By the Master's guidance does man shed his illusion :
His self in poise, he to the Lord is attuned. (I-Pause)
One caught in the Three Qualities to death is subject;
He meditates not on the Reality that made all:
To death and life unending is he subjected. (2)
A Preceptor devoid of insight sheds not illusion;
Discarding the essence is he involved in Daulity :
Entranced by poison, in poison is he absorbed. (3)
The Creation in *Maya*—illusion—is caught, taking it to be real;
Caught in Duality on the Lord it neglects to *meditate.*
Only one favoured by Divine grace the Supreme State attains. (4)
Divine Truth operates within the mind and without operates—
This Truth by no effort remains concealed.
To the enlightened is it spontaneously revealed. (5)
The devotee in truth is absorbed;
His egoism and *Maya*—attachment by the holy Word is burnt away.
The holy Lord Himself to the devotee grants union. (6)
By the Lord uttered by the holy Preceptor, *bestower of Bliss.*
The restless mind finds peace and poise.
From the holy Master's *guidance,*
Is enlightenment attained. (7)
The sole Creator is He, who creates and destroys.
No other is *His rival.*
Saith Nanak: This truth the devotee alone may realize. (8.6)

By the Master's guidance is obtained devotion above all value ;
One devoted to the holy Name is spontaneously in the Name absorbed;
His tongue chants ever the Name immortal—

Such joy in God is attained only by one by Him favoured. (1)
Meditate ever on the Lord of the Universe with your hearts :
Thus by the Master's guidance shall ye attain the Supreme State of Bliss.
(I-Pause)

As bliss enters the heart and enlightens it,
Man by the Master's guidance lauds the holy Treasury of noble attributes,
And turns himself into the humblest of God's slaves :
Ever amidst involvement with his family, his is the state of renunciation.
(2)
Rare is the devotee attaining liberation while alive—
Such a one alone finds the Supreme Blessing:
His Three Qualities effaced, his self is rendered a pause,
With the holy Lord is he spontaneously united. (3)
As in the heart is the holy Lord lodged,
One loses attachment for one's relations :
As is the mind pierced with devotion by the Preceptor's guidance.
To it comes poise;
With understanding of the Divine Law, the supreme truth it realizes. (4)
Thou art the Creator, none other I worship.
From devotion to Thee comes true exaltation;
By Divine grace alone may one laud Him;
From the Jewel-Name is the entire universe illumined (5)
By the Preceptor's guidance is the holy Word rendered joyful;
The heart in bloom is ever in devotion fixed.
By Divine grace is holy truth attained spontaneously.
By supreme good fortune is the holy Master found. (6)
Egoism, attachment and agony of foul thinking are annulled,
As God's Name, repository of noble attributes, in the heart is lodged,
By the Preceptor's guidance is enlightenment and the Lord's laudation inspired;
And the heart joys in resting at Gods' feet. (7)
He alone finds devotion whom He *thus* favours.
By the Preceptor's guidance grants He union through discarding of egoism.
Then is the holy Name in the heart lodged.
Saith Nanak: Thus is man spontaneously in eternal Truth absorbed.
(8.7)

In the Measure Gauri—Composition of Guru Amar Das

Through holy fear of God and poise,

Has the mind purified itself:
Through fixed devotion is it dyed in the holy Word.
And by submitting to the Divine Will is in its eternal abode lodged. (1)
Through devotion to the holy Preceptor is egoism lifted,
And the Lord, Treasure of Noble Attributes, attained.
(I-Pause)

The mind under fear of God through absorption in the Divine Word,
Is the true ascetic
The Lord immaculate pervades all places—
Through the Master's grace is union with Him brought about. (2)
To the humblest servant of the Lord comes *true joy*.
By such device alone is *sight* of the Lord attained.
Only through Divine grace is one to his laudation inclined. (3)
Cursed be long life denuded of devotion to the Lord's Name;
Cursed be the luxurious bed inducing the dark passion of lust after woman:
Those alone have lives fulfilled who find shelter in the holy Name.
(4)

Cursed be absorption in relations and family,
Whereby is devotion to the Lord neglected.
He alone is our true friend who lauds God's attributes:
None but the Lord's Name is my support. (5)
From the holy Preceptor have I attained the pure life and exaltation.
By meditation on the Lord's Name is all suffering effaced:
By absorption in the Lord's holy Name is found joy imperishable. (6)
By the Master's instruction have I learnt the truth of this living frame;
The flame of egoism's desire is extinguished.
All violence of mind gone, to compassion am I attached. (7)
The Lord by His grace alone confers the gift of devotion,
Rare is the devotee attaining this jewel *attained* by the Preceptor's guidance.
Nanak lauds the Lord unattainable and unencompassable. (8.8)
(PP. 229-233)

In Measure Gauri Bairagan—Composition of Guru Amar Das

By the grace of the one indivisible Supreme, Being Lord Eternal.
Those turning away from the holy Preceptor
Bear aspects God denying and evil ;
Ever are they chastised in bonds.
Never again attaining the human incarnation. (1)
Lord! Succour me, through Thy grace succour me ;

The Lord, inspiring the heart of meditation on divine attributes,
The seeker to holy company inclines. (I-Pause)
Such devotees are favoured of the Lord as follow the way of devotion;
Who discarding egoism take to the path of service
And die to the world's desires. (2)
He who gave body and life is our true Lord.
Evil it is to cast Him from one's thoughts—
Ever must He in the heart be lodged. (3)
Through devotion to the Name comes exaltation;
Through meditation on the Name too comes joy;
From the holy Preceptor is acquired devotion—
Through grace is the Lord attained. (4)
Those indifferent to the holy Preceptor whirl ever in perturbation;
Rejected of earth and heaven, are they in filth absorbed. (5)
The world drugged with attachment,
In illusion is lost;
Those by the Preceptor instructed,
The *Maya*-taint escape. (6)
Those devoted to the holy Preceptor bear true aspect of beauty—
Their filth of egoism shed.
Those dyed in the Divine Word are truly *made* pure
Through obedience to the holy Preceptor's Will. (7)
The Lord is the sole Bestower.
Through grace He alone brings about union.
Nanak, His servant, seeks His shelter—
By His grace shall He succour him.

(8.1.9.27)
(PP. 233-234)

INTRODUCTORY NOTE ON CHHANT (LYRICS OF DIVINE LOVE) IN GAURI PURABI MAHALLA III

(Composition of Guru Amar Das)

Like the other compositions bearing the same title *(Chhant)* of the authorship of Guru Amar Das or of any of the other holy Gurus, the lyrical characteristic is prominent in these verse-pieces. In the mystical tradition of India, which was adopted by the Gurus as their mould of expression for devotion and yearning for union with the Supreme Being, in these pieces the seeker-self is personalized as the loving female, separated from her lord who has been called away from home in pursuit of his vocation, which in medieval India would be carrying merchandise or soldiering. The imagery of love, separation and passionate yearning for union is woven into the texture of these lyrics. Their mode is parallel to the chaste tradition of the romantic poetry of India, which was composed in the rising vernaculars of medieval India during the centuries of Muslim rule. Incidentally, the Muslim mystics (Sufis) of India also caught on this mode, so that in the entire popular poetry of Indian Sufism, the mystical ardour is expressed through personalization of the seeker as the devoted female, the wife separated from the beloved-husband-to whose memory she is faithful. Such poetry, particularly with its high chaste and restrained expression in *Gurubani,* conjures up the image of the virtuous wife *(gribabadbu)* of a good family, with traditions of decent living in a well-organised community life.

This mode, which in Guru Nanak © in *Bara-Maha* Tukhari, Wadhans and Bilaval) finds a deeply passionate and ecstatic expression in Guru Amar Das is, as stated above, of a uniformly restrained character. The yearning, the pain of separation and the wished for joy of union are all expressed in language which does not concretize the experience of conjugal life, but maintains a symbolism, such as has entered the domestic-romantic folk poetry of the womanhood of the Indian countryside for centuries. The woman all through expresses herself as the chaste daughter-in-law of a respectable family or tribe, whose honour is in her keeping.

In the last group of these lyrics (which in the rendering have been called Quartets, there is a noble converse between the loving wife, pleading with the husband preparing to set out on a long journey, as the employee of some feudal lord of the medieval times, not to stay away from home amidst the perils of unknown ways and war. To her pleading to desist from his proposed sojourn, she lovingly exhorts him to seek joy in the Lord, that is, in prayer and meditation. This short piece, suddenly bursting upon the imagination with its dramatic character, is a rich paradigm for that ideal relationship of the family life which the Sikh people throughout their history, albeit brief, have ever held before themselves to guide their community living. Its loving tones have the effect of bringing about a synthesis between the conjugal tie and lyrical love.

A stylistic characteristic of Guru Amar Das's *Bani,* as seen, for example, in *Anand* and elsewhere, is the inverted repetition of a part of the second line into the third, creating a meditative, musical effect and depth of experience. This characteristic may be witnessed throughout this composition. In the English rendering it has not always been easy to reproduce it, though the attempt has been made so to render the lines with such as effect.

In the Measure Gauri Purabi-*(Chbant)*-Lyrics-Composition of the Third Apostle.

In the Name of the One Indivisible Supreme Being, Reality Eternal, Creator-*Purusba* Realized by Divine Grace.

BANI OF SRI GURU AMAR DAS

The First Quartet Opens

The devotee-female supplicates the Lord and on His noble qualities meditates:
The self, in separation from the Beloved Lord for a moment even,
Of life feels deprived.
Deprived of life it feels—
Without the Master's guidance is not attained the Divine Mansion.
Act ye on the Master's instruction,
And thus the fire of desire assuage.
The Lord holy-eternal is the sole Reality;
No other than He is real.
Without devotion to Him comes not joy.
Saith Nanak: Only such devotee-female are united,
As by the Lord Himself are granted union. (1)
Thou dear woman self.
By devotion too the Lord shall thy life's night pass restfully :
Happy shall be she that serves the holy Preceptor,
Enters upon devotion, and casts off egoism.
Casting off egoism, should she laud the Lord,
And ever be devoted.
Listen thou sister-friend, of heart devoted;
In the Master's Word immerse thyself.
By laudation of the Lord alone, shalt thou find love with the Spouse,
By devotion to the holy Name.
Saith Nanak : The woman wearing necklace of the holy Name
Alone shall win her Lord's love. (2)
Sire! The woman without the Beloved Lord, is alone in *the wide world:*
By Duality deluded without prop of the Master's Word.
Without the holy Lord who may save her, strayed through *Maya* —delusion?
In falsehood's ignominy caught, is she deserted by the Beloved,
From His mansion cast off.
When dyed in the Master's Word, by poise inspired,
Ever is she in *the Lord* absorbed.
Saith Nanak : Such a wife is ever in bliss,
Called by the Lord to Himself. (3)
Love! union comes when the Lord grants union Himself—
Who else may the union grant?
Beloved! who other than the beloved Master may the delusion lift ?
Mother mine! union comes when the Master the delusion lifts.—

Thus does the wedded woman find bliss.
Dark is *the world of those* without devotion to the Master.
Without the Master's guidance is the true path not found.
The woman finds bliss, dyed in the joy of poise,
By contemplation of the Master's Word.
Saith Nanak: The woman to the Lord is wedded,
Blessed by love and devotion for the Master. (4-1)

The Second Quartet Opens

Separated from the Beloved dear, am I in great distress—
Without the Beloved, how may I live?
Dear! Without the Beloved find I not sleep,
Nor find pleasure in wearing vestures.
Pleasure shall I find in dressing with the Beloved's approval,
As in the Master's teaching is the mind absorbed.
The woman serving the holy Master is of eternal wedded bliss—
Ever abides she by his side.
Through union made by the Master's Word does she find bliss with the Beloved,
And gains in her life profit of devotion.
Saith Nanak : The wife is beloved of her Lord,
Through meditation on the Lord's noble attributes. (1)
Dear! The wife devoted finds bliss with the Beloved:
Day and night is she dyed in joy by contemplation of the Master's Word.
As the Master's Word she contemplates and casts out egoism,
Union with the Beloved she finds.
Ever in wedded bliss and joy,
Is such a wife through devotion to the holy Name.
Those devoted to the Master hold ever *the cup of* nectar—
Their Duality cast out.
Saith Nanak: The woman devoted has found her Lord-Spouse—
All her sorrows ended. (2)
Dear! The woman, involved in *Maya*-delusion and avarice,
Of the Beloved grows forgetful.
False, in falsehood involved—
Deluded by the world's foulness foul she grows.
Should she on the Master's teaching meditate shall this foulness go,
And her human incarnation shall not be forfeited.
The Master's Word should she cherish, in truth be absorbed,
And cast out egoism;

The Lord's Name should she lodge in her heart—
Of these should her make-up be.
Saith Nanak: The woman seeking prop of the holy Name,
In poise shall be fixed. (3)
Beloved, be near me : Without Thee am I utterly helpless ;
Sleep visits not my eyes, nor sustenance do I relish :
Utterly without relish is sustenance, in sighs do I languish.
What joy in separation from the Beloved ?
The Master I supplicate : by his favour alone may union be found.
The Lord, Bestower of joy, Himself will make union—
To the devotee shall he grant His sight.
Saith Nanak : The woman devoted is of imperishable joy in matrimony:
Never shall she be widowed. (4.2)
(The Second Quartet closes)

The Third Quartet Opens

Dear ! The woman absorbed in the Lord's poise
Is by joy in him filled:
The Beloved, supremely beautiful, has charmed her,
Her duality in poise lost:
In poise her duality lost, the woman her Lord has attained,
In bliss with the Master's teaching.
This body of falsehood and evil is compact,
Upto the neck brimful of sin.
From devotion to the Master's teaching arises poise
Without devotion is foulness of mind not removed.
Saith Nanak : The woman shedding egoism
Gains the Beloved's favour. (1)
Dear ! The woman has found the beloved
Through the Master's devotion and love.
Her nights, dear ! in blissful sleep passed,
With the Beloved in her heart lodged:
With the Beloved in her heart, is she with Him united—
All her suffering gone.
Inside the heart's Mansion finds she bliss with the Beloved,
By the Master's teaching on Him meditating.
Day and night quaffing *Amrita* of the Name,
Her duality is removed.
Saith Nanak : The blessed wife with holy Truth has found union.
By the Master's love and devotion. (2)

Beloved Supremely cherished, The compassion bring *to Thy devotee*!
Thus does the woman supplicate, with the holy Word decked.
With the holy Word decked, her duality gone,
All her doings by the Master's *teaching* ennobled:
The holy Eternal, immanent through all time,
Through the Master's teaching has she realized.
The egoist, lust-filled, delusion-tormented—
To whom may he carry his wail ?
Saith Nanak : The egoist finds not poise
Without guidance of the Master, deeply cherished. (3)
Dear ! Raw, immature in years, unpractised in ways of the world,
Devoid of merit, is the Woman;
Inaccessible, immeasurable the Beloved:
Himself bestower of liberation.
Of faults granting absolution,
Beloved Lord of the devotee-woman,
All creation does He pervade.
Through love, devotion and yearning is He met—
This wisdom the holy Preceptor has granted.
One devoted to Him is in bliss night and day,
Ever in meditation on Him absorbed.
Saith Nanak : By poise of mind is the Lord-Spouse obtained—
The Woman so wedded has found all the Nine Treasures. (4.3)
(The Third Quartet closes)

The Fourth Quartet Opens

Dear ! Tempestuous is the Maya-lake, impassable—
How may it be crossed ?
Dear ! making God's Name the boat,
The Divine Word the pilot,
WIth the holy Word as Pilot, the Lord will Himself carry me across—
Thus may this impassable sea be crossed:
By attaining devotion through the Master's guidance,
May one die to the *lure of* the world.
In an instant does devotion to God annul sins,
Purifying the self.
Saith Nanak : The *sea of the world* may with devotion to God be crossed,
And iron turn into gold. (1)
Dear ! In lust are bound woman and man,

Neglecting devotion to God.
Man is deeply attached too relations, my self !
And in this waterless Maya-ocean is sunk.
Sunk in the waterless ocean,
Has he not realized the way to cross it over—
In the race of egoism is the world involved.
All that are born shall *one day* depart;
Only those guided by the Master's teaching shall swim across.
One Godward-turned meditating on God's Name—
Shall himself be saved, to his tribe bring liberation.
Saith Nanak : With the *holy* Name in the heart lodged,
By the Master's guidance comes union with the Beloved. (2)
Dear ! Nothing shall last but the Lord's Truth--
This world is like a juggler's show.
Dear ! Make firm thy devotion,
Let holy devotion be thy commerce.
Such holy commerce is high beyond man's understanding—
By the Preceptor's guidance is such wealth obtained.
Practise service, meditation, holy devotion,
Discarding egoism.
Of little understanding, thoughtless, blind—
Such are we :
The holy Preceptor on the way has guided us.
Saith Nanak : God's devotees by the holy Word are exalted,
By incessantly lauding Him. (3)
Dear ! All happens by His Will;
By the holy Word does He exalt.
Himself the holy Preceptor, Himself the Lord—
In all time He cherishes His devotees.
Age after age does He His devotees cherish,
Exalts and inspires in them devotion.
Himself is He all-knowing, all-seeing,
Himself inspiring devotion.
Himself Bestower of merit, annuller of evildoing,
The holy Name in the heart He lodges.
Nanak is a sacrifice time and again to the holy Eternal,
Whose Will is Supreme over all. (4.4)

(The Fourth Quartet Closes)

The Fifth Quartet Opens

Beloved Spouse ! Serve the Master,
Meditate on the Lord's Name:
The holy Lord is the true Spouse, with whom
Eternal bliss shall she find.
One should dedicate one's self to the holy Eternal
As madder full-boiled, yielding the fast dye.
The woman truly devoted to the Eternal,
Shall on her vestures have the fast vermilion.
Falsehood's pose remains not concealed,
However thick its alloy's layer.
Those given to, falsehood, their eulogies to falsehood are given,
To falsehood their devotion attached.
Saith Nanak: The Eternal is the sole Bestower,
Himself showering grace on *His devotees*.

(P. 311)

By egoism, evil thinking, Maya-poison and evil-doing
Is the World deluded:
By touch to the holy Preceptor does Divine grace come—
Egoism in pitch darkness in enveloped.
Saith Nanak : Himself He grants union
To whoso with love of the holy Word he inspires.

(P. 312)

Blind and deaf utterly one those coveting the world.
Caught in its din they hear not holy Word:
The God-directed chant the holy Word,
Their minds in it absorbed;
They listen to the Lord's Name uttered,
And in the Name are *Their minds* absorbed.
Saith Nanak : Each creature is like an instrument,
Played by the Divine *hand*.

(PP. 313-314)

The egoist, with vanity puffed up, realizes not the abode of true peace,
And each moment between pain and pleasure vacillates.
Called ever to the Divine mansion, he turns not thither—
How may he be accepted at the Divine Portal ?
One who realizes the Divine Mansion is exalted above the world,

And ever is in *prayer* with folded hands:
To such a one the Lord shows favour and turns his mind Godward,

Slokas

One denying the Mater finds not shelter anywhere.
Loser in this world and the next,
No rest he finds at the Divine Portal.
Occasion then may never again come to touch the holy master's feet.
One missing from the master's count shall have suffering unending.
The holy Preceptor malice bears towards none—
Whosoever he favours, to devotion he inspires,
Saith Nanak : Whoever has sight of him,
Is by Him granted liberation at the Divine Portal.

Couplets

The egoist unenlightened is foul of thinking and vain;
Inside is he full of wrath, at a losing throw his wisdom forfeited,
His doing all false, evil, sinful.
Worthless what he hears, worthless his utterance.
Blind and deaf he strays into the wilderness of *falsehood*.
Such is the egoist, purblind, in transmigration caught.
Without the holy Master's touch finds he no place with God.
Saith Nanak : He earns what for him is predestined.

(P. 314)

In the Measure Asa, Score 2-Composition of Guru Amar Das
In the Name of the Sole Supreme Being, Realized by Divine Grace

Only by supreme good luck is the Lord's sight obtained
Through the Preceptor's Word inducing true renunciation.
Albeit the Six Systems are everywhere pervasive
The philosophy that unites to God is inaccessible, endless. (1)
Liberation and attainment to the Supreme State come by absorbing the true Preceptor's system,
Whereby the holy Lord in the self takes abode. (I-Pause)
Through the true Preceptor's system does the world find liberation.
Liberated is whoever cherishes love and devotion to *God*.
Rare is the person who cherishes such devotion and love:
The holy Preceptor's system brings joy everlasting. (2)
Through the holy Preceptor's system is reached the Door of Liberation—
Whoever serves the holy Preceptor, is ennobled his whole tribe.

Liberation is not for one denying the holy Preceptor—
Deluded by evil propensities, chastisement he suffers. (3)
By the holy Preceptor's Word, the self gets joy and peace:
By Godward turning suffering touches him not,
Nor does death-dealing Yama touch him.
Saith Nanak: The devotee in the holy Eternal is merged.
(1.40)

By discarding egoism, in the Word one dies;
And by serving the holy Preceptor after renouncing self interest:
Thereby will the Bestower of all Blessing, devoid of fear abide in his self.
Only a rare one by good fortune in the holy Word is absorbed.
Garner good qualities, thus banishing evil from the heart;
And in the Word of the holy Preceptor be absorbed. (I-Pause)
Only one seeking good qualities will value them;
Through the immortalising Word shall he make God's holy Name manifest.
By the holy Word is one rendered pure;
And through good deeds is devotion acquired. (2)
Good qualities invaluable are hard to acquire,
Except when the immaculate self in the holy Word is absorbed.
Those meditating on the Name are highly fortunate,
Thus lodging for ever in their selves the Bestower of Merit. (3)
May I be a sacrifice to those garnering good qualities:
For this, laud qualities of the Eternal at His Holy Portal.
All blessing shall He bestow Himself.
Saith Nanak : Beyond power of utterance is the worth of His blessings.
(2.41)

Great is the Holy Lord's grace,
Who unites to Himself those long-separated from Him.
Such union does He Himself make:
His worth to Himself alone known. (1)
How may one compute the Lord's worth?
He is transcendent, inaccessible, unknowable.
Only by guidance of the Preceptor's Word may a rare one find Him.
(I-Paise)
The rare devotee alone the Lord's Worth may find through devotion:
Such bliss comes rarely to some through good fortune.
By meditating on the exalted Word is the devotee exalted himself.
Rare is the devotee with power to make the meaning of the holy Word manifest. (2)

One devoid of devotion is to suffering and maladies subject.
Only through the holy Master's touch is suffering relieved.
One without the Master's touch shall gather only suffering;
Grievous shall be the egoist's retribution. (3)
God's Name is sweet and delectable:
Those quaffing it are lost *in it*.
God himself may offer this draught.
Through the Master's grace alone may such joy be found.
Saith Nanak : Only those dying in the Name shall find liberation.
(4.3.42)

Unfathomable is the holy Lord,
Whose service brings joy and peace to the mind.
Those devoted to the holy Word without endeavour are *saved*.
At their feet I for ever bow. (1)
Those dyed in the Lord's dye,
Their suffering of transmigration annulled,
The Devine Portal they spontaneously gain. (I-Pause)
Any tasting the Divine Word experiences the holiest of joys—
The Lord's Name in his self is lodged.
To him is the Lord visible, filling all species;
Near and far he views *none else*. (2)
All talk and discourse *of God*;
But only those are united to Him to whom He shows grace.
By words alone may He not be found—
Only be the Preceptor's favour is He in the self lodged. (3)
The God-directed discard egoism,
Dyed in God's dye, their illusion is lifted;
Their contemplation the pure holy Word of God.
Saith Nanak : Through the Name are they ennobled. (4)
(4.43)

Those involved in Duality are caught in suffering:
Unattained to the holy Word, their life is a waste.
Only through devotion to the holy Preceptor does enlightenment dawn.
Let all beware of being in Duality involved. (1)
Only those attached to the Essence find acceptance *with God*-
Those that day after day meditate on God's Name
And through the Divine Word realize God as the Sole Reality.
(I-Pause)

Those involved with Creation shall unfulfilled remain;
Their blind deeds shall bring them retribution of the blind.
The ego-centred man is blind—
No resting-place shall he find;
A worm of ordure, in ordure shall he be absorbed. (2)
Devotion to the Master brings imperishable joy.
One lauding God in holy company,
And meditating on the Name Divine
Shall himself be saved and those related to him be also saved. (3)
One through the holy Word proclaiming Divine truth,
Saith Nanak : The Divine Mansion to him shall be revealed without effort, through the holy Word.
The God-directed bathe their limbs in the pure waters of the Holy Pool. :
Through such bathing their impurity of foul thinking and evil is cleansed. (4)
(5.44)

Death comes inevitably to egoists—
Ignominious is their end :
Caught in duality, their own life they waste.
Acquisitiveness brings them dishonour;
Meditating not on their selves,
In slumber of delusion they lie. (1)
He that loses His life in God's Word dies *nobly;*
Praise and dispraise to him are equal,
As by the Master instructed :
In this Age meditation on the Lord
Is the true benefit earned. (I-Pause)
Those without devotion rot and rot in the womb;
Attached to Duality, they make waste of their life.
The world devoid of devotion is in suffering's grip.
This truth the holy Master has revealed. (2)
The restless mind countless buffets receives;
Forfeiting this life's chance no rest it finds;
Caught in the womb, in filth it abides—
Such is the egoist's abode. (3)

May I be a sacrifice for ever and ever to the holy Preceptor,
Who through devotion merged *my light* into the eternal Light;
And has led me through the immaculate Word into the true abode of peace.

Saith Nanak : The true anchorite is one who subdues his ego. (4)
(6.45)

A *true* servant of God has effaced his pride of caste;
Seeking the holy Master's shelter has he dedicated himself body and soul.
The greatest honour is the holy Name in the heart to cherish:
Thereby is the Beloved Lord ever man's helper. (1)
The true servant is one who dies while alive;
Holds joy and sorrow alike,
And by Master's grace through the holy Word is saved. (I-Pause)

Man's actions from the primal hour are appointed—
Without meditation on the holy Word no resting-place is for man.
Good actions, divine laudation, lodging in the self the Name—
These be His gifts, that without fail He confers. (2)
Egoists in delusion are lost in the world;
Without the capital of devotion, false is their commerce.
Without capital what hope of gain?
The egoist deluded only wastes his life. (3)
The true servant is one serving the holy Preceptor;
Exalted his caste, great his renown.
Rising on the Master's ladder, highest of all he stands.
Saith Nanak : Greatness from *devotion* to the Name comes. (4)

False is the egoist's commerce
Never shall he attain to the Master's Mansion.
Involved in Duality is he caught in delusion;
Caught in attachment, is he whirled about in birth and death. (1)
See the cast-off woman's make-up
Any with mind involved with progeny, wife, wealth—
False, hypocritical and evil is his attachment. (I-Pause)
The woman by the Lord favoured is of everlasting bliss in matrimony—
The holy word her make-up,
Couched with her Lord in joy everlasting;
United with the Beloved, is she eternally blessed. (2)
The truly blessed wife is she who loves Truth,
And cherishes ever her Lord.
Ever is He present close to her gaze,
The Lord pervading all space. (3)
Neither pride of caste nor looks shall go with man in the Here-after;

Man shall be judged as are his deeds.
Through the holy Word alone is man made high and exalted.
Saith Nanak : Such a one alone is merged with eternal Truth. (4)
(8.47)

In devotion is the self without effort dyed.
Through holy fear of God is one absorbed in eternal Truth.
Devotion comes not without guidance of the Master, perfectly endowed.
Fallen in disgrace, egoists lament their *loss.* (1)
My self! Ever meditate on God and repeat *His Name:*
Thus wilt thou experience joy day and night,
And all thy desires be fulfilled. (I-Pause)
Through guidance of the perfectly-endowed Master is God, all-perfection, attained.
By lodging the holy Word and God's eternal Name in the heart,
Does man find purity of heart
And in the Holy pool has bath.
Those *bathing* thus are ever pure and in Truth absorbed. (2)
One thus purified shall have perpetual vision of God close to him,
And with Divine grace be filled.
Wherever such a one goes, vision of God shall he have,
And find, no bestower of boons is there except God. (3)
God is vast, ocean-like, a treasury overflowing.
With endless store of the noblest gems.
These God confers on such as have His grace.
Saith Nanak : The Lord confers these on whomsoever He wills (4)
(9.48)

The Master is the Ocean-ocean of truth.
Only through supreme good fortune may one serve the Lord;
Realisation too by His grace comes.
Service to Him is a boon coming through the Master's grace. (1)
Through realisation is found the jewel of enlightenment :
By the Master's grace is ignorance lifted;
Ever is *the mind awake,* and beholds Truth manifest. (1-Pause)
The holy Word burns away illusion and pride—
From the holy Master comes such realisation. (1)
By the Master's Word is known inner truth of the Mansion,
Transmigration is annulled and through absorption in the Name is poise found. (2)

The world is a process of birth and death;
The egoist unenlightened in smoke of *Maya*-illusion-is involved.
Much false slander he spreads—
Filth-worm, in filth absorbed. (3)
In holy company is found perfect enlightenment;
In devotion to the Lord is the Divine Word repeatedly uttered therein.
By resignation to the Divine Will is found everlasting joy.
Saith Nanak : Such a one in Truth is verily absorbed. (4)
(10.49)

Quintets in Measure Asa
Of the Composition of Guru Amar Das

He that loses himself in the holy Word is in everlasting joy,
And by the holy Preceptor is united to the Divine Essence.
Never does such a one die or suffer transmigration—
Through the holy Master's teaching in Truth is he absorbed. (1)
Those destined to devotion from the Primal Hour
Are ever in meditation engaged,
Being blessed with the highest devotion by the holy Master. (1-Pause)
Those whom the Lord unites unto Himself,
Inexpressible their depth of absorption in God.
Greatness on them has been conferred by the holy Master—
Exalted their state, in the Lord's Name are they absorbed. (2)
The Lord is absolute Master of His Will
In a brief hour does He make and unmake.
Those trying to discourse on God to others,
With all their praxis no place do they find *near God,* (3)
The Master units those with good deeds garnered.
To them is conveyed the holy Word and the Master's teaching.
Where the Word is, sorrows vanish.
Through the jewel-name is *the devotee.*
Spontaneously in Eternal Truth absorbed, (4)
No wealth greater than devotion is :
This comes to those by the holy Lord favoured,
The Lord immaculate in their mind lodges the holy Word.
Saith Nanak: Dyed in *the Name,* joy to them comes. (5)
(11.50)

Ritual dancing, orchestral music—
Nothing affects the mind, blind, deaf and impervious to devotion.

Inside it rage fire and storm of avarice and delusion—
Neither is the lamp lighted nor comes enlightenment. (1)
The God-directed through devotion have their selves illumined;
Their selves they view, and with the Lord are united. (I-Pause)
The true devotees dancing is to love the Lord;
His rhythm-beat is discarding the ego.
The holy Lord knows *true devotion from false.*
Through the holy Word is seen the Supreme Being in the self lodged. (2)
The God-directed cherish devotion in their hearts and love God—
With minds poised, on the holy Word meditating,
The true devotees, devotion and *praxis* is truth itself;
Devotion for show, ritual dancing to suffering leads. (3)
True devotion lies in dying while living ;
Thus shall one by the Master's grace swim across the ocean of worldliness.
By following the Master's Word is devotion rewarded,
And the Lord Himself in the devotees' self comes to abide. (4)
The Lord in His grace with the holy preceptor unites the devotee:
His devotion unshaken, his mind in the Lord is absorbed.
Noble is the repute of those *to God devoted.*
Saith Nanak : To those dyed in the Name *alone* comes true joy. (5)
(12.51)

In Measure Asa-score 2 In the Form Kafi-Composition of Guru Amar Das

In the Name of the Sole Supreme Being, Realised by Divine Grace
Through divine Will is found the true Preceptor, and Truth Realised.
He alone realizes the Lord in whose mind through the Master's grace
He be lodged. (1)
One Sole Master and Bestower of Boons I find, none other :
Should He get lodged in the heart by the Master's grace,
Is eternal joy found. (I-Pause)
In this Age the Divine Name alone is the annuller of fear.
Through the Master's teaching found.
The egoist purblind, ignorant, without devotion
Into Yama's clutches falls. (2)
Through a divine decree does he laud the Lord :
Faith brings joy *everlasting.*
Through a divine decree is found the blessing of human incarnation,
And noble enlightenment.

Nanak ! Laud thou the holy Name—
By Godward turning may liberation come. (4)
(pp. 360-366)

IN THE MEASURE ASA—COMPOSITION OF GURU AMAR DAS—ASHTPADIYAN
(Octets)-Score 2

In the Name of the Sole Supreme Being, Realized by Divine Grace
In the holy Pool of Thy Name are contained all Scriptures;
At Thy feet lies holy Ganga.
Human understanding can compass what has roots in the Three Qualities.
Thy *truth* is all wonder, *unknowable.* (1)
Nanak, His slave meditates on His feet:
Thereby emanate from Him the ambrosial Words. (I-Pause)
Thirty-three crore gods are all Thy servants—
So are miraculous powers and practitioners of *pranayam.*
None His truth can describe:
What can one contemplate *of it* and utter ?
All Thy creatures bear the Three Qualities and arise from the Four Sources.
Only by Thy grace may one attain the Supreme State,
Through uttering the inexpressible truth (3)
Thou art Creator of all existence—
What power has any one of Thy creatures ?
Only by Thy glance of grace may one merge in the Truth. (4)
The whole evanescent Creation Thy Name utters—
Yet only those favoured by Thee, by the Master's prompting, realize Thee—
The egoists in ignorance remain steeped. (5)
On Brahma descended the four Vedas that he studies and meditates upon—
Yet even poor Brahma realizes not the Divine Ordinance,
And is subject to retribution in heaven and hell. (6)
To each Age was given its lord, who incarnated, the Creator has lauded:
Even these have not encompassed Him-What may man utter of His *extent*?
(7)
Thou art all-holy; all-holy Thy Creation—
Only by Thy grace may one utter holy Truth.
Those enlightened by Him, spontaneously in the Name are absorbed.
(8)
(1.23)

The holy Preceptor my illusion ended;

And lodged in my mind God's Name immaculate :
From contemplation of the holy Word has come everlasting joy. (1)
Hear my self, the essence of holy truth:
The Bestower alone knows the way—
The treasure of devotion only through the holy Preceptor is attained.
(I-Pause)

Great is the bliss of the holy Preceptor's touch,
That assuages the fire of avarice and desire,
Whereby attuned to God-intoxication, man may ever laud Him (2)
None without the holy Master's aid gets realization—
Maya illusion-and Duality continue to entangle man.
By Godward-turning are found devotion and the Divine Word. (3)
The greatest of austerities, the essence of all such, is the Master's service.
Thereby is lodged the Lord in the self,
Annulling all sorrow;
And the devotee, all-pure, appears at the Holy Portal. (4)
By serving the Master comes awareness of the three worlds;
He alone attains the Lord who his own self realizes :
By contemplating the holy Word is the Divine Mansion attained. (5)
Service of the holy Preceptor liberates the devotee's whole tribe.
By cherishing the holy Name in the heart,
At the holy Mansion attains he great honour. (6)
Supremely fortunate are those prompted to the Master's service—
Ever are they engaged in devotion and meditation on the Name.
Their whole tribe through devotion is liberates. (7)
Nanak utters this truth after contemplation :
Cherish in the heart ever God's Name.
Those dyed in devotion to God attain Liberation's Door. (8)
(2.24)

Each one by desire is impelled;
Only one realizing the Divine Ordinance is of desire rid.
Whole worlds in sleep of desire are involved—
Only those wake up who *by God are awakened.* (1)
The holy Preceptor realization of the Name has imparted—
Desire goes not without devotion *to God.*
Through devotion alone fulfilment comes.
In *Kaliyuga* the meritorious deed is the holy word to realize;
To shed pride is true devotion.

The holy Master's service finds approval *with God*.
Have realization *of God* who of desire is the Creator. (2)
What to offer him who the holy Word imparts,
And by his favour lodges the Name in the self ?
In gratitude offer him this head,
Your ego shed,
One realizing the Divine Ordinance finds joy everlasting. (3)
God is the sole Master of His will;
And by means of the holy Master in *the mind* lodges the Name.
He sets astray as well as shows the *true way*.
By the holy Word is one in Truth absorbed. (4)
Holy is the Word, holy the sacred texts;
Through holy Teachers is it uttered age after age.
The egoist goes astray in illusion and false beliefs.
All without the Name are of sense bereft. (5)
The same *Maya* pervades all three worlds;
Fools with all their learning get only confirmed in Duality.
Excess of ritual brings nothing but suffering.
Service of the holy Teacher all joy brings. (6)
Contemplation of the Name is delectable amrita:
One subduing the ego, everlastingly enjoys it;
By Divine favour is one *given* spontaneous joy.
By dyeing in the Name comes everlasting love of Truth. (7)
Recite holy texts and on the Divine Word meditate;
Recite holy texts with heart denuded of egoism,
Recite holy texts in spirit of fear *of God* and love of Truth.
Nanak! lodge in thy heart the Name by God-given enlightenment. (8)

(3.25)

(pp. 422-424)

IN THE KAFI TUNE, IN THE MEASURE ASA-COMPOSITION OF GURU AMAR DAS

In the Name of the Sole Supreme Being,
Realized by Divine Grace-Score 8 Ashtpadiyan (Octets)

From the Preceptor comes tranquility, who assuages the fire of desire;
From the Preceptor comes devotion and high exaltation. (1)
Brother mine! Ever meditate on the Name solely:
Seeing the world burning in flames, have we run to it for shelter.

(1 Pause)

For the preceptor comes enlightenment,
And contemplation of the Supreme Essence,
By the Preceptor's instruction have we found a resting-place.
And overflowing treasure of devotion. (2)
By the Master's guidance come meditation on the Name and realization of true knowledge;
By the Master's guidance come devotion and divine laudation,
And limitless filling of self with the holy Word.
By the Master's guidance comes joy that no sorrow admits;
By the Master's guidance come subduing of the ego and purification of mind. (4)
By the Master's touch are eliminated egoism and awareness of the three worlds;
Comes vision of the pure Divine Light pervasive
And merging of light into Divine Light. (5)
Through the holy Master's instruction is understanding exalted;
Coolness and peace falls on the self,
And joy through devotion is found. (6)
Only by the Divine glance of grace is the perfectly endowed Master found :
Then are annulled sin and evil-doing.
And sorrow and failure. (7)
In his hand alone lies exaltation—
He alone *devotion* to the holy Name prompts.
Saith Nanak: As the wealth of devotion finds place in the self,
Comes *true* greatness.

(IV. 26)

Listen, my self! Lodge God in the heart :
Thus, brother; will He grant *thee* union.
Ever practice sincere devotion,
Fixing the mind on the holy Eternal. (1)
On the Name solely meditate!
Thus wilt thou find joy, brother!
Remove egoism and Duality—
Thus will come supreme exaltation. (1-Pause)
Gods and sages hanker after devotion—
It comes not without the Preceptor's guidance.
Brahmin-scholars who study *Scriptures* and astrologers—
Its mystery eludes them. (2)
All He disposes *as He wills*—

This mystery no one can spell.
Bliss comes as He grants—
This truth the Master has revealed. (3)
All Creation in His power lies
Who pervades all.
Whom may one revile?
None other is there. (4)
The Divine Ordinance is the same for all;
By the same dispensation are all governed :
Himself has He put man's mind in a whirl,
And cast in it avarice and evil inclinations. (5)
Some has He guided Godward. and with enlightenment endowed:
Devotion too is granted them that their selves enriches. (6)
To the enlightened all existence is vision of Eternal Truth—
Truth have they realized.
No delusion misleads those who with Truth are enlightened. (7)
With them the five Evils in restraint abide.
Saith Nanak : Without the holy Master's guidance are these not subdued;
Egoism by contemplation of the holy Name is subdued. (8)
(V.27)

All boons within lie; nothing may outside *be sought* :
All these by the preceptor's favour may be obtained, should the mind's doors be thrown open. (1)
Brother! *by guidance* of the Preceptor is the Lord found,
Within is Treasure of the Name, revealed by the perfectly-endowed Master.
This the seeker after the Lord may obtain,
And the jewel of contemplation find.
Should he open his mind, with deep insight may he view the Treasure of Liberation. (2)
Within are innumerable mansions, where resides the self;
Thus shall he find his heart's desire,
Never again to enter on transmigration. (3)
This boon the jewel testers have got, by enlightenment granted by the Master.
This boon is the invaluable wealth of devotion, that rarely by the Master's favour comes.
What use seeking this boon without? (4)
Within is it found.
The whole world lost in delusion wanders,
The egoist into ignominy falling. (5)

The anchorite, false, leaving his own home, at others' homes begs—
Like a thief shall he be caught,
And indifferent to devotion, shall buffets receive. (6)
Those enlightened about their selves, brother are blessed:
Within their selves God they realize by the Master's great favour. (7)
God is Himself Bestower and Enlightener—
Who else may help ?
Nanak! Meditate thou on the Name—
Thereby obtain honour at this Holy Portal. (8)

(VI.28)

Sweet is the taste of knowing the self :
Those in love with Truth,
By tasting of divine juice have found liberation. (1)
The holy Lord immaculate, in the pure heart abides:
By enlightenment given by the Master may He be lauded;
Thereby may one, set in poison, practise renunciation. (I-Pause)
Without listening to the holy Word is the self not revealed—
The world is blind *without such vision*.
By the enlightenment given by the Master is the mind illuminated--
The Name at the last, will be man's true saviour. (2)
God's devotees practise devotion solely ;
Devotion their daily practice:
In their hearts, on their lips is the holy Name—
Through devotion the holy Word they contemplate. (3)
Exaltation comes from listening to the name and from devotion to it:
One for ever lauding the Name, by *its aid* attains the Mansion Divine. (4)
From the Name is the self illuminated, and great renown obtained;
From the Name comes bliss,
With the Name lies *true* shelter. (5)
Without devotion honour comes not to any—
The egoist into disgrace falls.
Such in Yama's demesne in bonds are chastised—
Their lives a waste.
From devotion comes to all, inspiration to service;
Through the Master is the Name realized.
From devotion to the Name comes faith and exaltation. (7)
Devotion comes on whomever He confers.
By the Master's teaching is the Name realized.

Saith Nanak : All *existence* to the Name is subject—
Devotion to it by supreme good fortune comes. (8)
(VII.29)

A woman abandoned attains not her lord's mansion,
Nor knows the bliss of conjugal life
Her speech lacking in sweetness, her manner arrogant—
All her delight is in other attitudes. (1)
How may the mind be subdued?
By the Master's grace may it be restrained, and by getting enlightenment return to its true abode. (I-Pause)
The happily-wedded wife is by the Lord Himself decked through prompting to love :
Such follow the Master's will—
With *devotion to the holy* Name, with poise of mind, are they decked. (2)
These ever have bliss with their Lord,
To the blessed conjugal couch invited;
Attached in love to the Beloved,
Having with him joy of union. (3)
Enlightenment is make-up inexhaustible,
Imparting to the noble woman true beauty.
Such a one is truly blessed in family life,
With *devotion to the holy* Name with poise of mind are they decked. (4)
The happily-wedded wife is blessed with love by the Eternal Master, inaccessible, limitless.
Such their holy Master serve in sincere, devoted love. (5)
The blessed wife decks herself with a necklace of noble qualities;
Her person scented with love;
Inside her mind the jewel contemplation. (6)
Those dyed in devotion are exalted—
From the holy Word comes noble birth and honour.
Those without devotion are truly low-caste, filth-worms. (7)
The whole world in pride is involved.
Without the holy Word this malady goes not.
Saith Nanak : Those dyed in the Name are of pride rid,
And in the Eternal merged. (8)
(VIII.30)

Those dyed in the Eternal are truly pure-ever pure their renown.
In this life are they lauded everywhere,
After death age after age renowned. (1)

My self ! Finely dyed, take thou the *holy* dye of truth:
One dyed in the beautiful Word of *God* loses never its shine.
(I-Pause)

We are low, soiled, pride-filled, by lure of duality impelled:
The Master's touch, the *true* philosopher's stone,
Into gold has transmuted us;
With the everlastingly pure gleam endowed. (2)
Without the Master's *touch,* no one is dyed—
From the Master's touch alone comes the dye.
Those dyed in the Lord's fear and love
Are in His attributes absorbed. (3)
Without the Lord's fear the dye will not catch,
Nor will the mind be purified:
Ritual without such fear is false;
No resting-place for such *with God.* (4)
Those alone are noble dyed whom He so destines,
In holy company *casting them* :
Such company by the perfectly-endowed Master is inspired,
Merging *the seeker* spontaneously in truth. (5)
Without holy company each is as a beast,
Of the Creator ignorant:
Without the Name each an evil-doer. (6)
Others there are who purchasing merits, bargain away evil qualities—
Endowed by the Master so to do spontaneously.
By service of the Master is found devotion,
That in the self is lodged. (7)
For all creation there is One Sole Bestower,
Setting each to an appointed task :
Saith Nanak : Those to devotion appointed are ennobled,
And through the holy Word merged in God. (8)
(IX.31)

The whole world hankers after *finding devotion* to the Name,
This comes only to those favoured by grace.
Without devotion all *life* is suffering—
Only those in whose selves is lodged the holy Name have joy. (1)
I seek shelter with Thee, who art illimitable, gracious:
Exaltation by devotion is through the perfectly-endowed Master found.
(I-Pause)

In the variegated Creation of God, One Sole Reality is pervasive within and without.
His ordinance alone operates in all happenings;
Who else may one approach for help ? (2)
To some Thou givest enlightenment; others in ignorance remain—
This solely in Thy power lies.
Some by Thy *grace* are to Thee united;
Others with false hearts from Thy Portal are drawn off. (3)
Some from the primal hour are immaculate,
Set by Thee to devotion:
From the Master's service comes joy *to those* enlightened through the holy Word. (4)
Some involved in filth, evil-doers,
Without wisdom, thought and restraint,
Wander aimlessly in life. (5)
Those favoured by His glance of grace alone are with devotion blessed;
Inspired by purity, content and restraint, their self the immaculate Word into their ears pours. (6)
From study one arrives not at understanding of God's extent:
From the master alone is realized His greatness,
Through enlightenment given by the holy Word. (7)
Man ! Purify *the mind* and body, and the Divine Word contemplate.
Saith Nanak : In this frame *lies* the treasure of the holy Name,
That through illimitable devotion to the Preceptor is acquired. (8)
(X.32)

One dyed in truth is the blessed wife—
The Master's Word her make-up:
In her self has she found her Lord by contemplation of the holy Word.
(1)

By devotion to the Lord, man's good deeds,
Of sins get him absolved:
The woman in the Lord has found her husband, in the union brought about by the Master. (I-Pause)
Some *wives* see not their Lord even though by their side,
In illusion of Duality involved.
How may those abandoned find Him ?
In agony are their nights passed. (2)
Those in whose selves is lodged truth through pure deeds,
Daily *their Lord* in spontaneous love they serve,
And in the Eternal are merged.

The woman abandoned is lost in illusion, through false words and evil doing:
Not cherishing their Lord, in empty couch in agony they *lie.* (4)
One sole Lord alone is real; beware of the mind in illusion being led astray;
Let the woman learn this of the Master and serve Him,
And lodge holy truth in her self. (5)
The blessed wife is united everlastingly with *her* Lord, sacrificing pride and egoism:
With her Lord is she ever united,
Finding joy in holy union with Him. (6)
Those craving for worldly possessions get at last nothing:
The wife abandoned is not admitted inside her Lord's Mansion,
Her life ending in regrets. (7)
One sole Lord there is, in Him alone be absorbed;
God's Name in her mind should she lodge. (8)
(XI.33)

Those tasting Amrita are perpetually blessed to enjoy it :
The holy Lord is above need, without even a sesame grain of need. (1)
Holy Amrita is raining, falling on the tongue of the God-directed:
Their hearts ever in bloom;
Perpetually they laud the Lord. (I-Pause)
Egoists are ever like the woman abandoned, wailing at their doorstep—
Never have they had joy in their Lord,
Receiving what for them is recorded in the primal hour. (2)
What is sown by the Master's direction yields the crop of Truth—
The holy Name their article of commerce:
On those engaged in earning such profit,
Are conferred treasurefuls of devotion. (3)
Those God-directed are as the ever-blessed wife,
Decked with God's fear and devotion—
Ever in enjoyment of their Lord, bearing in their hearts truth. (4)
May I be a sacrifice to those *blessed with* joy of their Lord—
Ever are they by their Lord's side,
Their ego discarded. (5)
Happy their mind and body, radiant their visages
Through love of their Lord ;
In the blessed couch have they joy with their Lord,
Their egoism and desire annulled. (6)
Graciously has He returned to my home by the Master's limitless favour;

The blessed wife has found her Lord,
The Sole Divine Being. (7)
The *Preceptor,* maker of union, has the self with the Lord united,
And of all sins got it absolved.
Saith Nanak : Speak to Him what will win His favour. (8)
(XII, 34)

From the holy Master comes merit, should the Lord bless one with such union:
Arises perpetual meditation on the Name and enlightenment appears. (1)
My self ! Lest thou think the Lord is far—
Behold Him ever by thee;
Ever He listens, watches, in the holy word pervasive. (I-Pause)
Those recognizing their selves by the Master's guidance,
Single-mindedly on God meditate;
Ever are they in enjoyment of their Lord,
And from devotion to the holy Name get bliss. (2)
And my self ! None the *true* friend is-contemplate the holy Word;
Rush to God's protection, and the Door of Liberation attain. (3)
Listen to the holy Word, contemplate its import,
In truth be absorbed:
By the holy Word subdue egoism,
And find joy in the Holy Mansion. (4)
In this age only from devotion to the Name comes glory;
None without the Name is exalted.
The glory of Maya lasts four days
And quickly vanishes. (5)
Those indifferent to the Name are dead,
Die they must;
Never have they had joy in God,
And in filth are absorbed. (6)
Some by His grace He to Himself unites,
By perpetually to devotion inducing them:
Truth their practice Truth their *way of life,*
In Truth are they absorbed. (7)
Without *guidance of the holy Word* it hears not, sees not—
Blind and deaf, the world is in illusion.
Those without the Name shall suffer;
Devotion to the Name through His favour comes. (8)
Those absorbed in the holy Word are pure and approved *of God.*
Saith Nanak : Never are they forgetful of the Name;

Know, at the Eternal Portal they abide. (9)

(XXIII.35)

From devotion to the holy Word are the saints known;
Fulfilled are their utterances.
Discarding egoism and putting faith in the holy Name,
True union they find. (1)
By *devotion* to the Lord's Name is one honoured:
Blessed is the birth of such;
By all are they venerated. (I-Pause)
From egoism and avarice arise caste arrogance,
Violent wrath and pride.
Only when egoism is subdued through the holy Word,
Is light merged into Divine Light. (2)
Through union with the holy Preceptor is my life blessed;
I *thereby* found the holy Name, *repository* of the Nine Treasures,
And everlasting fullness of store. (3)
The merchants of the commodity, lovers of the Name, come *for it;*
One attuned to the Master finds this wealth of meditation on the holy Word. (4)
Pride-blown egoists understand not devotion:
From the primal hour are they doomed,
Their life forfeited on a gamble. (5)
Without love of God, no devotion can be nor joy of body :
From this is found the value of holy love,
Devotion to the Master and poise of mind. (60
Whomsoever He guides to devotion,
Through contemplation of the Divine Word *enters* on it :
Then in the heart abides solely the Name of God,
With Egoism and Duality *subdued.* (7)
Devotion to the Name is the caste and status of God's devotees;
Himself He ennobles them;
Ever are they under His shelter—
He fulfils them as it may please Him. (8)
Strange is devotion to God,
Revealed through the master's teaching.
Saith Nanak : With the Name lodged in the heart,
Through *God's* fear and devotion are *God's devotees* by the Name ennobled. (9)

(XIV.36)

Those deluded by *worldly* delights,
Without the Name, in suffering are involved;
Uninstructed they remain by the holy Master's great self,
Without true enlightenment. (1)
My mind deluded ! Taste thou of God's joy and delight therein.
Involved in worldly tastes art thou straying, making a waste of the life.
(I-Pause)
In this Age God's devotees, *living* in purity,
In the holy Name remain absorbed.
Nothing without good fortune is obtained;
No more can man say. (2)
One who has the true vision of his self, and dies by the holy Word,
And casts away evil thinking from his mind—
Should he run to shelter with the holy Preceptor,
The gracious Lord *his sins* forgives. (3)
Without devotion to the Name no joy comes,
Nor is suffering cast off;
This world in Maya-delusion is lost,
Involved in illusion of Duality. (4)
The woman cast off knows not the joy of her Lord's *love*—
What good her make-up ?
Such are ever burning in suffering,
Deprived of the joy of couching with their Lord. (5)
The blessed wife, by casting off egoism, has her Lord's Mansion attained.
Such with the Master's Word are decked,
And with their Lord are in union. (6)
Man involved in the *blinding* dust of Maya-delusion
Has put off thought of death from his mind;
Such egoists die and are born time and again;
And, dying, are with ignominy treated at Yama's Portal. (7)
Those by the Lord favoured are with Him united,
By contemplation of the holy Word.
Saith Nanak : Those absorbed in the Name,
Bear radiant faces at the holy Lord's Portal. (8)
(XV.37)
(pp.424-430)

In the Measure Asa-composition of Guru Amar Das-Acrostic in the Name of the Sole Supreme Being Realized by Divine Grace

A,K = All creation is destined ultimately to fall prey to death

R=Man stores up evil deeds, and falling into evil courses neglects doing good. (1)

My self ! How *strangely* oblivious art thou of the final reckoning; Know that reckoning, must one *day* render. (I-Pause)

S,N. = Remembrance of God thou hast not, nor meditation on the Name.

Chh. = Ignorant one! day and night art thou declining. How mayst thou escape yama's grip. (2)

B = Ignorant one; devoid of realization, in illusion is thy life wasted.

Unmeriting art thou called;

On thy head shall rest the burden of other's sins. (3)

J = Ignorant one ! thy light has been taken away-At the end as thou leavest this world regret shall *haunt* thee.

Neglectful of meditation on the One Supreme Word, In transmigration shalt thou whirl. (4)

Thou Brahmin, Learn first what may befall thee; Instruct not others in false teaching.

First shall the noose close round thy neck, then round those of thy disciples. (5)

S. Ignorant one thou hast discarded restraint in accepting offerings unjustified:

Thy master's daughter is like thy own—

In taking such of offering hast thou made a waste of thy human incarnation. (6)

M.=Ignorant one ! The great malady of pride has deprived thee of all sense:

In thy inner self hast thou not meditated on God, and hast hankered after worldly things. (7)

K. Ignorant one ! Involved in lust and violence hast thou wandered along in life—

In covetousness caught, hast thou forgotten God.

Despite much learning and discoursing to *others*.

Without realization, art thou into disgrace fallen. (8)

T, Th=Ignorant one ! In darkness of wrath art thou burning;

Whatever spot thou touchest by thy presence is fouled.

Sh, D -Ignorant one ! Thou goest seeking offerings from door to door,

But hast not asked God for the true boon of *devotion*. (9)

P-Ignorant one : this shall not take thee across, caught in thy fraud.

Fool ! The holy Lord has himself put thee under a curse—

Such is thy destiny. (10)

Bh. Ignorant one ! in the ocean of worldliness shalt thou sink, involved with Maya:

Know, whoever by the Preceptor's grace realizes the One Sole Supreme Being,

In an instant shall find liberation. (11)

W=Ignorant one ! Know that thy turn to depart is at hand,
Yet the Lord hast thou neglected.
This opportunity never again shall come—
Into Yama's grip shalt thou fall. (12)
Jh. Ignorant one ! All sorrow shall vanish,
Shouldst thou just listen to the holy Master's teaching.
No preceptor is like the holy Preceptor.
One without the Preceptor is known as evil. (13)
Dh = Ignorant one ! Thy restless mind restrain:
Know, inside thee lies a treasure.
One devoted shall quaff the Lord's nectar,
Inexhaustible till eternity. (14)
G=Ignorant one ! On the Lord meditate—
Not by word-mongering is He found.
Cherish in thy heart the Lord's holy feet—
Thus may thy past sins by forgiven. (15)
H=Meditate, thou ignorant one ! on the Lord's teaching,
That may bring thee eternal joy.
Learning of the Godless brings suffering abounding—
Without the holy Master's *guidance* liberation shall not come, (16)
R=Ignorant one ! Meditate on God pervading all hearts.
Those realizing God, through the Master's grace,
Shall ultimately have realization of the Absolute. (17)
Lord ! Unknowable, inexpressible is Thy extent.
Saith Nanak : Those *blessed with the holy* Preceptor's touch
Have their reckoning annulled. (18)
(18.2)
(pp. 434-35)

In the Measure Asa-Composition of the Guru Amar Das—
Chhant (Lyrics) - Score 1
In the Name of the Sole Supreme
Being Realized by Divine Grace

In my home is *sung* the holy epithalamium.
By the holy word embellished.
Union of the Bride and Bridegroom has come about,
By the Lord Himself arranged:
Arranged by the Lord Himself by lodging Truth in the Bride's heart,
By devotion inspired;

WIth make-up of the holy Word, decked with truth,
Ever shall she have joy of her Lord in love.
Only by sacrifice of egoism is obtained the Divine Bridegroom,
With joy in God in the heart lodged.
Saith Nanak: With the Divine Word is she decked,
Her entire life fulfilled. (1)
The woman involved in Duality in illusions is lost,
With the Divine Bridegroom not blessed.
Such a woman, devoid of merit—
Here life is a sheer waste.
A sheer waste is the life of this egoist woman,
Immature, delinquent
In sorrow pining.
From service of the holy Preceptor comes joy everlasting,
And abiding union with the Beloved.
To see the Beloved is her heart in bloom, full of joy.
Saith Nanak: The woman neglectful of the Name in delusion is fallen:
Union with the Beloved alone brings joy. (2)
The woman the Beloved has realized, by her side;
This union the holy preceptor has granted.
Her heart with Him is united through *devotion to* the holy Word;
Through constant devotion is her agony assuaged.
The holy Word her agony has assuaged,
The heart has found peace,
Joy in the Lord has she tasted in her being.
In union with her Beloved does she feel joy everlasting,
In noble discourse learnt from the holy Word.
Brahmin scholars and those with vows of silence have made study of scriptures to exhaustion:
Liberation have they not found through sectarian rites.
Saith Nanak: without devotion is the world mad—
The holy Lord by His Word to Himself unites *all.* (3)
Joy has come into the woman's heart by union with the Beloved Lord.
Saturated is she with joy in the Lord,
Through the imperishable Word of the *holy* Master.
Through the imperishable Word has she with the Beloved found union—
Ever meditating on His qualities in the heart lodging them,
As in the couch bedecked she finds joy with the Beloved.
In union with Him are her faults effaced.

From the home where God's Name is constantly remembered,
Eternally rises the song of joy.
Saith Nanak: To be dyed in the Name is to find perpetual bliss—
In union with the Lord lies all fulfilment. (4)
(1-6)
(pp. 439-440)

IN THE MEASURE ASA-COMPOSITION OF GURU AMAR DAS—CHHANT (LYRICS)-SCORE-3

In the Name of the one Indivisible Supreme Being,
Realized through Divine Grace.

My loved friends ! Practise ye devotion to the Lord;
Serve ever the Master; acquire *thus* the blessing of devotion.
To the Lord devote yourselves, that it may please Him :
Should you follow your own will, the lord's pleasure shall you in no way win.
Hard is the path of devotion and love—
Rare is the person that finds it from the Master's door.
Saith Nanak : Only such as by the Lord are favoured,
Are inspired to set their hearts on devotion. (1)
My self, practising renunciation,
To whom art thou exhibiting this renunciation ?
Those lauding the Lord ever raise a paean of joy.
Practise renunciation sincerely-to the Lord all is known—
He pervades water and land.
By the Master's guidance is His Ordinance realized.
Those realizing the Ordinance are blessed fully with joy.
Saith Nanak: He is the true anchorite who is ever in the Lord absorbed.
(2)
My mind run wherever thou wilt; the Lord ever is by thee.
My self ! All cleverness discard;
On the holy Master's Word meditate:
Ever is He by thy side, even when for a moment should thou on Him meditate.
Therewith shall thy sins of successive briths be annulled.
And at last shalt thou attain the supreme state.
By the Master's inspiration on the Eternal meditate,
That thou mayst to Him be attached.
Saith Nanak : My mind ! In whatever direction thou run, ever is the Lord by thee. (3)
By the holy Master's touch is the wandering *mind* set at rest,

And in its own sphere abides :
Its commerce the holy Name; on the Name it meditates,
And in the Name is absorbed.
As by the holy master's touch is the wandering mind set at rest.
Perfect absorption it attains.
Therein are *served* victuals of Amrita, and melody of peace arises,
Whose sound the whole world proops.
Therein play innumerable instruments,
Casting perpetual bliss,
And the mind in the Eternal is absorbed.
Says Nanak : By the holy Master's touch is the wandering *mind* set at rest
And in its own sphere abides. (4)
My self ! In aspect art thou Divine effulgence :
Thy own exalted origin realize !
My self ! The Lord is ever by thee;
Listen to the holy Master's teaching and live in bliss.
One who realizes his origin shall realize too the Lord,
And enter into the Mystery of life and death,
As by the Master's grace he realizes the Sole *Creator*.
Disappears attachment to Duality,
As the mind finds rest, the fanfare of joy arises,
And with the Creator one finds acceptance,
Saith Nanak : My self ! In aspect art thou Divine effulgence :
The *exalted* origin realize ! (5)
My self ! With pride art thou stuffed;
With pride ever laden.
Maya the delusion-monger has deluded Thee—
Thereby dost thou in transmigration whirl about.
Stupid self ! ever absorbed in pride,
In the end must thou repent.
The maladies pride and desire grip thee,
Thy life wasted.
The egoist realizes not that in the Hereafter must he repent.
Saith Nanak : My self ! With pride art thou stuffed;
With pride ever laden. (6)
My self ! Be not conceited that thou knowest aught—
By the holy Master's teaching get humility.
Inside thee is arrogant thinking—
WIth the holy Word wash it off;

Before the holy Preceptor *stand* in humility—
Think nowise thou art anything.
Through pride is the whole world burnt—
Beware lest thou make ruin of thyself.
Act as the holy Master guides;
Obey the Master's instruction.
Saith Nanak : Discard egoism; thus obtain thou joy;
My self ! In humility abide.

(VII)

Blessed is the hour wherein the holy Preceptor I met,
And the mind with devotion to the Lord was filled.
Supreme joy and peace then came over me,
And mind and body were full of bliss.
Then entered the Lord my mind and came in self to abide;
All evil qualities were discarded.
As willed the Lord, good qualities manifested themselves,
By the holy Preceptor embellished.
Those *alone* have found approval *with the Lord*.
Who repeatedly have meditated on the Sole *Holy Name*,
And discarded feelings of Duality.
Saith Nanak : Blessed is the hour wherein I met the holy Preceptor;
And the mind filled with *devotion* to the Lord.

(VIII)

Diverse of God's creatures in delusion are lost—
The Lord Himself in delusion has involved them.
Involved in the attitude of Duality, from egoism they act.
The Lord Himself in delusion has involved them,
Put them on the false path-for such no help !
Lord! Thou alone knowest if they fare well or ill—
Thou the Creator of this cosmos.
Mighty is Thy Ordinance,
This the rare God-directed person realizes.
Saith Nanak : What help for these poor creatures,
Whom Thou Thyself hast in delusion cast ?

(IX)

My holy Lord ! Holy is Thy greatness.
Transcendent Absolute, immeasurable Lord art Thou—
Inexpressible Thy might.

Whoever has Thy holy might lodged in the mind,
For ever lauds Thee.
Those *alone and Thee* as are by thee favoured;
To the holy External is their self attached.
Those by Thee united, in Thee by the Master's *guidance,* are absorbed.
Saith Nanak : My holy Lord ! Holy is Thy greatness.

(X.27.5.2.7)

(pp. 440-442)

IN THE MEASURE GUJARI-COMPOSITION OF GURU AMAR DAS-SCORE 1

In the Name of the Sole Supreme Being, Realized by Divine Grace
Cursed be the life devoid of love for the Lord;
Cursed be activities leading away from the Lord,
And engaging the mind in Duality. (1)
My self ! The holy preceptor serve, whose service love for the Lord inspires,
And takes the mind away from all else.
With the mind fixed on God, fear of old age vanishes,
And man attains the state of eternal life.

(I-Pause)

From love of the Lord has arisen a unique peace
Behold the greatness of such devotion!
By effort of the self is egoism eliminated, leaving the mind pure,
Merging light into Light. (2)
All seek such a holy Preceptor, but without good fortune is he not found.
Only as one steps away from the line of falsehood,
Does everlasting joy come (3)
Saith Nanak: To such a Master what service to render ?
To lay before him one's life!
To keep in mind the holy Master's will:
Himself will he show grace. (4)

(1.3)

Serve solely the Lord!
Forsake service to any other.
Service of the Lord brings fulfilment of the heart's desire.
Service other than the Lord's is a waste of life.
To the Lord is my love *dedicated*;
The Lord my way of life!
The Lord is mine;

His account my sole discourse!
By the holy Master's grace may my heart in devotion be absorbed!
Such is the end *I seek* in the Lord's service.
(I-Pause)

The Lord my scriptures, my relation, my brother!
For the Lord hunger;
With the Lord's Name is my mind filled;
The Lord my relation, to succour me at the end. (2)
Other than the Lord all wealth is false,
Accompanying man not at death.
The Lord my treasure, to go with me;
Ever to accompany me.
False is one who to the unreal attaches himself,
And from falsehood acts.
Saith Nanak: All happens as the Lord wills;
None this mystery can express. (4)
(11.4)

Devotion to God's Name is hard in this world to attain—
By the preceptor's help alone is it attained.
Without the Name liberation comes not—
Let *whoever wishes* try other means., (1)
May I be a sacrifice time and again to the holy Master;
By the holy Master's touch is the Lord lodged in the mind lodged,
And therein comes to abide. (I-Pause)
As is the Lord's fear induced in the mind,
Arises dispassion to the world:
By such dispassion is the Lord found;
Ever after is the self in the Lord absorbed. (2)
Truly liberated are those that their minds *impulses* overcome,
Whereafter it wanders not;
In everlasting absorption abides and of the three worlds has awareness.
(3)
Saith Nanak: By the Preceptor's touch is *the desciple himself* exalted to be the Preceptor.
Behold, such is the Lord's will.
Such a *miracle* the Creator alone may bring about,
And merge light into Light (4)
(III.5)

All repeat God's *Name*:
Mere utterance brings not attainment of God:

Should God be lodged by the holy Preceptor's favour in the mind,
One may have the blessing. (1)
One whose heart is caught in love of God.
Forgets Him never;
Ever from the depth of his self does he utter God's Name. (1-Pause)
Those with hearts full of hypocrisy
And called *holy* for their outward show—
Never is their desire assuaged; (2)
In regrets shall their end be. *(6)*
Should anyone *bathe* at innumerable bathing spots,
His heart's pride may still not go:
One with attitude of Duality not overcome,
Must be the Celestial Judge be chastised. (3)
Only by good fortune may one attain the *spiritual state*,
Rare is the person realizing God by the Preceptor's direction.
Saith Nanak: Only one overcoming his egoism
To the Lord may be united. (4)
(IV.6)

One forfeiting pride shall attain peace and poised understanding.
He is *truly* pure who through the Preceptor's guidance realized the Lord,
By fixing his devotion at His feet. (1)
My self! without understanding ever with Lord mediate;
Thereby shall all thy desires be fulfilled.
One trough the Preceptor's favour attaining joy in the Lord,
By quaffing it shall get everlasting bliss. (I-Pause)
One by union with the holy Preceptor makes himself the philosopher's stone;
Thereby must he be venerated.
All venerating him shall be rewarded:
From his teaching shall come realization of holy Truth. (2)
One without spiritual merit shall not be venerated;
Nor without enlightenment shall he guide others.
A purblind ignorant man dubbed holy Master—
Whom can he guide along the spiritual path ? (3)
Saith Nanak: Without God's glance of grace nothing may be attained—
He confers *devotion* on whomsoever he favours;
Through the Preceptor's favour does He confer merit,
Filling the mind with His Name. (4)
(V.7)

In the Measure Gujari—Composition of Guru Amar Das—Quartets

Enlightenment arises not in Banaras nor is lost there:
Only by union with the holy Preceptor,
As enlightenment arises, does man get realization., (1)
My self! Listen to the Lord's discourse,
And in the mind lodge the holy Word:
With thy understanding in poise,
Will illusion leave thy mind. (I- Pause)
Lodge the Lord's holy feet in the heart—
Thereby shall thy sins be annulled.
By subduing thy mind compounded of senses,
Shouldst thou lodge at God's holy water-edge. (2)
The mind ego-directed, is thoughtless,
Bereft of understanding;
Not realizing the Lord's Name, ultimately must it depart repenting.
Thus has the holy Preceptor instructed. (3)
The mind is Kashi, all holy water-edges and Scriptures.
The sixty-eight water-edges shall ever be by his side,
Who in his heart the Lord has lodged. (4)
Saith Nanak: By meeting the holy Preceptor is the Divine Ordinance realized,
And the Sole Creator in the self lodged.
Whatever pleases Thee is *holy* Truth;
And in Truth is absorbed. (5)
(VI.8)

Thou Brahmin! Listen to the One Holy Name of limitless worth,
This is true teaching.
Whatever is learnt from feelings of Duality—
All such learning must bring torment everlasting. (1)
Bow at the Lord's feet, thereby attain realization of the Divine Word;
Taste with thy palate the joy in God—
Thus alone shall thy mind be purified. (1 Pause)
With contentment of mind attained by the holy Master's touch,
All desire for ever is annulled.
With the Name invaluable attained,
None goes into another's home to *beg*
The egoist's speech and words betoken not realization :
Whoever by God-given wisdom has his mind enlightened,
Attains God's name. (3)

Despite Scriptural learning still thou dost not realize God,
And goest about wandering:
The a truly foolish person is one who realizes not his self,
And for truth bears no love. (4)
The holy Creator Himself has deluded the world—
In this nothing can man say.
Saith Nanak: He does what pleases Him;
As is His will. (5)

(VII.9)

(Pp. 490-492)

Gujari Mahalla III-Score I

(The following hymn occurs in the measure Gujari in the section containing *Ashtpadis* (Octets).

These are made up of eight verses each, though as in the one given below, there is a variation and the number of verses is ten.

The theme here, as in many other places in the *Gurubani*, is a critique of the ritual prevalent in various creeds, particularly because of its being devoid of spiritual and ethical content. All ritual of whatever creed, according to the teaching of the holy Gurus, leads away from the spirit of true religion, which consists in subduing the impulses that keep the mind restless and take it away from the pursuit of liberation. Devoid of the ethic spiritual urge, ritual is lifeless and a hindrance in the way of a truly religious life. It must, therefore, be abandoned and all ritual observances be transmuted into a search for enlightenment and the higher life.

Ritual dancing in temples before deities is herein the theme. Not dancing as indulged in by those seeking thereby to propitiate certain deities (e.g., Krishna, Shiva and the goddess Durga), but devotion of God (symbolically called dancing to the tune of God) is the truly religious act. In Var Asa V, Guru Nanak has made a scathing criticism of religious mimes of the Vaishnavite sect of Krishna worshippers indulging in ritual dancing called ras-lila, seeking to recreate through dance the life of Krishna. False, according to Guru Nanak, is such ritual. Pointing to the mockery of such mimicry, Guru Nanak thus expresses the essence of true religion:

God's servants serve Him through righteous doings;
In the cool night are their hearts full of ardour for God,
In the Master's meditations lies the true teaching of religion :
By his grace does he bring about liberation of the devotee.

In studying, therefore, the following hymn,
this background and line of spiritual thinking
should be kept before the mind.

In the Measure Gujari-Composition of Guru Amar Das—Score.
In the name of the Sole Supreme Being, Realized by Divine Grace
May my ritual dance be the dance *of devotion* by my mind,
And by the holy Preceptor's favour subduing of the self.
One keeping the mind in poise alone funds liberation,
And attains the heart's desire. (1)
Dance thou, my mind, before the Master :
One dancing by the Master's direction attains bliss,
And sheds Yama's terror in death. (I-Pause)
The true devotee is one dancing by God's direction,
By him inspired with devotion in Himself.
He Himself sings *hymns of devotion* to the deluded mind
And on the true path guides him. (2)
By constantly dancing does the devotee cast off Maya :
No stupor seizes him in Shiva's abode.
The world's dancing and frolicking is in Maya-sleep ;
Singing of other than God :
With egoism no devotion can be. (3)
Holy men, the world-renouncing sages by meditating enlightenment—
All to God's will dance.
Accomplished yogis, practitioners of yogic exercises,
In their absorption too, to God's will dance,
That by the Preceptor's prompting meditate *holy* wisdom. (4)
Continents and the entire cosmos, the Three Qualities—
All in absorption in Thee dance.
All creation, the four-fold sources of life
All in obedience to Thy will dance. (5)
Only those favoured by Thee dance the *tune,*
By devotion to the holy Word inspired by the Preceptor's prompting.
Those submitting to the Divine ordinance.
Are the *true* devotees and have vision of holy Truth., (6)
True devotion in absorption in the Eternal lies
No devotion without service can be.
Only by dying to the world and contemplation of the holy World.
Does one to Truth attain. (7)
Many in the world dance for worldly gains:
Rare is the person realizing the Essence.

Only such by the Preceptor's favour attain to it
As have your grace. (8)
Forgetfulness of the Eternal even for an instant is time spent fruitlessly.
Meditating on *Him* with each breath brings on forgiveness as lies in His will. (9)
Those alone to *Thy will dance* as by Thee are favoured,
And by the Preceptor's prompting the holy Word contemplate.
Saith Nanak: Such alone abide in eternal bliss
As by your glance of grace are favoured. (10.1)
(P. 506)

Gujari-ki Var Mahalla III
Var in Measure Gujari-composition of Guru Amar Das

(Musical Direction): To be sung to the tune of the Var of Sikandar and Birahim
In the Name of the Sole Supreme Being,
Realized by Divine grace
Slokas M.III.
The world in acquisitiveness is consumed
Knowing not the *true* way of life;
Only by obeying the holy Master's will does one attain to the *true* station of life.
Those whose hearts in *devotion* to God's feet are absorbed,
Find the life everlasting.
Saith Nanak! As by His grace God lodges in the self,
By the holy Master's inspiration do men find lasting poise.
Composition of Guru Amar Das
Inside man is doubt, the source of suffering,
Heaping on the head pain through worldly pursuits.
Those involved in the sleep of Duality wake never
From love and attachment to the world.
Never meditating on God's Name, nor contemplating the holy World—
Such is the egoists' conduct.
Not attaining devotion to the Lord's Name,
Wasted is their life.
At the end in ignominy Yama chastises them.
Pauri (Stanza) His essence He created when no other existence was there—
Himself His counsellor, acting at His will.
Then existed neither heaven nor the nether world, nor the three worlds.
Then was He Himself, formless—no creation then existed.

Doing as pleased Him—
None existed besides Him. (1)

Sloka

Eternal is the Lord;
Revealed through living the holy Word.
Death touches Him not—
Beyond the transmigratory circle lying.
Ever must He be served, who all existence pervades.
Worthless is the service of any other, subject to birth and death.
Fruitless is the life of such as know not their Lord,
And are to anther devoted.
Saith Nanak: Incalculable is the chastisement inflicted on such by the Creator. (1)

Couplet

Meditate on the holy Name,
Everywhere in truth pervasive.
Saith Nanak: One approved of God alone through realizing His Ordinance.
Is with the Truth rewarded.
One making false utterance, falsely acting,
Without realization of the Ordinance,
Is blind, insincere. (2)
Pauri (Stanza): He set in motion union and separation
And thereby laid foundation of Creation.
By His Ordinance formed He the Creation,
And his own Light merged into universal Light.
All light emanates from the Light Divine,
By the holy Preceptor's word rising.
Brahma, Vishnu and Shiva,
Are each set by Him to an appointed task.
Of Maya he created the root,
As well as bliss of the Fourth State. (II)

Slokas

Meditation and austerities are of value only, should they win the Lord's favour.
Man achieves exaltation through the holy Preceptor's pleasure.
Saith Nanak: *This comes to one* who, discarding the self, is in the holy Lord absorbed. (1)

Couplet

Rare is the person that the holy Preceptor's teaching absorbs:

This, Nanak! comes to whomsoever the Lord Himself exalts. (2)

Pauri (Stanza)

Maya-delusion is ignorance, stubborn and of great power.
With a heavy load of stone of sin, how may one swim ?
With everlasting dye of devotion on man,
The Lord may carry him across.
Through the Preceptor's Word, and discarding of egoism and evil thinking,
May the mind be rendered pure.
Through meditation on the Lord's Name, Himself He may carry across *the devotee.* (III)

Slokas

Kabir! Narrow is the Gate of Liberation—small as the tenth of a mustard-grain.
May self, turned an elephant intoxicated.
How mayest thou go through it ?
Should a holy Teacher be found who by his favour may show pleasure,
The Door of Liberation may then becomes wide,
Permitting easy ingress and egress. (1.3)
Saith Nanak: The Door of Liberation is narrow in the extreme-
Whoever grows small may cross it.
In egoism is the mind grown gross—
How many it pass through ?
Through the holy Preceptor's touch is egoism lifted,
And the self with Divine Light filled.
The self is everlastingly liberated.
When in supreme peace absorbed. (2)

Pauri (Stanza)

The Lord, after creating the universe, under His own power has kept it.
By intellectual feats is the Lord not attained:
This is straying about in illusion.
By the holy Preceptor's touch does one die to the world,
And through realization is in Truth absorbed.
Through the holy Word is egoism removed,
And union with the Lord attained.
He is All-knowing, All-powerful, (IV)

Slokas

Cursed is a life without love of the Lord,
And lodging the holy Name in the mind:
What gain in the world to such?

False is Maya's wealth—
In an instant is its illusion removed.
As from one's hand it drops,
The body to ashes turn and the limbs wither away.
Those to the Lord devoted,
Have in their heart abiding joy.
One meditating on God's Name in joyful ecstasy
Is ever in devotion absorbed.
Saith Nanak: The Lord has entrusted *to me* such treasure,
As in the self absorbed abides.
Of such the dye is blazing,
Shining evermore. (1)

Verses
Maya the she-serpent is holding the world in its coils,
Gobbling up whose serves it.
One turning snake-charmer by the Master's guidance, crushes it.
Saith Nanak: Such alone are saved
As to truth are devoted. (2)

Slokas
To One Sole Lord are all creatures subject,
With each ever abiding.
Saith Nanak: One turning away from His Ordinance,
Even though near remains from His alienated.
Those alone are obedient to His Ordinance,
On whom His glance of *grace* falls.
In obedience to the Ordinance lies *eternal* joy,
As such a one is like the loved wedded wife. (1)

Couplet
One indifferent to the Lord is like the wife burning away in sorrow the whole night,
Bereft of His love.
Saith Nanak: Those are the happily wedded wives
Who give love to the beloved Lord-Spouse. (2)

Stanza *(Pauri)*
Viewing the world over,
The Lord I find the Sole Provider.
By Man's effort nothing comes;

The Lord alone is the Judge of actions.
Through the Preceptor's Word comes the Lord in the heart to abide;
And thus arises Enlightenment spontaneously.
As is slaked the fire of desire,
The self in the Ambrosial Pool is bathed.
The Lord, supreme in greatness,
Imparts by grace the power of holy utterance. (IV)

Sloka

What love has the spirit for the body
Which it leaves behind itself, lying prostrate ?
Man nourishes it by evil effort,
Although in the end it forsakes him.
The body is like blinding dust—
Ask the wind, where is the dust *flying with it*? (1)
One with Maya-deluded ego is in transmigration ever whirled about.
Saith Nanak: I sought not to know the Lord's Ordinance,
Whereby in the truth I could be absorbed.

Couplets

The wealth of devotion is alone lasting—
All other wealth is evanescent.
Neither thief nor highwayman may snatch this wealth.
This holy wealth with the self is united, and with it abides.
From the Master, perfectly endowed is it obtained,
The egoist of it remains deprived.
Saith Nanak : Blessed are the merchants
Whose gain is the wealth of devotion. (2)

Stanza *(Pauri)*

The Lord is supreme, mighty,
Holy and unfathomable.
The entire universe to Him is subject:
All the visible expanse is His.
The inalienable, stable wealth *of devotion*
Is by the Preceptor's grace obtained.
Through Divine grace comes the Lord in the self to abide,
As the Preceptor, conqueror *of evil* is met with.
Those nobly-endowed *alone* laud the Lord,
Immortal, changeless, perfectly supreme. (VII)

Sloka

Accursed in the life of those that repudiating joy in God.
Act evil and sin, rising from egoism.
The egoists of darkened soul are gripped by Maya-delusion,
Lacking true enlightenment.
To such comes not joy in this world or the next;
There they end full of regrets.
Through the Preceptor's grace do the rare devotees meditate on the Nam—
Their egoism banished.
Saith Nanak: Only one so destined
To the Preceptor's teaching submits. (1)

Verses

The egoist is like the lotus turned upside down,
In devotion and meditation lacking ;
Seeking egoistic power always,
Unholy is all his praxis.
His mind not saturated with devotion,
His utterance lacking in holy joy.
Such incline not towards holiness,
In falsehood lying all their delight;
Saith Nanak: Such is the Lord's dispensation—
The egoists sink through their falsehood;
God's devotees are saved through meditation on the holy Name. (2)

Stanza *(Pauri)*

One lacking enlightenment is in transmigration whirled about;
Lacking devotion to the Preceptor,
Full of regrets is his end.
Through divine grace is the holy Preceptor found,
When egoism is discarded.
Then is all desire annulled,
With joy in the self abiding;
And with a devoted heart,
Man ever lauds the Lord. (VIII)

Sloka

The world reverse one to the Preceptor devoted;
The praxis supreme above all is attainment of devotion.
Thus come peace and calm to abide in the self,

And in the heart joy everlasting.
Of such the sustenance and vesture is holiness,
And through devotion comes to them greatness. (1)

Couplet

My self! Listen to the Master's teaching,
Whereby thou mayest find the Lord, Repository of all Graces.
With the Lord, Bestower of Joy abiding in the self,
Are egoism and pride banished.
Saith Nanak: When by His grace is such *devotion* attained,
One is in a perpetual state of meditation. (2)

Pauri (Stanza)

In the devotee are created truth and calm of soul and purity :
With hypocrisy and evil banished from the mind,
The self attains victory thereby,
Immersed in holy light and spiritual joy,
With dark impulses banished.
One day by day lauding the Lord,
Holy virtues shall in him be manifest.
Of all creation of One Sole Bestower, and true Helper. (IX)

Sloka

A truth Brahmin is one who the Supreme realizes,
And is ever in the state of devotion.
Such would be he, who under the Preceptor's guidance cultivates truth and self-discipline.
His malady of egoism shall vanish,
Such would he be should he laud the Lord,
Garner good qualities—
His light shall be merged in Divine illumination.
In this age rare are the enlightened ones,
Who annulling egoism are in the Supreme merged.
Saith Nanak: Contact with such as meditate ever and ever on the Lord's name,
Brings joy imperishable. (1)

Couplets

In the egoist unenlightened person's mind lies hypocrisy,
And on his tongue runs falsehood.
Hypocrisy pleases not the Supreme Lord—
Ever does all that happens pour into his sight and hearing.

One influenced by duality setting out to instruct mankind—
His action by *Maya*-delusion is impelled.
Such action brings everlasting suffering,
And unending travail of transmigration.
His doubts not annulled,
In filth is he absorbed and merged.
On whoever the Lord's grace falls,
Is to the Preceptor's teaching inclined :
Such a one meditates on the Lord's Name and lauds it—
The Name brings him ultimate release. (2)

Pauri (Stanza)
Those induced towards obedience to the Lord's will,
Are the prefect ones of this world;
Meditating on the *holy* Supreme World,
Serve they the Lord.
Those Lord's servitors,
And devotees of the holy Word.
Those casting off their egoism *alone* attain to the Divine Mansion.
Saith Nanak: Through the Preceptor's guidance,
Meditating and bearing God's Name is their selves,
Are they *with Him* united (X)

Sloka
Of those Godward-turning is the mind inspired to meditation.
The melody of perfect peace *from them* arises
And the mind in the holy Name absorbed,
Once Godward turning is ever in joy in God dyed,
And with love of the divine inspired.
Such a one sees solely the Lord, hears solely the Lord,
And with joy of love of the Lord is inspired.
Saith Nanak: By Godward turning is enlightenment attained.
And darkness of ignorance lifted,
Those visited by divine grace since the primal hour
Are alone inspired by turning to the Master on the Lord's Name to meditate. (1)

Couplets
One serving not the holy Master,
And without love of the holy Word;
Meditating not on the holy Name—

What good his birth?
Everlastingly is he whirled in transmigration,
Rolling in ignominy in *worldly* filth.
Such a one, attracted to false acquisitiveness,
Reaches not the goal.
Saith Nanak: Those Godward-turning.
Swim across,
Should by the Lord they *with Himself* be united. (2)

Pauri (Stanza)
God's devotees *shine in beauty* at the Holy Portal,
By the Divine Word sustained;
By devotion to the Lord inspired
Are they tense with love of Him.
Ever abide they dyed in the Lord's love,
Their Palate tasting of joy in God.
Blessed in the birth of those by the Master enlightened,
Lodging in their selves the Lord.
Crowds of those without the Master's guidance go about wailing,
Through attachment to duality ruined. (XI)

Sloka
In the *dark* Kali Age have the devotees of God, the treasury of realisation gained,
And from the Lord the highest state obtained.
Through devotion to the holy Preceptor may man lodge the Lord's Name in the mind,
And ceaselessly in meditation engage.
By *absorbing* the Preceptor's Word may one practise renunciation *even* as a householder,
And burn away attachment and egoism.
Such a one is saved himself and saves also the whole world—
Blessed in the mother that bore him.
Such a hoiy Preceptor comes the way only of one,
In whose destiny this is recorded in the primal hour.
God's servant Nanak is a sacrifice to his Master
Who guided along the right path one by delusion gripped. (1)

Couplets
Mankind by *Maya* of the Three qualities is attracted,
As is the moth by the lamp consumed,

The priest neglectful of his duty looks with coveting eyes for lucre,
Prying who has offered what.
With thoughts of duality he studies falsehood—
God has from the Name alienated him.
Yogis, wandering mendicants, *sannyasis,* all are deluded—
Swollen with egoism and pride.
They accept not simple food and clothing as alms;
In obstinate crazes have they wasted their life.
Out of all these that perform alone has poise and wisdom obtained.
Who through Godward-turning has on the holy Name meditated.
Saith Nanak, servant of God: To whom may one complain,
Since all happens as the Creator has willed. (2)

Pauri (Stanza)
Maya—delusion, lust, wrath and egoism—
All are evil spirits.
These are Yama's subjects,
Heavily chastised by him.
Egoists attached to duality along, Yama's path are pushed:
In Yama's demesne are they chastised in bonds,
None their wailing to hear.
Whoever finds favour with the Lord is with the holy preceptor united—
Through the Preceptor does liberation come. (XII)

Sloka
Pride and attachment by their delusions have consumed the egoists
through and through.
These hold in their coils those that in delusion are to duality attached.
Burnt by the Master's Word, do they leave hold of man:
Then are body and mind rendered pure,
and God's Name in the mind takes abode.
Saith Nanak: The Lord's Name is *Maya's* teaching. (1)

Couplets
For numerous *Yugas* has the self wandered about:
When poised, then does its wandering cease.
The Lord has willed that it wander thus,
By creating the mime and show of *maya*.
By divine grace is the Preceptor found,
And the self, God-absorbed, finds poise.
Saith Nanak: By its own prompting is the self instructed—

Then it neither dies nor is destroyed. (2)

Pauri (Stanza)

Vast is this citadel of the human body—
By a chain of fortunate happenings it is obtained,
Himself tasting all delectation.
Himself too is He inaccessible,
unsoiled, a *yogi* from all attachments separated.
He acts as lies in His pleasure;
All shall happen as He Wills.
By meditating on the Lord's holy Name,
Is separation from Him annulled. (XIII)

Sloka

Wonderful is His prompting to devotion,
To holy Truth by the Master's teaching.
Wonderful is His laudation,
Whose essence by Godward-turning the rare spirits realize.
Wonderful is the Divine Word, holy and true,
Whereby union with truth is obtained.
Saith Nanak: In the attitude of wonder is the Lord attained,
And through grace obtained. (1)

Couplets

The tongue expressing wonder and ecstasy is by the holy Word exalted.
Through the holy Word is union with the Lord attained.
Supremely fortunate are those whose tongue to such ecstasy gives utterance.
Those in wonderful ecstasy shine in spiritual beauty,
By all creation revered.
Wonderful! Wonderful!
Such wonder by grace is obtained :
Saith Nanak: Those attaining it are at the Holy Portal exalted. (2)

Pauri (Stanza)

In the citadel of this body barred by door-panels of adamant,
Abide falsehood, evil and pride.
Those lost in delusion,
The egoists, blind and ignorant, are of sight bereft.
By praxis and ritual is truth not found,

Ritualists have tried this to exhaustion.
These gates of adamant by the Master's Word are flung open,
By chanting the Lord's Name.
The Lord is tree of nectar :
Whoever quaffs it
Is filled never again to hunger. (XIV)

Sloka

In lauding the Lord the night of life in joy is passed;
In lauding the Lord lies imperishable joy, mother mine
In lauding the Lord is devotion to Him formed.
Only one visited by divine grace such laudation utters.
One lauding the Lord shall be exalted.
Saith Nanak: Those lauding God abide by His Holy Will. (1)

Couplets

Holy is the utterance of laudation,
Attained after deep search by the Preceptor's guidance.
The devotee utters laudation through the holy Word,
From a heart full of ecstasy.
In laudation is found the Lord,
Without travail by seeking Him through the Preceptor.
Saith Nanak: Supremely fortunate are those
That from their heart on the Lord meditate. (2)

Pauri *(*Stanza)

My self, greatly covetous,
Ever art thou in covetousness immersed,
And deluded by Maya and desire dost run in all directions.
In the Hereafter shall not be *with the great* name and high caste—
The egoist, *to these attached,* shall only get suffering.
His tongue has tasted not of joy in the Lord ;
Joyless is his utterance.
Filled are those that have tasted the nectar through the Preceptor's teaching. (XV)

Sloka

Laud solely the Lord who is eternal and unfathomable.
Laud solely the Lord who is bestower of *noble* qualities,
And giver of poise to the mind.
Laud solely the Lord who pervades all Creation.

Laud solely the Lord who is Provider of all.
Saith Nanak: Laud the One Sole Supreme Being,
By the holy Preceptor revealed.

Couplets

Those devoted to God are in laudation ever engaged ;
The egoists die of swallowing poison:
To such appeals not Divine laudation;
All their life in suffering passed.
Those devoted to God quaff nectar,
And with devoted hearts utter laudation of God.
Saith Nanak: Those lauding the Lord,
Are the pure ones—
Knowledge of the Three Worlds is to them revealed.

Pauri (Stanza)

Should the Lord so will, the Preceptor is found,
From whom comes prompting to service and devotion.
Should the Lord so will, in the mind is He lodged,
And joy unsought is tasted.
Should the Lord so will,
Comes joy and everlasting gain.
Such are exalted on thrones in the Court Divine,
And *abide* ever in their own abode.
Those alone submit to the divine will
Who the true Preceptor have found. (XVI)

Sloka

Those endowed by God with enlightenment alone laud Him.
With laudation is the mind purified and egoism cast out.
The devotee lauding Him constantly has his desires fulfilled.
Those lauding Him have the true splendour,
And with the Lord are united.
May my heart ever raise laudation, and my tongue ever utter the Lord's praises!
Saith Nanak: May I sacrifice body and mind to those that engage in lauding the Lord. (1)

Couplets

Behold! Holy is the Lord; His Name immortality confers.
Those devoted to Him have been rewarded,

May I to them be a sacrifice !
Laudation of the Lord is the treasury of all merit—
Whosoever is blessed with it has joy of it.
Land and sea are filled by laudation—
This blessing by Godward-turning is found.
It behoves the Master's devotees ever to laud the Lord :
The Lord Supreme is thereby pleased.
Saith Nanak: One lauding the Lord from his heart,
Shall not by Yama's minions be tormented (2)

Pauri (Stanza)
Holiest of the holy is the Lord; holy the Divine Word.
From the holy Preceptor comes awareness of Truth.
Whereby is man merged spontaneously into truth.
Such are ever awake, sleep overpowers them not;
In the waking state is their sight *of life* passed.
Holy are those that by the wisdom given by the Preceptor taste of joy in God.
None ever found *truth* without the Preceptor's teaching.
Those ignorant of it have by death without a trace been swallowed.
(XVII)

Sloka
Utterance of laudation of the Lord is the Formless Lord's *one self*,
Supreme over all.
Inaccessible and unfathomable is such laudation,
With the holy Eternal identical.
Laudation is the Lord Himself superior to desire,
Is Almighty.
In laudation lies the immortal Divine Name—
By devotion to the Preceptor found.
Inclination to laudation from destiny and divine grace comes.
Saith Nanak: Inclination to laudation from devotion to the Preceptor comes,
From unceasing meditation. (1)

Couplets
Peace and poise come not without devotion to the holy Preceptor;
No other recourse is there for man.
However may one such acquisition desire,
It comes through destiny solely.
Those full of covetousness and evil,
Are through duality lost.

Of such the transmigration ceases not;
In egoism they suffer.
Those devoted to the holy Lord remain not unfulfilled.
Such are not by Yama summoned,
Nor undergo *his* torments.
Saith Nanak: Those devoted are saved.
Into the holy Word merged. (2)

Pauri (Stanza)
The true bard *of God* is one devoted to his Lord ;
Standing at His door he serves Him,
The Divine Word contemplating.
The Bard shall attain lodgement at the Portal and Mansion Divine,
Bearing holy truth in his heart.
Great is the bard's vocation in contemplation of the Lord—
By the Lord is he saved. (XVIII)

Sloka
Even a milkmaid in a rude tribe born,
As devotion to the Lord grows is her,
By contemplating the Master's Word
Ever on Him meditates.
One by the holy Master instructed,
Is by fear of God inspired:
Such a one alone is a lady of noble lineage.
Only one by the Creator favoured realizes the essence of her Lord's command.
One not so endowed is ill-taught, ill-mannered,
And is by her Lord cast off.
Through fear of God come purity and chastity of limb;
With mind illuminated and understanding exalted,
Through meditation does one acquire great merit.
One who is fixed in fear *of God* abides ever in such fear,
And acts under such fear—
Shall find joy and exaltation in this life
And liberation in the Hereafter.
Through fear of God is attained the Lord without fear,
And union with the Light Infinite found.
Saith Nanak: One pleasing Lord is alone well-born—
Such merit only by divine grace comes. (1)

Couplet

Let me for evermore laud the Lord—
May I be a sacrifice to Him!
Saith Nanak: Cursed be the tongue that lauds other than the One Supreme Lord. (2)

Pauri (Stanza)

Incarnations of God, endowed with part of His essence,
Yet were subject to duality;
Kingly state they kept and into states of joy and sorrow were involved.
Shiva and Brahma, despite their devotion, have found not God's truth.
The Lord, without fear and form, is inaccessible :
Through devotion to the Master is He revealed.
In that state intrude not sorrow and separation,
And the devotee in poise is fixed amidst the changing world. (XIX)

Sloka

All these forms visible *to the eye* are evanescent:
One realizing *the truth* of this alone finds acceptance *with God.*
Saith Nanak: One to himself attaching value is a fool, barbarian. (1)

Couplet

The mind is an elephant, the Master the elephant-trainer ;
Enlightenment is the goad,
Whereby is the beast driven.
Saith Nanak: The elephant unguided by such goad
Shall ever into the wilderness stray. (2)

Stanza (Pauri)

Pray I to Him who has created me;
By devotion to the holy Master have I found all fulfilment.
By meditating on the Lord's Name immortalizing
In holy company,
All sorrows vanish.
Saith Nanak: By attaining the wealth imperishable of God's Name,
All my sorrow has vanished. (XX)

Sloka

Like the cultivator rain-starved,
In the field with high mounds.
I look to the high heavens *for rain.*
Should the woman be truly devoted,

Her Lord must visit her.
Thou cloud *of grace*! Rain if thou wilt—
Why delay thy shower ?
Nanak is a sacrifice to those who by the Master's favour.
Realize Him in their selves. (1)

Couplet
That which pleases is truly sweet:
One who shows favour is alone a friend.
Saith Nanak: The true devotee is one whose *mind*
He Himself illuminates.

Pauri (Stanza)
This is Thy servant's prayer to thee :
Thou art the Sole Lord,
Protector at all times:
On Thee I meditate.
All creation is Thine,
That Thou dost pervade.
Those traducing Thy servant
Are by Thee destroyed.
Nanak! Leave sorrowing and live without anxiety
By worshipping at His feet. (XXI)

Sloka
The whole world, gripped by desire, in the end dies—
Desire leaves not man ever.
Saith Nanak: Through devotion to the holy Eternal
Are all desires fulfilled. (1)
He who created them shall take them away.
Saith Nanak: Nothing shall last but the Divine Reality.

Stanza (Pauri)
He Himself created the universe with its elaboration;
Himself is He Master of Wealth, Himself the merchant;
Himself to the store;
Himself the ocean and the boat;
Himself is He the helmsman.
Himself the Master and disciple—
Himself shall he reveal the anchorage.
Nanak, thou servant of God!

On His Name meditate!
Thus will thy sins be annulled.

(XXII)
(pp. 509-517)
(Found correct)

Note on Gujari-ki-var Mahalla III

The Var (philosophical and devotional composition) in Measure Gujari, unlike some other composition of this nature is totally the composition of Guru Amar Das. Hence, in its different portions, the authorship has not been indicated, although in the text of the Scripture this has been done. This composition consists of 22 verse-units, all structured on a uniform pattern, though the different constituents of the composition as a whole show a variety in length. The different component parts—the Slokas, those designated in the translation as 'Couplets' and Stanzas (Pauris) are in the accepted nature for these genres. The Pauris, particularly, which is the name for a stanza with a uniform rhyme scheme, has later been composed with an immensely powerful flow and effect by the Savant, Bhai Gurdas. The *Pauri* became the pattern also for the later narrative and the disquisitional compositions of a secular character in Punjabi poetry. The influence of this tradition may particularly be seen in the shorter poems of Bhai Vir Singh, the great poet of Sikh renaissance of the 19th-20th centuries.

The themes in *Gurubani* are all through the same, following the original pattern set up by Guru Nanak, whose vision and terminology may be seen throughout the holy *Granth,* in its regional language-mixtures, which are mainly central and western Punjabi and Braji Hindi. With this cherished uniformity and continuity of a tradition may, however, be seen the touch, in each holy author, of his particular personality and emphasis, along with preference for stylistic patterns. According to the Sikh philosophical postulate, it is one sole spirit manifest in all the ten Apostolic personalities of the Gurus. Yet, their humanity which they have themselves taken care to emphasize as against the claim to divinity or superhumanness of some other teachers, may be seen to shine through what may be called the 'signature character' of their compositions. This characteristic in each case has to be discovered and defined by the sensitive critical faculty operating with the utmost reverence for an emotional identification with the compositions themselves.

In the measure Gujari, there is another Var of the composition of Guru Arjun Dev. In the Var under study here, the emphases are, warning to man against being involved with Maya or the phenomenal show of things, with duality or attachment to the world, to being forgetful of the Supreme. Duality is the philosophical concept wherein the reality of Maya or objective material nature is firmly held, and man tends to turn materialist. Among the images most strongly cherished and repeatedly employed by Guru Amar Das is that of the devotee as the faithful wife, sensitively obedient and responsive to the will of her Lord, and blessed with the joys of conjugal life. The materialist, whose mind is fixed on the world, is like the woman whose conjugal faith is weak or doubtful, and who is cast off by her lord. The theme of the devotee as the yearning, ardent female finds a rich emotional expression in Guru Nanak's compositions. In Guru Amar Das, this theme finds a somewhat abstract treatment, which nevertheless embodies a deep spiritual experience.

Another theme ubiquitous in *Gurubani*, but reiterated with particular emphasis by Guru Amar Das is Divine Grace. This grace expresses itself in several ways, particularly in prompting the mind to devotion, in bringing about the devotee-seeker's union with the perfectly-endowed, holy Preceptor (Guru, Sati-Guru) without whose guidance man may flounder about in doubt and his inclinations may not find anchorage in faith and poise, which is the Source of Liberation and cessation of the transmigratory circle. Only the Preceptor's *Shabda* (Word, Essence of teaching) is liberating in inclining the seeker to Bhakti (devotion). The theme of the supreme importance of the holy Preceptor and of thanksgiving to God for His grace in blessing the devotee with the touch of the Preceptor finds the strongest and most reiterated expression in Guru Amar Das's compositions.

Towards the end of this Var occur some highly appealing images :_ There is the group of Stanzas (XIV to XVIII) in which ecstatic divine laudation (Wahu-Wahu) is the theme. Such expression of laudation is the very essence of devotion and is the source of liberation. Following these is the representation of the devotee as *Dhadi* (the bard) singing praises of his Lord, finding through devotion, entry to the Divine Portal and Mansion and finding poise as his reward. This image occurs also elsewhere in the *Gurubani*. There is then in Stanza (XIX) a very striking image, that of the Gujari (milkmaid) who despite her rude, unlettered origin and lineage, by devotion to her Lord and cherishing holy fear may be exalted to noble ladyhood. Such also is the devotee who through obedience and faith may be exalted to sainthood from ordinary human clay. Holy fear of God is another of the themes emphasized in the *Gurubani*, particularly in Guru Nanak's compositions.

Another image is that of the elephant, guided by the god. This goad is God's holy fear, and the elephant-driver is the Preceptor (Guru) inspiring the seeker with such fear. Lastly, there is the image of the cloud, symbolizing Divine Grace, which comes, as the devotee seeks it through supplication and prayer. The composition closes with the image of the unity of all beings—the Creator being immanent in all forms, as the Master of wealth, the merchant and the store; Himself the Ocean, the Boat and the Helmsman, revealing the anchorage to the human individual tossed about in the waves of doubt and involved in Duality.

In the Measure Wadhans—Composition of Guru Amar Das—Score 1

In the Name of the Sole Supreme Being, realized through Divine Grace

With the mind impure, all *man's actions* are impure;
With cleansing of the body is the mind not purified.
The world in illusion is fallen; rare is the person who of this has realization. (1)

My self! Meditate solely on the *holy* Name *of God*:
This treasure the holy Master on me has bestowed. (1-Pause)

Should one learn to perform yogic postures and control the senses,
Even so impurity of the mind is not removed and filth of egoism not cast off. (2)

The mind is not controlled by any discipline except seeking shelter with the holy Preceptor:
Contact with the holy Preceptor turns the mind away from the world:
Inexpressible is this state. (3)
Saith Nanak: One who dies into the holy Preceptor's Word,
She *thereby* find *true* life;
Thus will the impurity of covetousness be cast off
And the mind purified. (4) (1)
By Divine grace comes devotion to the holy Preceptor,
By grace alone comes such devotion.
By grace is the mind subdued and is purified. (1)
My self! Meditate ever on the holy Eternal:
With meditation on the Sole Lord shalt thou find joy,
And never again by suffering be visited. (1-Pause)

By grace does one find life after *death to the world;*
By grace is the holy Word in the mind lodged.
By grace does one realize the Divine Ordinance,
And is therein absorbed. (2)
May the tongue burn that has tasted not of joy in the Lord !
The tongue absorbed in worldly joys, in duality, finds only suffering. (3)
The Lord's glance holds all Creation alike,
Himself too He has made distinctions.

Saith Nanak: Contact with the holy Preceptor brings fulfilment,
And exaltation through devotion.

(4) (II)

Maya—illusion is a duststorm;
Without the preceptor's *teaching* comes not illumination:
Those engaged in contemplating the Word *alone* have realization;
Mankind, in Duality absorbed, is lost. (1)
My self! Guide thy actions as the Preceptor has instructed;
One ever absorbed with the Lord,
Shall *alone* attain the door of Liberation.

(1-Pause)

God is the Sole Treasure of Merit;
One finds it only when He confers it.
Without devotion the world from God is alienated.
Through the Preceptor's Word alone comes union. (2)
Those that have sought possessions in the world have at last been effaced;
Nothing with them has lasted.
True through the holy Preceptor is found;
Thus is one in the holy Nam, absorbed. (3)
This body is full of desire—
Light without the flame *of realization*.
Saith Nanak: In bondage is the egoist;
Turning towards the Preceptor he obtains liberation.

(4) III

Ever radiant is the face of the devoted wife,
Who from the Preceptor has acquired poise;
Ever is she blessed with her Lord's love,
By shedding off all egoism. (1)
My self! Meditate ever on God's Name:
The holy Preceptor *thus* has given me realization of God. (I-Pause)
The wife deserted is piteously wailing, cast off from the Lord's Mansion:
Caught in duality, her face turns hideous,
And in the Hereafter gets suffering. (2)
The woman with merit ever on her Lord's merits meditates,
And lodges in her heart the holy Name;
The woman lacking merit ever in suffering wails. (3)
One sole Lord and Master of all is He;
Inexpressible His greatness.

Saith Nanak: Himself has He made beings from Himself separate,
Then to devotion prompted. (4) (IV)

The holy Name immortalizing is ever joyful;
True joy in the Preceptor's Word lies;
The holy Word brings absorption in peace and poise—
This by the Lord in the heart is lodged. (1)
The Lord out of grace has made *for us*
union with the holy Preceptor;
And by prompting of the Master, perfectly-endowed, has come meditation on God's *holy* Name. (I-Pause)
Brahma who uttered the text of the Veda,
Yet remained caught in maya-delusion;
Shiva with his enlightenment, yet in dark passion and egoism is involved. (2)
Vishnu is ever incarnating himself—
When may he bring liberation to the world ?
Those instructed by the Preceptor, dyed in God consciousness—
Their darkness of illusion is lifted. (3)
Devotion to the holy Preceptor brings release;
One by him instructed *alone* finds liberation.
Those dyed in the holy Name are the true anchorites,
And the Door of Liberation attain. (4)
One sole Truth pervades all creation,
And upholds all.
Saith Nanak: I cherish not other than the sole Lord,
Who is the compassionate ruler of all.
(5) (V)

From the Preceptor come holy discipline and realization of the Essence;
From the Preceptor comes prompting to meditation on the holy Eternal. (1)
By the Preceptor's instructions, my self! on the *holy* Name meditate,
Which shall for ever uphold thee.
(I-Pause)

The holy Lord alone is the honour and exaltation of the true devotee;
To the devotee the Lord alone is the true friend. (2)
Whoever He favours alone turns to devotion,
And exaltation finds. (3)
The devotee lives the true, holy Word.

Saith Nanak: The devotee brings to his whole clan liberation.
(4)(VI)

My tongue is spontaneously absorbed in joy in God.
By meditation on the holy Name, content of soul is found.
Meditation on the holy Name brings joy imperishable :
May I ever be a sacrifice to the holy Preceptor!
(I-Pause)

By meditating solely on God the eyes look not covetously,
And the mind is content, with duality gone. (2)
Through the holy Word and God's Name comes joy to body and limbs,
And fragrance of the Name in the heart is lodged. (3)
Saith Nanak: Only those with the writ of good fortune recorded on the forehead,
Find renunciation spontaneously through the Preceptor's word.
(4) (VII)

Devotion to the Name comes solely from the perfectly-endowed Master,
And absorption in the holy Word and holy Truth. (1)
My self! By submission to the Preceptor,
Seek thou wealth of the Name.
(I-Pause)

Through the Preceptor's Word cast off impurity of mind,
And lodge therein the immaculate Name *of God*. (2)
In illusion does the world wander about;
Whirled in transmigration and by Yama chastised. (3)
Saith Nanak: Fortunate are those that on the Lord's Name meditate,
Lodged by the Master's grace in their merits. (4) (VIII)

Egoism and devotion are to each other opposed,
Abiding not together:
With egoism no devotion may be practised,
And the mind unsatisfied remains. (1)
My self! Meditate on the Lord and practise the Preceptor's Word:
Through submission is attained the Lord and egoism cast off.
This body is egoism-filled;
From egoism has proceeded all incarnation.
Egoism is a great sand-storm,
All realization clouding. (2)
With egoism goes not devotion, nor the divine will realized;

In egoism is the self bound, and the
Name in the mind not lodged. (3)
Saith Nanak: Contact with the holy Preceptor casts off egoism
And the truth in the mind lodges.
Then does one practise truth, live truth,
And through devotion in the holy Eternal is absorbed.
(4) (IX)
(pp. 558-560)

In the Measure Wadhans—Composition of Guru Amar Das—
Ashtpadiyan (Octets)
In the Name of the Sole Supreme
Being, Realized through Divine Grace
To listen to the holy texts, in tunes inspiring devotion;
And contemplation of the holy Word;
Lauding the holy Eternal unceasingly—
Such is my blessing and good fortune. (1)
My self! Be thou a sacrifice to the holy Name.
Shouldst thou be God's humblest servant,
Then mayest thou *devotion* to the holy name attain., (I-Pause)
With the tongue truthful, dyed in truthfulness,
Body and mind are rendered pure.
Laudation of other than the holy Eternal
Makes a total waste of one's life. (2)
Raising crops of truthfulness,
By planting seed of truthfulness, is the truest commerce :
Earning thus the profit of prayer,
Thy stores with the wealth of devotion shall be full.
To make truthfulness one's food, truthfulness too the wear ;
To seek shelter with God's Name—
Such blessings by divine grace comes;
In the Divine Mansion one finds abode. (4)
Those whose birth is holy, an holy their departure—
No more in transmigration are caught.
By Godward-turning are they reckoned pure at the holy Portal,
And into the holy Eternal are absorbed. (5)
May I be a sacrifice to the holy Preceptor, who thus has endowed me:
With pure heart and mind to raise holy laudation,
With attitude of sincerity to chant praise of the Eternal. (6)

Blessed is the occasion and the hour in which devotion to the holy Eternal is formed,
With sight turned pure, speech purified,
And the pure gaze is cast on all Creation. (7)
Saith Nanak: Union has come about as the holy Eternal has made it:
Himself He unites *the devotee.*
He keeps Creation as it pleases Him;
His own pleasure He fulfils. (8)

How may the mind wandering in all directions raise divine laudation?
As the senses overpower it and lust and violence oppress it. (1)
Spontaneously let the chant of laudation rise!
Devotion of God's Name is in this era rare
Quaff ye the joy in God through wisdom by the Preceptor granted. (I-Pause)
As through realization of the holy Word is the mind purified,
The Lord is lauds;
As by wisdom given by the Master is knows itself,
In its own abode it settles. (2)
My self! Sing ever the Lord's praise, dyed in devotion to Him.
The Lord immaculate confers joy imperishable;
From Him find fulfilment. (3)
By seeking shelter with God were we exalted from a low state,
God in His greatness saved from sinking
One heavy as a stone. (4)
By enlightenment given by the Master did we turn from poison into Amrita;
As fragrance *of devotion* settled within us,
From a bitter root did we turn into sandalwood. (5)
The human incarnation is a rare gift;
Only by earning it does one find it.
By great good fortune is the holy Preceptor met,
And meditation on god's Name found. (6)
Egoists deluded seek poison:
There human life a waste:
God's Name, unending ocean of joy, and the holy Word,
To them have not appealed. (7)
All utter God's name by their tongue;
Few lodge is in their heart.
Saith Nanak: Those in their heart lodging it,

Liberation and release attain. (8)

(11)

(pp. 564-565)

In the Measure Wadhans—Composition of Guru Amar Das—
Chhant (Lyrics)
In the Name of the Sole Supreme Being,
Realized by Divine Grace.

Dear girl-child! with beauty on thee from the dye of thy Lord's love;
Dear child! attuned to the holy Word,
Hailing bliss of thy Lord's love through thy devotion;
Thou art chaste, loving wife, by the holy word ennobled,
These with sincere love in thy heart, cherished by the Lord,
For Him dost bear *fervent* love.
By sacrifice of egoism hast thou found thy Beloved—
By absorption in the Master's Word.
Thou with love, bearing devotion in thy heart.
Saith Nanak: To such a woman the Lord Himself grants union—
By the holy Lord is she cherished. (1)
Thou woman of little merit! See thy Lord is ever by thy side.
Dear girl! those that love their Lord,
Have sight of Him pervasive everywhere.
Pervasive everywhere, see Him before their eyes,
Unchanging through the ages.
The simple, raw girl-child *through loving* Him shall get His love,
Who rewards *good* actions.
The wife tasting of joy in God, uttering for Him words of laudation,
Shall in the Divine Pool remain immersed.
Saith Nanak: The woman favoured of the Lord
Is one who ever keeps the holy Word in mind. (2)
Dear girl! Go and ask those happily-wedded:
They are the ones who their egoism have shed.
Dear girl! Those not shedding egoism,
Of the Beloved's command are not aware.
Those shedding egoism have the Beloved found,
And have frolicsome joy.
Such a wife ever is in joy, with mind fulfilled,
Ever lauding the holy Name.
Blessed is the woman with devotion in her heart,

Who finds joy in devotion.
Saith Nanak: The woman bears ever a joyful heart
Who with truth is decked. (3)
Dear girl! Discard thy ego, and by the Master's will abide:
Thus dear girl! wilt thou ever have bliss with the Beloved Lord,
And abiding place find in thy true home.
One abiding in her true home and raising words of holy laudation,
Imperishable conjugal bliss shall enjoy,
With the Beloved playful, in prime of youth—
Cherished ever by her Lord.
Thus will she bear bliss with the Divine Lord,
Bearing on her forehead marks of fortune,
Ennobled by the holy Word.
Saith Nanak: The woman shall have joy in the Lord,
Should she by the holy Preceptor's will abide.
(4) (1)

All business accomplished with the Master's instruction,
with poise of mind, is good.
Day by day must one the Name expound,
And as reward quaff the joy in God:
By ever expounding the Name in devotion to the Lord,
The reward shall come of joy in God.
Garner merit, discard evils and have the true vision of the self;
By the wisdom and exaltation by the Master given.
Quaff joy in the holy Word.
Saith Nanak: Devotion to the Lord is a wonderful experience,
Come to the rare beings that are divinely-directed. (1)
The crop of devotion to God is sown in the mind;
In the self it sprouts.
Abiding in thy self, quaff thou this joy,
And in poise of mind garner this profit.
This profit got in poise of mind by lodging the Lord in the mind,
Is truly worthy of praise.
Let the devotee lodging God's Name in the mind,
The Essence of the Master's teaching realize.
Egoists engage to exhaustion in farming and trade—
Their desire still unfulfilled remains.
Saith Nanak: in the mind sow the holy Name—
Thus will you get exaltation through the holy Word. (2)

Those alone engage in holy commerce—
Who on their forehead bear the jewel of good fortune.
By the Master's teaching the mind finds poise,
And through the holy Word practises renunciation.
Such bear marks of good fortune on their high forehead;
Through truth practise they renunciation.
And in holy thought are *their minds* dyed.
Bereft of the Name the whole world is mad—
Through the holy Word *alone* is egoism discarded.
Devotion to the holy Word brings *true* wisdom,
And from the Master's teaching comes bliss of devotion.
Saith Nanak: As is found the holy Word, annuller of *Yama's* terror,
Through good fortune recorded on the forehead,

Does man devote himself to the Lord. (3)
True farming and trade lie in *obeying* God's will—
From obedience comes exaltation.
By the wisdom granted by the Master is God's will realized—
Through obedience to the Divine Will comes union with God.
Our united through obedience finds poise
In the unfathomabie Word of the Master.
True exaltation from the Master comes:
The truth taught by him brings exaltation.
By discarding egoism is attained the Annuller of *Yama's* terror,
And through devotion to the Preceptor comes union with God.
Saith Nanak: By uttering the Name immaculate, inaccessible, unknowable,
In the Divine Will is one merged. (4. II)

My self! Meditate ever on Eternal Truth;
Thus wilt thou abide in happiness in thy own place—
Yama and death then shall not have power to touch thee.
By meditation on the holy Word shalt thou not be touched by the noose of death and Yama;
Thy mind ever shall be dyed in truth and purity,
Thy transmigration annulled,
The world in illusion of Duality is lost;
Caught in egoism, is in the grip of death and Yama.
Saith Nanak : Listen, my mind! On Eternal Truth ever meditate; (1)
My self! Inside thee lies the rich store—
Seek not for anything without.
With this enjoy thy fill,

And guided by the Preceptor, abide in God's glance of grace.
By the Preceptor guided, my self! Abide in God's glance of grace,
Inside thee is thy true friend, God's Truth.
The egoists purblind, bereft of enlightenment.
Lost in duality are undone.
Without devotion none release shall find,
But shall by yama and death be bound.
Saith Nanak: inside thee lies the rich store,
Seek not for anything outside. (2)
My self! With the invaluable blessing of *human* birth,
Some in the commerce of truth engage;
Their holy Lord they serve—their minds filled with the holy Word inelucatable.
In their minds the word ineluctable.
With devotion in the Name, find they the Nine Treasures.
Egoists by Maya—delusion—are gripped;
By suffering tormented, in duality end they in ignominy.
Those subduing egoism and in the holy Word absorbed,
Deep-dyed in truth abide.
Saith Nanak: Invaluable is the human incarnation—
This truth the holy Preceptor has revealed. (3)
My self! Those serving the holy Preceptor are truly fortunate.
True anchorites are those who the senses subdue.
Such the true anchorites; their minds on truth fixed.
Their Essence they realize.
Fixed deeply in truth their understanding,
By the Preceptor's teaching spontaneously they utter the holy Name.
Some lust after woman, seek attachments of Maya;
Egoists and those asleep to truth—these are the unfortunate ones.
Saith Nanak: Those with fixed minds serving the Lord,
Are the immensely fortunate ones. (4, III)

Hold commerce in jewel-commodities as by the holy Preceptor instructed.
True profit and gain in devotion to the Lord lies,
In merging one's qualities into the divine entity.
Merged in the Divine shall he be whom He Himself so instructs—
In the world *true* gain in devotion lies.
Without devotion no joy shall come.
In duality must one meet with ignominy;
Through wisdom given by the Preceptor must one seek shelter in the Name.
The commodity of *devotion* to the Name profit unfailingly brings.

To whomsoever God to such commerce sets.
Hold commerce in jewel-commodities as by the hold Preceptor instructed. (1)

Maya-attachment is utterly the source of suffering—
A losing trade:
Through falsehood to swallow poison—
Abounding evil from this arises.
Much evil thus arises; abode of doubts is the world;
Those without devotion meet only with ignominy.
Scholars who study Scriptures only hold disputations;
Know, without realization comes not *true* joy.
For those caught in attachment to Maya,
Transmigration shall not cease.
Attachment to Maya is the source of suffering;
Losing is this trade. (2)
In the Court Divine the spurious and genuine *conis*,
All shall be tested.
The spurious ones shall from the Portal be cast off,
Wailing as they lie.
These thoughtless barbarians as they lie shall wail.
Egoists—their life a waste has been.
Poisonous is Maya that the world has deluded—
Its votaries have cherished not the holy Name.
Egoists in setting up against God's devotees,
Meet only suffering in the world.
Know that the spurious and the genuine shall at the Holy Court be tested. (3)

All that happens is by His Will;
To whom may man complain?
He sets each a task as it pleases Him—
As lies in His might.
He sets each to tasks as it pleases Him—
None is in *himself* a hero or a coward.
The source of universal life,
Bestower of rewards for deeds—
In His Will alone lies deliverance.
Saith Nanak: By grace of the Master is egoism cast off,
And exaltation through the Name achieved.
All happens as He wills,
To whom to complain ?

With none else lies power. (4, IV)

Devotion to the Lord's Name is the true bargain, the true commerce.
By wisdom given by the holy Master is commerce in the Name conducted,
Whose value is immensely high.
High the value of this holy commerce—
Only the supremely fortunate are therein engaged.
Within and without are they dyed in devotion;
Their minds in the holy Name centred.
Only one on whom grace falls, this truth finds,
By contemplating the Master's Word.
Saith Nanak: Only those dyed in the Name,
Those holding commerce in holiness find joy.
Egoism and Maya are impurities—
One indulging in such is spoiled.
By the Master's teaching is the mind rendered pure,
And the palate tastes of joy in God.
The palate of joy has taste,
The heart is drenched therein,
By contemplation of the holy Word.
Inside lies a well with Amrita overflowing,
By the holy Word does the water-carrier draw it out.
Whoever has Divine favour in *pursuing* truth engages.
My tongue! Ever utter God's *Name.*
Saith Nanak :Those dyed in the Name are the truly pure;
All others with egoism's filth are spoiled. (2)
Scholars, astrologers all shout—
Into whose ear want they to pour their noise?
Soiled by Maya-attachment, their commerce is in Maya.
Of Maya their commerce, to worldliness are they attached—
In transmigration would they suffer.
Poison-worms, in poison are they rolling,
And in filth absorbed.
One's actions are as pre-destined—
None has power this to efface.
Saith Nanak: Those dyed in the Name find joy—
Others only in ignorance and folly shout. (3)
With the mind in Maya-delusion dyed,
All discrimination disappears.
With the mind dyed through the Master's teaching,

The dye of duality is washed off.
With the dye of duality gone, is the mind in truth absorbed,
And with truth are the stores filled.
One enlightened by the Master alone has realization,
And is with truth exalted.
By Divine favour alone is union with God found—
Nothing else may one speak of this mystery.
Saith Nanak: Those without *devotion* to the Name are in delusion lost;
To those dyed in the Name comes joy. (4) (V)

Listen, my self! The world is *caught* in transmigration;
By truth shall all in the end be determined;
The holy Eternal alone may in His grace grant liberation—
Then shall transmigration cease.
Transmigration shall cease and Truth determine all:
By *following* the Preceptor's teaching shall exaltation be found.
Those dyed in holy truth and in pose absorbed,
Absorbed in poise shall abide.
The holy Eternal have they loved and in their selves lodged;
Dyed in the holy Word—in the end shall they be absolved.
Saith Nanak: Those dyed in the Name, in truth are absorbed.
Never again shall they wander in transmigration. (1)
Attachment to Maya is madness;
The world caught in duality is lost.
Love of father and mother is all attachment;
In attachment is the world caught.
In attachment caught, for none the consequences of deeds can efface.
He who created the universe,
Is alone the Doer—
None His equal.
The egoist purblind in agony struggles to exhaustion—
Peace comes not without *absorption* in the holy Word.
Saith Nanak: Bereft of the Name , are all astray;
In Maya—delusion lost. (2)
Finding the world burning have we rushed to seek the Lord's shelter,
Praying to the Master, perfectly endowed: save us;
Grant us true merit.
Save us under your shelter,
Grant merit by *devotion* to the Lord's Name—
None like to Thee is bestower.

Supremely fortunate are those in devotion engaged,
With faith fixed in the Sole Supreme Being abiding through all time.
Those practising celibacy, charity, austerity,
Without the Preceptor's guidance attain not the supreme state.
Saith Nanak: Realization of the holy Word to such is granted
As under God's shelter put themselves. (3)
All realization in man from God emanates—
No other source of realization is there.
Thou who art within and without—
Realization by Thy gift is granted.
When by Thy gift is realization granted,
No other wisdom pleases.
Through the Preceptor's teaching is joy in God tasted.
Holy is His Portal; eternally holy,
Through the holy Word is He revealed.
As exaltation by the holy Preceptor is granted.
The devotee in his self finds his lasting abode.
Saith Nanak: Those dyed in the Name, alone attain to the Divine Mansion—
Their wisdom is the highest of all manner of wisdom.

(4) (VI)

(pp. 567-572)

Note on Lyrics in Raga Wadhans

The preceding compositions are called *Chhant* which in the *Adi Granth* stands for a composition (hymn) with certain lyrical features. Guru Amar Das and his successor Guru Ram Das, whose *Chhants* followed those of Guru Amar Das, have in the style of their expression certain characteristics which make their compositions vibrate with a lilt, and undulating rhythm and a musical sinuosity. The end-phrases in one line will be caught up in the next, to form part of a new line. This repetitive feature produces the quality of inspired meditation. There is prominent internal rhyming and verbal resonance. These features are revealed best in the study of the original text, but some attempt has been made here also to give a reflection of it in the translation. This feature is particularly characteristic of Guru Amar Das's *Anand* in the measure Ramkali, which is made up of inspired meditations in its 40 stanzas. The first five stanzas and the *finale* of *Anand* form part of the daily morning and evening service in Sikh congregations. While studying the *Chhants*, therefore, attention may be directed to the feature pointed out here.

Preceding Guru Amar Das's *Chhants* are Guru Nanak's. Those are in a shorter measure. In the latter half, this composition develops pronouncedly lyrical and musical features. The quality of repetition of phrases for effect in producing atmosphere is found there also. The last two stanzas particularly are rich in beauty of imagery. The Lord as Beloved is featured as of inexpressible beauty, resplendent like the idealized figure of Krishna, darling of the milkmaids. The seeker-self is pictured as stepping about in consciousness of love as the dancing waves of the Ganga, while the beloved's gait is compared to that of the majestic elephant, in the approved Indian poetic mode.

Guru Amar Das's *Chhants* are six in number, each forming a quartet of lyrical stanzas, having an enveloping theme and internal continuity in the experience conveyed.

The composition following, like the one preceding, is also of the character of a 'lyric,' although it is not so designated. It has even in a higher degree the characteristic of verse-music. Each stanza begins and closes with the same line—the last line having some minor verbal variation. All through, except at the end, the image of the married woman persists, who is faithful to her Lord or is neglectful of Him. Conjugal happiness and bliss come to the faithful, while the unfaithful shall find nothing but suffering and misery in a kind of widowhood.

In these hymns we have an inspired vision of the aged Guru Amar Das, who came to occupy the apostolic seat at the age of seventy-three (1552). He has left behind a large volume of sacred poetry, characterized by spiritual ecstasy and verse-music.

In the Measure Wadhans—composition of Guru Amar Das.
In the Name of the Sole Supreme Being, Realized through Divine Grace

Laud ever the holy Lord, in whose power lies all.
Never shall the woman be widowed, nor go into mourning.
Into mourning never shall she go;
Ever in enjoyment of bliss, shall she be admitted inside *her Lord's* Mansion,
Should she realize the Beloved as the Rewarder of Deeds.
Noble as Amrita shall her utterance be.
The well-endowed wife revolves ever in her mind her Lord's merits,
And ever thinking on Him never shall she feel sorrow of His separation.
Laud ever the holy Lord, in whose power lies all. (1)
By the Word is the holy Lord realized—
Himself He makes union.
The woman casting off her egoism,
It in her Beloved's joy dyed.
Her egoism cast off, never shall death touch her,
As through the Master's teaching she realizes, no other is there.
Of such a woman shall all desires be fulfilled;

Her heart in joy drenched, with the Master,
Life of the world, is she united.
Dyed in joy of the holy Word, youth-intoxicated,
Into her Lord's clasp is she taken,
By the Word is the holy Lord realized—
Himself He makes union. (2)
Who are such as the Lord have realized ?
Knowledge of this shall I seek from God's devotees.
Those devoted to him, casting off egoism—
The holy Beloved is with them spontaneously united.
The holy Beloved is found through living the truth,
When is the woman in the holy Word dyed,
never is such a one widowed.
Ever in conjugal bliss, her self in perpetual absorption abides:_
The Lord everywhere is pervasive;
Holding Him perpetually in her sight,
Ever has she bliss of Him.
Who have the Lord realized ?
This shall I from God's devotees find. (3)
Those from the Beloved separated shall find union too,
Should they at the holy Preceptor's feet fall.
The holy Preceptor ever is gracious-
All evil thoughts he burns out with the holy Word.
Burning out with holy Word evil thoughts,
Duality he banishes,
And in holy Truth is the seeker-female *left dyed*.
Through the holy Word comes joy imperishable,
And ego-illusion vanishes.
Saith Nanak: With the Beloved immaculate, giver of joy imperishable,
The Master through the holy Word grants union.
Those from the Beloved separated
shall find union too,
Should they at the holy Preceptor's feet fall.
(4) (1)

Listen, spouses, of the *holy* Word!
Serve the Beloved by contemplating the holy Word.
The woman of bad ways realizes not her Lord,
And bereft of Him, wails as Him she disregards.
One that through tears remembers Him, ever lauding His merits,

Never shall she suffer widowhood.
By submitting to the Preceptor's teaching is He known,
Through the holy Word realized,
And thus is one absorbed in devotion to the holy Lord.
Those not realizing their Beloved, Rewarder of Deeds,
Are false, ruined by their untruth.
Listen, spouses of the holy Lord !
Serve the Beloved ever by contemplating the holy Word. (1)
The world that comes and goes has He created.
Those ruined through Maya-illusion are in transmigration whirled around.
In transmigration whirled, evil in them arises.
The *world* bereft of realization is ruined.
Without realizing the holy Word is the Beloved not found,
Such a waste their lives, and caught in falsehood and evil, their destiny bewail.
What use wailing over the Beloved's loss !
He is life of the world-
Only those wail that of the Lord are unmindful.
The world that comes and goes has He created. (2)
The Beloved is eternal, holy, perishing never.
The woman of poor understanding, forgetful of Him
Caught in duality, suffers widowhood.
Suffering widowhood in duality, in Maya, delusion she suffers,
Her years ending, her limbs declining.
All that is born, must pass away,
Only those caught in duality *feel pangs* of suffering.
Forgetful of inevitable death at Yama's hands,
The world in Maya's pursuit struggles,
With mind in greed and covetousness absorbed.
The Beloved is eternal, holy, perishing never. (3)
Some wail, from the Beloved cast off-
The blind ones, not knowing He is by their side.
By the Master's grace is the holy Beloved found—
Let the woman ever contemplate Him.
Let her the Beloved contemplate
Ever is He by her side—
Only the egoist thinks Him far.
Those not realizing, the Lord is ever by them,
Their life is ruined, and is to them of no avail.
Saith Nanak: The woman shall find her Lord,
Should she for ever contemplate Him.

Some wail, from the Beloved separated
The blind ones not knowing He is by their side.

(4) (II)

Those from their beloved Spouse separated wail—
The holy Beloved is ever by my side.
Those that have realized that departure *from the world* is inevitable,
Serve the holy Lord and ever in mind keep Him,
Ever keep they His Name in mind; the holy Lord is ever with them:
Devotion to Him brings joy.
By the holy Word borne in mind is fear of death annulled,
And transmigration ceases.
The holy lord of the holy Name casts His glance of favour on them.
Those from their beloved spouse separated wail-
The holy Beloved is ever by my side (1)
Supreme over all is the Lord *I* seek—
How with the cherished Beloved may I find union?
Spontaneous became the union when made by the holy Preceptor,
With the Beloved kept ever in mind.
As is the Lord cherished in live in the heart,
Through the holy Preceptor is His sight obtained.
Frail is the vesture of Maya-illusion, which worn, makes the feet
unsteady *in the way of God*.
Holy is the vesture dyed in the dye of the Beloved,
Which worn, fulfils all desire.
Supreme over all is the Lord—
How with the Beloved may I find union ?
With realization of the Holy Lord was I blessed,
And the sinful beings of the world disregarded.
Ever have I joy with the Beloved,
By contemplation of the holy Word.
By contemplating the holy Word art thou in bliss, woman!
By touch of the holy Preceptor hast thou found the Beloved.
Dyed in joy in thy heart is thy mind in ecstasy of peace.
All thy tormenting suffering is gone.
By dedicating body and soul to the Master,
Is the mind with devotion filled.
As was desire and suffering eliminated,
With realization of the holy Lord was I blessed,
And the sinful beings of the world disregarded. (3)

In the world created by the Lord,
Without the Master's guidance all is pitch dark.
The Lord brings about union, makes union Himself,
And Himself He inspires devotion.
Inspiring devotion *Himself*, that is the commerce of spiritual poises,
By the Master's guidance grants He fulfilment of life's aim.
Blessed is the birth of one who his egoism casts off,
And at the holy Portal is adjudged pure.
Through devotion to the Name, saith Nanak,
Is the heart illumined with the jewel of realization.
In the world created by the Lord,
Without the Master's guidance all is pitch dark.
(4) (III)

This frail body is now by old age gripped:
Those saved by the Master are alone saved—
All others are born and die and are in transmigration caught.
In transmigration caught, others are born and die—
Full of regrets they leave the world;
No joy without *devotion to* the holy Name comes.
Only for deeds done in life comes the reward;
The egoist in ignominy ends.
The vale of death is utterly dark, storm-tossed,
Friendless is the self there.
Frail is this body, now by old age gripped : (1)
With realization by the holy Preceptor granted,
This frail body shines as gold.
As Maya-illusion is lifted,
The self in the holy Name is merged.
As is the self in the Name merged and sings Divine laudation,
Comes joy of union with the Beloved.
Then comes the state of perpetual joy,
As is egoism lifted.
I fall at the feel of those *holy* persons
That cherish in the heart God's Name.
With realization by the holy Preceptor granted,
This frail body shines as gold. (2)
Laud the holy Eternal by the wisdom by the holy Preceptor granted.
Those without the Preceptor's *guidance* in illusion are lost—
In the Hereafter shall they find no honour.

In ignominy in the Hereafter, full of regrets for evils done,
Suffering to their share shall fall.
Those dyed in the Name in vermilion shall be decked,
And have joy in their beloved Husband's clasp.
None great as He--
Inexpressible is His greatness.
Laud the Eternal by the wisdom by the holy Preceptor granted. (3)
I touch the feel of those that the holy Eternal have lauded.
Such are true and holy--
Their touch all impurity removes.
Their touch all impurity removes, like bathing in the holy pool.
In poise of mind.
The holy Preceptor in the secret has instructed me,
Of the holy Name immaculate, inaccessible.
Saith Nanak: Those so instructed are in devotion ever engaged,
And in holy truth merged.
I touch the feet of those that the holy Eternal have lauded. (4) (IV)
(pp 582-585)

Wadhanis-ki-Var, Composition of Guru Ram Das.
(To be sung to the tune of Lallan Bahliman)
In the Name of the Sole Supreme Being, Realized through Divine Grace.
Sloka (Compositions of Guru Amar Das)
Those dyed in the holy Word are the great souls.

In their hearts is borne the holy Name.
Truth they garner, ever living by *guidance* of truth
And love of the holy Name.
Ever abide they pure; impurity touches them not, by Divine grace.
Saith Nanak: May I be a sacrifice to such
As meditate ever on God. (1)

Couplet (Composition of Guru Amar Das)
I look him to be a swan, and so followed him,
Had I known it was a wretched crane,
Never would I have touched him. (2)

Couplet (Guru Amar Das)
Seeing the swans swimming, the cranes too felt like imitating them.
The wretched cranes were drowned,
Head thrown downwards and feet raised aloft. (3)

Pauri (Stanza)—Composition of Guru Ram Das
Thou art the Sole cause and Source of *all things,*
Thou hast Thyself made Creation.
Thou art the Sole Formless Absolute, none else.
Thou art of Almighty; all Thou willst happens.
Unsolicited dost Thou confer boons on all Creation.
Raise ye all aloud the shout:
Hail *the Lord* who has blessed the tongue with His holy Name!
(I)

Sloka (Compositions of Guru Amar Das)
All Creation to fear is subject: the Lord alone is without fear.
Should the Lord by devotion be lodged in the mind,
Fear enters not there.
Foes and suffering approach not there,
Nor can any such touch it.
The devotee is firm-fixed in the thought,
To *submit* to whatever He does.
Saith Nanak : Himself He shall save
His servant's honour.
And fulfil his objectives. (1)
Verse (Composition of Guru Amar Das)
Some of our friends are about to depart,
Others already have departed:
Those that remain must depart too.
Those indifferent to devotion to the holy Preceptor,
Their life and death in regrets are enveloped.
Saith Nanak: Those dyed in truth never *from God* get alienated, Through devotion to the holy Preceptor are they in Him absorbed. (2)

Pauri (Stanza) Composition of Guru Ram Das
Happy is meeting such noble souls as have inside them *love* and God that merit brings.
Happy is meeting the cherished holy preceptor,
Who egoism has cast out of *ourselves*.
Blessed be the perfectly-endowed holy Preceptor, who through divine instruction
All creation has uplifted.
My devotee friends! Meditate ever on God's Name,
That shall carry you across the ocean of worldliness.
The holy Master has imparted Divine instruction—
May I be a sacrifice hundreds of times to him! (II)

Sloka (Composition of Guru Amar Das)
In service and submission to the holy preceptor lies the essence of all joy,
Whereby comes exaltation in this world and at the Divine portal liberation.
Such service lies in adopting truthful doing, truthful wear,
And in the holy Name seeking shelter.
In holy company is Found truth,
And love of the holy Name.
In the holy Word lies the *source* of joy imperishable,
And being judged holy at the Divine portal.
Saith Nanak: Devotion to the holy preceptor comes by grace of the Creator. (1)

Couplets (compositions of Guru Amar Das)
Serving other than *the holy preceptor* is a shame on life and living.
Such a one discarding Amrita, to poison is attached—
Poison his gain and poison his capital:
Poison his food and wear;
Poison the morsels in his mouth.
Here such a one finds suffering,
And in death in hell abides.
Egoists with face blackend, know not the holy word-
Ruined through lust and wrath.
Devotion to the holy preceptor they discard,
Their stubbornness nothing accomplishes.
Bound in Yama's demesne are they chastised;
None to hear their entreaties.
Saith Nanak: One earns what in his destiny is recorded.
For the devotee his abode in the holy Name is *destined*. (2)

Pauri (Stanza): Composition of Guru Ram Das
Devote yourselves, devotees of God! to the holy Preceptor
Who in our mind firmly fixed God's Name.
Devote yourselves day and night to the holy Preceptor
Who has inspired meditation on the Lord of the universe.
Have vision each moment of the holy Preceptor
Who has shown the path *leading up to God*.
Fall all at the feet of the holy Preceptor,
Who has the darkness of illusion lifted.
Bless ye all the holy Preceptor
Who has shown the way to the treasure of devotion to God. (III)

Sloka (Composition of Guru Amar Das)
The holy Preceptor's touch all desire removes.
This goes not by forms of ritualism:
One so involved meets suffering that from door to door drives him,
And in the Hereafter is severely chastised.
In him is not formed poise, that contentment would bring.
To desire from stubborn egoism is to court suffering.
Better than the ascetic pose is the householder's life,
Wherein is practised charity.
Those dyed in the holy Word have realization,
Those caught in duality in illusion lie.
Each earns what is recorded—
Nothing more can man say.
Saith Nanak: Truly noble are those the please Him,
Whose honour He keeps up to the last. (1)

Couplets (Compositions of Guru Amar Das)
Devotion to the holy Preceptor brings joy imperishable,
And the suffering of transmigration lifts;
All apprehension gone, in peace does the mind abide.
Inside us lies the holy pool of Enlightenment:
Thus has the holy Preceptor instructed.
With impurity gone is the mind purified,
By bathing in the Pool of Immortality.
The pure-minded meet the pure-minded
Out of love for the holy Word.
In their selves find they God-consciousness,
Merging their light into the Light *Divine*.
Hypocrisy to Yama and death must fall prey;
Those practising these in ignominy are dragged away.
Saith Nanak: Those dyed in the Name, through devotion to the holy Eternal are saved. (2)

Pauri (Stanza)—Composition of Guru Ram Das.
Be you seated in holy company
Where God's Name repeated utterance finds.
Raise God's Name in poise of heart—
Cast not off the essence of *devotion*.
Meditate ever day and night on God's *Name*—
Thereby shall ye find succour at the Portal Divine.

He alone shall find the holy Preceptor perfectly-endowed,
On whose forehead is recorded the writ in the primal hour.
Boy ye all before the Master,
Who the divine Discourse has raised. (IV)

Sloka (Compositions of Guru Amar Das)
Union of devotees with devotees has come about,
Who with love for the Preceptor are inspired.
Together have they meditated on the beloved Lord,
In true devotion of heart:
Through the Master's Word unfathomable have they found poise from within themselves.
Such noble souls, whom the Creator has brought together,
Never from *one another* are separated.
Some have got not the love of the vision—
Indifferent to contemplation of the Word.
Those alienated through love of duality—
What further separation for them ?
Friendship with egoists is hollow, passing.
Such love in an instant snaps,
And to evil leads.
Those without devotion to the holy Eternal,
Devoid of love for the Name—
What worth cultivating friendship with such,
By the Creator Himself sent astray ? (1)

Verses (Compositions of Guru Amar Das)
Some there are that ever remain constant—
Ever may I be a sacrifice to them.
May my body, mind and substance to them be a sacrifice;
May I ever humbly at their feet bow.
By their touch comes poise to the mind,
And thirst and hunger disappear.
Saith Nanak: Those dyed in the Name are ever in joy,
By centring their meditation on the holy Eternal. (2)

Pauri (Stanza)-Composition of Guru Ram Das).
May I be a sacrifice to the Master
Who on the Lord has discoursed.
May I be a sacrifice ever to the Master,
Who on the way to devotion to the Lord has instructed me.
That beloved holy Master is by me ever,

Succouring me in all places.
I ever hail the holy Master who has to me granted knowledge of the Lord.
May Nanak be a sacrifice to the holy Master,
Who instructed me *in devotion to* the holy Lord's Name,
And thus my mind's desire fulfilled. (V)

Sloka (Compositions of Guru Amar Das)
The world caught in flames of desire, is burnt away,
And in agony is crying:
With the holy Master's cooling touch, never shall fire touch it again.
Saith Nanak: None escapes *Yama's* terror,
Except by contemplation of the holy Word. (I)

Couplets (Compositions of Guru Amar Das)
Ritualism quenches not the flame of desire—
Nor ends its anguish:
Beating the hole kills not the snake—
Thus without fruit is the ritual practice of the faithless.
Through devotion to the holy gracious Master is the Word in the mind lodged:
Then are mind and body in poise and peace.
And the fire of desire quenched.
With egoism gone, is the imperishable supreme joy attained.
He alone practises holy renunciation who to truth is devoted.
Never is such one by anguish visited—
God's Name to satiety fills him.
Saith Nanak: Laudation comes not without *devotion to the* holy Name:
Such a one in egoism remains absorbed, (2)

Pauri (Stanza) (Composition of Guru Ram Das)
Those meditating on the holy Name of the Lord,
Attain joy illimitable
Fruitful is the life of those that hunger after the holy Divine Name.
Those meditating on God, by the Master instructed,
All their sorrows vanish.
Those alone are devotees and true disciples,
That cherish not the least desire for *other than the Lord.*
Blessed is the Master of such as of the divine
Fruit of Immortality have tasted. (VI)

Sloka (Composition of Guru Amar Das)
In Kaliyuga is Yama of the terrible aspect operative;
Under divine command he acts.

Those saved by the Master are liberated;
The egoist he chastises.
By Yama's command is the world bound—
None to restrain him.
By devotion to Him who set Yama to his task,
By Godward turning, suffering comes not.
Saith Nanak: Those to the Master devoted
With purity of heart,
Are by Yama *himself* served,

Couplets (Composition of Guru Amar Das)
This body is of maladies full—
Without the holy Word suffering *arising from* egoism goes not.
By the holy Master's touch is one rendered pure,
As the Lord's Name in the mind is lodged.
Saith Nanak: By contemplation of the holy Name,
Bestower of Joy,
Sorrows spontaneously vanish. (2)

Pauri (Stanza) (Composition of Guru Ram Das)
May I ever be a sacrifice to the Preceptor,
Who instructed me in *devotion to* the Lord, life of the universe.
May I sacrifice my body in particles to the Master,
Who uttered to me the Name of the Lord, Destroyer of Evil-doers.
May I be a sacrifice to the Master,
Who has emancipated me from the poisonous malady of egoism.
Mighty is the grace of the holy Preceptor
Who eliminating evil,
In virtue instructed me.
Only those find the holy Preceptor,
That bear the record of such good fortune on their forehead. (VII)

Sloka (Composition of Guru Amar Das)
Those that have died to the world are the true devotees;
Only those God-directed in devotion engage
In the primal hour have they been blessed with the wealth of devotion,
That none can efface.
In their mind is lodged the Sole Eternal Lord,
Treasury of Noble attributes.
Saith Nanak: Those by divine blessing united *with Him* never again are alienated. (1)

Couplet (Composition of Guru Amar Das)
One without devotion to the holy Master
Poor world his thinking be.
Not knowing the Essence of the holy Word,
Is he deluded by Maya-poison.
One bereft of divine wisdom, in ritual remains absorbed,
To duality attached.
Unaware of their unreality, are the ego-filled,
And by Yama in ignominy get chastised.
Saith Nanak: With whom else may man seek succour ?
The Lord alone is Bestower of Grace. (2)

Pauri (Stanza)—Composition of Guru Ram Das
Thou art the Creator, all knowing;
All creation is Thine.
Thou with Thyself dost unite those that please Thee—
What power has the poor creation?
Thou art Almighty, holy Creator.
Beloved! Those alone are united with Thee,
That win Thy favour, by the Master instructed.
May I be a sacrifice to my holy Preceptor
Who has revealed the truth of the Lord inaccessible. (VIII)

Slokas Composition of Guru Amar Das)
Only the jeweller's trained eye may judge of jewels:
Of jewels the benighted ignorant fool knows not the value.
The Master's World is the jewel—
Of this the jeweller alone may judge.
Those with mind unawakened are ego-filled:
They are born and they die,
Ignominy their destiny.
Saith Nanak: He alone the jewel may acquire,
Who by the Master's instruction is with these in love.
Ever does he utter the holy Name—
Devotion to God his life's sole concern.
By Divine Grace is the Lord in the heart lodged. (1)

Couplets (Composition of Guru Amar Das)
Those that to the holy Master have not devoted *themselves,*
And loved not the Lord's Name—

Deem not such to live:
Death for them is by the Creator destined.
Caught in the great malady of egoism,
From duality they act.
Saith Nanak: The ego-directed are dead while living—
In forgetfulness of the Lord fall they into suffering. (2)

Pauri (Stanza (Composition of Guru Ram Das)
The whole world venerates him who bears purity in his heart.
May I be a sacrifice to one bearing in his self the wealth of the holy Name.
True wisdom lies in meditating on the Lord's holy Name.
Of all Creation is the Lord succourer—
All he cherishes,
Through enlightenment by the Master granted,
In all manifestation is viewed the Supreme Self. (IX)

Sloka (Composition of Guru Amar Das)
Without devotion to the holy Preceptor, the self in bonds *remains,*
And acts from egoism.
Without devotion to the holy Preceptor, beings find not rest from *transmigration,*
And in death and life whirl about:
Without devotion to the holy Preceptor, man's utterance all joy loses,
And the holy Name abides not in the mind.
Saith Nanak: Those without devotion to the holy Preceptor,
In Yama's realm are chastised in bonds,
And leaves this world with faces blackened. (1)

Couplet (Stanza) (Composition of Guru Nanak)
Burn the way of life that turns the mind away from the Beloved Lord.
Saith Nanak: Pure is the love wherein is maintained devotion to the Master. (2)

Pauri (Stanza) (Composition of Guru Ram Das)
Serve the Lord, the sole Bestower,
On Him alone you meditate.
Seek alone of Him fulfilment, and get your heart's desire.
To seek other than Him is shame and disgrace.
One serving the Lord has the true reward achieved—
All his desires fulfilled.
Nanak is a sacrifice to those
That ever from their hearts on the Lord's Name meditate. (X)

Sloka (Composition of Guru Amar Das)
With His devotees is the Beloved pleased:
Himself has He inspired in them devotion.
On His devotees has He conferred true kinship;
Over them has the holy Lord erected a canopy.
Those serving the holy Preceptor ever are in bliss, every pure:
Not such have true royalty as make violent clashes,
And in transmigration are withheld.
Saith Nanak: Those devoid of devotion in disgrace abide,
Honour coming to them never. (1)

Couplets (Composition of Guru Amar Das)
Joyless is listening to discourses,
Devoid of devotion to the Master's holy Word.
From devotion to the holy Preceptor, in the mind is the holy Name lodged,
And illusion and fear of Yama vanish.
In the holy Preceptor's image is the seeker made,
His heart to the holy Name devoted.
Saith Nanak: From devotion comes exaltation,
And honour in the hereafter at the Divine Portal. (2)

Pauri (Stanza) (Composition of Guru Ram Das)
The Master's disciples, with minds full of devotion to the Lord,
To venerate the Master congregate:
In ecstasy in the holy Name they hold commerce,
And profit of the holy Name carry away.
Radiant are the faces of the true disciples—
At the Lord's Portal find they favour.
The holy Preceptor is the grain heap of devotion to the Lord;
By supreme good luck is the disciple therein granted a share.
May I be a sacrifice to the disciples,
That at each step on the Lord's Name meditate. (XI)

Slokas (Composition of Guru Amar Das)
Saith Nanak: The Name is a treasure, found through the holy Preceptor's guidance,
The egoists, ignorant of this treasure lying in their homes
In blindness howl and bark. (1)

Couplets (Composition of Guru Amar Das)
As pure gold is life that to the holy Name is devoted:

Thus is found the pure light immaculate;
All illusion and Yama's fear through the holy Preceptor's guidance vanish.
Saith Nanak; Those devoted to God find joy imperishable,
And absorbed in God—and they true anchorites. (2)

Pauri (Stanza) (Composition of Guru Amar Das)
Blessed are the disciples whose ears have listened to the master's teaching.
Those meditating on God's holy Name—
Shattered are their egoism and illusion.
None but God's Name is the true friend—
Thus have God's devotees contemplated.
Those enjoying the Lord's pleasure,
The holy Preceptor's guidance accept.
Those guided by the Preceptor,
Meditating on the holy Name,
Are in God's love deep-dyed. (XII)

Sloka (Composition of Guru Amar Das)
The egoist is craven, misshapen—
Without devotion comes not respect.
Ever is he engaged in seeking gain;
Even in dream finds he not joy.
Saith Nanak: Only those seeking the Master's guidance are saved;
Else, in bonds they suffer. (1)

Couplets (Composition of Guru Amar Das)
The God-directed bear noble aspect at the Divine Portal,
By living the Master's Word;
Poised within, are they ever in joy,
And are at the Holy Portal honoured.
Saith Nanak: By the Master's guidance is the Divine Name learnt;
In holy Truth are those so enlightened, absorbed. (2)

Pauri (Stanza) (Composition of Guru Ram Das)
Prahlad instructed by the Preceptor, through meditation on the Lord, attained the supreme state;
Through holy instruction Janak fixed on God's Name his mind.
Through holy instruction Vashishta discoursed on divine teaching.
Brother! None ever found devotion to God without the Master's guidance.
The Lord makes Himself manifest to the devotee by the Preceptor's guidance. (XIII)

Sloka (Composition of Guru Amar Das)

One devoid of faith in the holy Preceptor and love for the holy Word,
Never shall find happiness, even after hundreds of transmigratory circles.
Saith Nanak: Through devotion the holy Eternal
Is by the Master's guidance spontaneously followed. (1)

Couplets (Composition of Guru Amar Das)
My self! Seek a guide whose service shall annual transmigration's suffering.
Thus shall illusion disappear,
And egoism through the holy Word be consumed:
The wall of falsehood be demolished,
And in the mind truth shall be lodged.
The mind in poise and joyful the heart,
And thus shalt act with truth and moral discipline.
Saith Nanak: By supreme good fortune is the holy Preceptor found,
Should the Lord so please. (2)

Pauri (Stanza) (Composition of Guru RamDas)
One subject to the Lord's rule is of the whole world overlord.
On none need he depend.
The Lord, *ruler of the Universe,* shall make him liege-lord of the world.
From man's rule may one escape—
How may one the Lord's rule escape?
The Lord abiding in the devotees' hearts is the mightiest of all,
Who has subjected to them all recalcitrant rebels.
By divine grace is the greatness of devotion attained—
Rare are those that by the Preceptor's guidance on the Lord meditate.
(XIV)

Sloka (Composition of Guru Amar Das)
Those devoid of devotion to the holy Preceptor are ruined—
Their life gone waste.
In Duality lies great suffering—
Those caught in it are in transmigration whirled;
Living in filth, through numerous births they pass.
Saith Nanak: Those devoid of devotion shall suffer Yama's chastisement,
And leave this world in regrets. (1)

Couplets (Composition of Guru Amar Das)
In the Universe is One sole Male—
The whole creation females.
All creation He pervades, yet is by any untouched—

In His mystery inaccessible.
The perfect Master alone reveals Him;
From the holy Word is knowledge of Him obtained.
Those serving this mightly Male acquire *true* heroism.
By the holy Word have they consumed their egoism.
None His rival; none His tormentor or foe,
Imperishable His rule, ever abiding.
Ever His devotees serve Him, lauding His *noble* attributes.
Nanak is in ecstasy, beholding might of the Eternal Lord. (2)

Pauri (Stanza) (Composition of Guru Amar Das)
Those cherishing the Lord's Name ever in their hearts,
The Lord is their Saviour.
The Lord's Name is our father, mother, helper and friend,
With the Lord's Essence is our commerce,
With His Essence our counsel—
His Reality ever our cherisher.
The Lord's Essence company lovingly sought,
His Essence our tribe, our family.
The holy Preceptor on Nanak has conferred blessing of the Lord's Name;
In this life and next is the Lord His saviour.
(XV)

Sloka (Composition of Guru Amar Das)
Those blessed by the holy Preceptor utter ever the Lord's laudation.
The Lord's Name, annuller of sorrow, in their mind is lodged.
In the holy Word are they merged.
Liberated themselves, to their tribe too they bring liberation.
Those making obeisance at the Master's feet,
The Supreme Creator, pleasure have won.
Humble Nanak is the Lord's slave—
May He in His grace from ignominy save him. (1)

Couplet (Composition of Guru Amar Das)
In egoism lies trepidation;
In trepidation is the life of such passed.
Egoism is the supreme malady;
One caught therein is in transmigration whirled.
Those so predestined,
With the holy Preceptor's *touch* are blessed.

Saith Nanak: Such by the Master's grace are saved—
Their egoism by the holy Word consumed (2)

Pauri (Composition of Guru Ram Das)
The Lord's Name is our Lord unknowable, inaccessible, Eternal Creator of the Universe.
The Lord's Name we serve; Him we worship—
In the Name is our mind dyed.
None supreme over the Lord's Name to our sight—
The Name our saviour at the last.
The Master gracious has instructed us in the holy Name—
Blessed by the Master's progenitors.
Ever bow I to the holy Preceptor,
Whose touch on me realization of the Lord has conferred. (XVI)

Sloka (Composition of Guru Amar Das)
One neglecting to serve the great Preceptor
And devotion to the Divine Name;
Without finding joy in the holy Word—
In transmigration shall remain whirling.
The egoist purblind contemplates not the purpose of his birth.
Saith Nanak: only those favoured with His grace find liberation. (1)

Couplets (Composition of Guru Ram Das)
The holy Master alone is wide awake—
The rest of the world in slumber of attachment and desire is involved.
Those devoted to holy Master are *truly* awake,
Dyed in *devotion* to the holy Name, of noble attributes.
The egoist purblind contemplates not the Lord,
And caught in birth and death is effaced out of existence.
Saith Nanak: By the Master's guidance
Such engage in contemplating the holy Name,
For whom in the primal hour the writ has so run. (2)

Pauri (Composition of Guru Amar Das)
The Lord's Name is for us the feast of delicate viands,
That consumed, fills us wonderfully.
The Lord's Name is our vesture *fine*,
Which worn, leaves us covered and contented ever,
The Lord's Name is our trade and commerce,

To which the holy Master has appointed us factor.
Of the Lord's Name have we rendered the accompt,
Releasing us of submitting to Yama's accounting in the Hereafter.
Rare are those who by the Master's guidance
Have the Lord's Name contemplated :
In the primal hour has the writ for them so run.
(XVII)

Sloka (Composition of Guru Amar Das)
Ignorant and blind is the world,
Engaged in acting from a motive of duality :
What from duality is done,
Brings in suffering rushing to the body.
By the Master's favour is found joy,
Should life by the holy Word be guided ;
Act by dictates of the holy Word,
And ever contemplate the Name Divine.
Saith Nanak: Man acts as willed by the Lord—
This divine secret none may expound. (1)

Couplets (Composition of Guru Amar Das)
In our home lies perpetually the treasury of the holy Name,
Of devotion are our stores full.
The Lord ever is man's *succourer*
One the self perpetually bestowing favours.
Those favoured of the Lord. laud Him ever
In the Master's Word illimitable.
In the Master's Word they chant of might in all Ages.
Thus shall the self ever be in joy,
And in poise abide.
Enlightenment by the Master granted,
Is the jewel,bestower of liberation.
Saith Nanak: Whoever the Lord favours finds this,
And at the Divine Portal is judged pure. (2)

Stanza (Composition of Guru Ram Das)
Blessed is the devotee who makes obeisance at the holy Master's feet;
Blessed is the devotee who has uttered the holy Name of the Lord Creator.
Blessed in the devotee whose heart revels in listening to the Lord's Name:
Blessed is the devotee who by the Master's service is guided to utter the Lord's Name.

Ever bow I to the disciple who, submitting to the Master's guidance,
Has his teaching followed. (XVIII)

Sloka (Composition of Guru Amar Das)
None found *the way* to God by forced praxis—
All such have practised fruitless ritual.
In forced *praxis* all such adopt various grabs,making vain efforts.
Caught in duality, only suffering is their lot.
The pursuit of occult powers is worldly attachment—
The holy Name thereby finds not lodgement in the heart,
From the Master's obedience is the mind purified,
Ands darkness of ignorance lifted.
Saith Nanak: Thus is the jewel of Enlightenment (1)
Within the self formed.

Couplets (Compositions of Guru Amar Das)
One finding not joy in the holy word,
Or devotion to God's Name.
Joyless his utterance,
In ignominy he abides.
Saith Nanak: One gets recompense for deeds done-
This none has power to efface. (2)

Pauri (Stanza) (Composition of Guru Ram Das)
Blessed is our holy preceptor, immaculate being,
Whose touch has on us conferred peace and poise.
Blessed is our holy preceptor, the Lord's devotee,
In obedience to whom our mind to God's Name is devoted.
Blessed is our holy preceptor, God-enlightened,
By whose teaching friend and foe to our gaze look alike.
Blessed is our holy preceptor , our true friend,
Form whose *guidance* devotion to the holy Name in us is inspird.
(XIX)

Sloka (Composition of Guru Nanak)
In the home is the wife pining for her Lord far away,
Ever thinking of Him:
Union with Him may soon come about,n should her love be sincere.
(1)

Couplet (Composition of Guru Nanak)
Saith Nanak: False is all utterance without true love :

One with such a mind shall utter words of praise,
Only as benefits come (2)

Pauri (Stanza) (Composition of Guru Ram Das)
The Creator is Himself the preserver of all creation :
To those devoted to Him the holy Name is their immortalizing force :
With this are they filled—their hunger satisfied.
One sole being pervades all
To rare devotee is He visible.
Nanak, servant of God, seeking His shelter has found bliss.
(XX)

Sloka (Composition of Guru Amar Das)
The whole world has sight of the holy Preceptor :
His mere sight brings not liberation;
This comes from devotion to the holy Word.
Impurity of egoism goes not without devotion to the Lord's Name.
To come he grants union by grace,
Purifying them of duality and evil-doing.
Nanak! Die thou *to the world* by the holy Master's sight,
By devotion to him. (1)

Couplets (Composition of Guru Amar Das)
The purblind unenlightened ignorant fool
Has engaged not in obedience to the holy Preceptor :
Caught in feelings of daulity, has he fallen into suffering,
And in agony wails.
What prompted him to neglect *obedience* to the Master,
At departing from life has it not benefited him.
Saith Nanak: In following the Master's teaching lies true joy—
From Divine grace alone comes liberation. (2)

Pauri (Stanza) Composition of Guru Ram Das)
All that happens from Thee emanates
None else is there to whom we may complain of Thy doings.
The Lord's is the Voice, His the Call;
On land and water is He pervasive—
Himself the Saviour and Destroyer.
My self! Seek thou shelter with Him.
None but the Lord has power to bring death or grant life—
My self! Free thyself, therefore, from all anxiety.
In all states, my self !

While rising, sitting, sleeping,
On the Lord's Name meditate.
Saith Nanak, servant of God—
Thus by the Master's guidance may one attain the Lord. (21 (4)

(pp. 585-594)

In Measure Sorath — Composition of Guru Amar Das—Score in the Name of the One Indivisible Supreme Being, Realized by Divine Grace. (Quartets)

(The First Quartet Opens)

Such devote themselves to Thy service as in the holy word find joy.
Those discarding egoism have by the Master's grace found purity ;
Ever lauding the attributes of the holy Lord,
Through listening to the Master's Word are they exalted. (1)

Lord ! Just as children are we, seeking Thy shelter—
Thou who art the sole Reality,
Supreme Being without a second. (Pause)
Those with *minds* wakeful alone find the Lord,
By the holy Word annulling egoism.
God's devotees, even though householders, are as anchorites,
By contemplating the essence of Enlightenment.
Through obedience to the holy Preceptor find they joy ever lasting,
Cherishing the Lord ever in their hearts. (2)
The mind in all directions wanders,
Through duality ruined.
The egoist unelightened contemplates not God's Name—
His life gone waste.
Only by the holy Preceptor's touch *is the blessing* of devotion found,
And illusion of egoism lifted. (3)
God's holy devotees live purity
By contemplation of the Master's Word.
The holy Lord grants to them union Himself,
Through the Truth in their hearts lodged.
Saith Nanak: By devotion have I obtained the pure state and
enlightenment—
In this alone lies our wealth. (4.1)

(The First Quartet Closes)

The Second Quartet Opens

On his devotees has He conferred the wealth of devotion—

The Lord's Name is the holy wealth.
Inexhaustible is this wealth of the Name,
Beyond all value.
Those possessing this wealth bear radiant faces,
As the holy Lord they find. (1)
My self! By listening to the Master's Word is the Lord attained;
Those ignorant of the Word are into illusion fallen,
And at the Divine Portal chastised. (Pause)
Five are the robbers lodged in this body—
Lust, violence, avarice, attachment, egoism.
The Amrita they carry off—this the egoist realizes not.
At the last, none to his rescue shall come.
Blind is the world, blind its ways—
Without the Master's *guidance* all is darkness. (2)
Man through egoism and avarice is ruined ;
Nothing in the end shall accompany him ;
Those divinely-guided alone the Name contemplate,
Ever bearing in mind the Lord's Name.
The holy Word and divine laudation they chant,
By God's glance of grace blessed. (3)
Enlightenment given by the holy Master is the mind's imperishable light,
Supreme ruler over heads of monarchs.
God's devotees in devotion are ever engaged day and night.
Devotion to God their true wealth
Saith Nanak: By contemplation of the holy Name *alone* comes liberation;
Those dyed in the Name alone find the Lord. (4.2)

(The Second Quartet Closes)

Third Quartet Open

Only through humility of obedience is the Lord attained,
By discarding egoism.
Joy in God is His devotees' sole course,
Ever lauding Him.
Ever are they dyed in the holy Word in ecstasy unbroken, In the Lord absorbed (1)
Lord! Holy is Thy glance *of grace :*
Shower favour on us Thy servants, cherishing us. (Pause)
In laudation of the holy Word lies my life;
By the Master's guidance is Yama's terror ended.
Supremely beautiful is the holy Lord—

In devotion to Him lies the heart's delight.
One absorbed in the holy Word, the holy teaching,
Is alone in the mind ever awake. (2)
The Lord, unfathomable fount of perennial joy,
Inexhaustible is His reality.
From obedience to the holy Master
Is the Lord, annuller of sorrow, in the heart lodged.
Then are mind and body made pure,
In everlasting joy absorbed,
With illusions shattered. (3)
God's way is a hard path—
The rare devotee contemplating the Master's Word,
This may find,
Should he be immersed in God's dye,
Be by the Word inspired,
And discard egoism and evil-doing.
Saith Nanak: Such a one is dyed ever in the holy Name,
That through the holy Word purifies. (4-3)
(The Third Quartet Closes)

The Fourth Quartet Opens

Lord! Ever may I laud Thee while breath fills this frame ;
To be forgetful of Thee for a moment, an instant,
Is to me like an age.
Brother! Ever were as ignorant, unawakened—
The Master's Word to us has brought light. (1)
Lord! grant to us illumination Thyself.
Lord! May I be a sacrifice to Thee!
To Thy Name may my life be dedicated. (Pause)
Into the holy Word have we died *in flesh* :
From the holy Word have found life after death;
From the Word found liberation.
By the Word are mind and body made pure,
And the Lord in the heart lodged.
The Word is the Master Bountiful, wherein is the heart dyed,
In the Lord absorbed. (2)
Those ignorant of the Word are deaf and blind.
Fruitless their sojourn in this world !
Without joy in the Lord, wasted is their life—
Ever are thy in transmigration whirled:

Egoists ignorant, with minds in darkness enveloped. (3)
Himself the wilder of His might, brother !
Himself He guides along the right path—
Non His will to share.
Brother! The writ recorded in the primal hour none may efface—
His will alone prevails.
Brother! In Nanak's mind is the holy Name lodged—
Nothing else therein abides. (4.4)

(The Fourth Quartet Closes)

3

Guru Ram Das

(b. 1534; d. 1581)

Guru Ram Das born on September 24, 1534 in Chuna Mandi, Lahore. His father Hari Das, who belonged to Sodhi caste was a petty trader. His mother, Anup Kaur who was named Daya Kaur, after her marriage was a lady given to the life of devotion and prayer. Hari Das also had a religious bent of mind. The parents being very poor, Ram Das even as a child, had to supplement the income of his father by selling boiled grams. The Sikh chroniclers state that once his poor mother sent him with a basketful of boiled grams to sell; but he gave them to a company of holy men. The story shows that Ram Das had a large heart, sharp sensitivity to the sufferings of the people. When still a small boy, his dear mother passed away. When he grew to be seven, his father expired. Orphan as he was, grandmother (mother's mother) took him to her village Basarke. There also he had to pass his days in poverty and shortages. His straightend circumstances did not demoralise him rather quickened his intellect, bred in him courage and made him serene and sober. The handsomeness of his physique coupled with the sterling qualities of mind made (Guru) Ram Das a rare personality at once lovable and charismatic. This was the reason that people at Basarke loved and adored him. According to Bhai Sahib Singh "Guru Amar Das who came to Basarke to condole with the grandmother of Ram Das at the death of her son-in-law, developed deep affection for the boy and even after he left for Khadur Sahib (A.D. 1541) he used to come to Basarke and pat the boy."

Ram Das lived at Basarke for five years. He lived on what he earned by selling the boiled grams. At the age of twelve, he along with his grandmother left for Goindwal to settle there.

According to Bhai Sahib Singh, (Guru) Amar Das who was deputed by Guru Angad Dev to found a new city of Goindwal on the bank of the river Beas invited Ram Das along with other relatives to settle in the city. In fact Guru Amar Das had started taking interest in the welfare of Ram Das since he first met him at Basarke. At Goindwal, Ram Das began to live a life dedicated to the Guru's cause. He would do any job for the Guru and the cause which he championed. He had the sacred privilege of seeing personally Guru Angad also. He addressed himself zealously to understand the meaning of the sacred compositions of the Gurus in all their import as also their cause. He acquired mastery over the diction, poetic art and mythology. He learnt science of music which he made use of in his compositions of different hymns. Through service and contemplation, he mastered his senses and different propensities.

In A.D. 1552 Guru Angad Dev passed on his apostolate to Amar Das instead of his sons who did not come upto his expectations because they were not as devoted to his cause as Amar Das. Ram Das, who at that time was living at Goindwal could very easily understand that in order to qualify for apostolate one had to acquire requisite merit and fitness.

Accordingly (Guru) Ram Das exerted to the best of his capacity and ability to acquire the same. Guru Amar Das struck by the manifold qualities of Ram Das decided to marry his dear daughter, Bibi Bhani, with him and the marriage was solemnized in A.D. 1553.

Giani Gian Singh says that the marriage took place in A.D. 1542, i.e. to say when Bibi Bhani was in the sixth year of her age. A probe into the matter would dispel the fog hiding the truth. The view of Gian Singh is unfounded for two reasons; firstly, the Guru did not favour child marriage and secondly the sequence of the fact belies the assertion. It is said that the Guru, on seeing the boy, exclaimed "Jetha is the right type of the boy. I was in search for my daughter." Obviously, the Guru meant that the Guru was of a reasonable age and endowed with certain qualities required of good husband and certainly Jetha was not a child. Moreover, Jetha accompanied a band of devoted Sikhs who went to Goindwal to render service in the construction of Baoli. Since all records speak that the construction of Baoli was started in A.D, 1552. Hence it is reasonable to assign the end of A.D. 1552 or the beginning of A.D. 1553 as the time for the marriage of Bibi Bhani.

After his marriage Jetha stayed with his father-in-law and was closely associated with the ministry. He put on record many an incident connected with the struggles that his Master with his opponents, and as such his writings are a good source of information in respect of contemporary affairs.

Jetha commanded full confidence of the Guru and this was the reason that he diputised the Guru on his behalf in the court of Akbar and accompanied the Guru when the latter went on a long journey to Hardwar to acquaint the people with his mission. The Guru was so much impressed by Ram Das that in A.D. 1574 he got down from his seat, seated Jetha thereon and placed five paise and one account before him as a mark of handing over Guru Gaddi to him.

Mohri, the youngest son of Amar Das reconciled himself with the succession of Guru Ram Das, but Mohan, the eldest one, resented this act of his father, retired in indignant silence to the solitude of his own room, where he remained all his life. Rama, the elder son-in-law also acquiesced in the choice made by the Guru.

Consolidation and Transformation

On the assumption of the pontificate, Guru Ram Das shifted his residence to the present site of Amritsar to avoid any possible unpleasantness with the relatives of the last Guru so that he might find peaceful time to work on his plans. He was a powerful personality. Whosoever came into his presence, was impressed. His songs moved all. In the hymus composed by him, God was adored and love-sickness of the soul was voiced. The melted even the stony hearts. His words, mighty, simple and touching went deep into the hearts of listeners. He infected visitors with the Love of God deep rooted in his heart. He composed a large number of soul-elevating hymns. The poetry of Ram Das flows like a stream of love whose cooling melody yearns for the beloved and sings the magic-spell of his glance. It is put in the mouth of the Bride of God, she pines in her longing for more glimpses of Him and still one more. The Master's divine music thrilled the soul of a whole people and his song had the might of bringing about a revolution in one's outlook.

Apart from composing hymns and preaching Guru's Gospel, he took steps to strengthen the organisation of the Sikhs. The following is the account of the steps he took in this direction.

Foundation of Chak Guru or Ram Das Pur (Amritsar)

The most notable achievement of the Guruship of Guru Ram Das was the laying of the foundation of the city Ram Das Pur, which is now called as Amritsar. But there is no concensus of opinion as to when its foundation was actually laid. According to Macauliffe, when Akbar paid a visit to Guru Amar Das for the first time, he made a grant of land to Bibi Bhani, the daughter of Guru Amar Das. Shortly afterwards, the Guru asked Ram Das to shift to those lands and excavate there two tanks—Santokhsar and Amritsar. In this way, Guru Ram Das started the work during the life time of Guru Amar Das.

Ibbetson, Conningham, Archer and M'Greger, however, hold the opinion that the grant of the land on which the city of Amritsar developed was made by Akbar to Guru Ram Das, and it was the latter who founded the city "Sikhan De Raj Di Vithia" also supports this view. M'Gregar states that Akbar was much impressed by the hallowed personality of the Guru and issued an order that "a certain portion of ground should be granted to Ram Das which was accordingly done, and the ground thus bestowed, being of a circular farm was named 'Chakkar Ram Das.' According to the Amritsar District Gazetteer, the pool which formed the nucleus of the city, had been a favourite resort of Guru Ram Das. In 1577, he obtained grant of the site together with 500 bighas of land from the Emperor Akbar on payment of Rs. 700 Akbari to the Zamindars of Tung who owned the land. It may here be explained that none of these writers is a contemporary of Guru Amar Das and Ram das; yet the account given by the District Gazetteers and European travellers seems to be true on two counts; firstly, their account is in consonance with the Sikh tradition and secondly the basis of Macaulliffe's view i.e. Suraj Parkash is unreliable because it gives confused, at places self contradictory account of this event.

From the above, it is evident that the present city of Amritsar was built on the land which was granted by Akbar to Guru Ram Das and he started the excavation work near about A.D. 1577. After some time Guru felt that it was difficult to direct the work of excavation from Goindwal and as a sequel to it, he left for the new place. Prof. Puran Singh gives another reason in this context. According to him, the Guru shifted to the new site because he did not want to come into clash with the Muslims and the orthodox Hindus of Goindwal who were feeling soar over the ever-increasing influence of the Guru.

According to G.C. Narang "small huts were built near the bank for the Guru and the Sikhs. A few more huts were raised to accommodate the visitors. As a result of all this, a small town in the neighbourhood of the tank grew up and it began to be called 'Chak Guru' or Ram Das Pura. He invited men of 52 trades to take up their residence there and to open their business in the Guru's Market which is still known as "Guru ka Bazar.' The city, in the course of time grew to be the biggest centre of trade in the Punjab."

As regards the excavation of tanks, he had, in the beginning, undertaken to dig two tanks—Santokhsar and Amritsar. But after some time he felt that it was extremely difficult to complete both these projects simultaneously on account of the paucity of funds. Hence, the Guru suspended the work on Santokhsar and asked his followers to concentrate their attention on the tank, known as Amritsar (tank of Nectar). Bhai Budha and Bhai Selho who were the most devoted Sikhs were assigned the job of supervising the projects. According to Macauliffe "it was felt by the Guru and Bhai Budha that they must procure ample funds if they wanted to complete the whole work within a short span of time. Consequently, the Guru chalked out a plan to disseminate Guru's teachings on a larger scale which was also the remedy for the financial difficulties, for it would arouse devotion in the hearts of disciples who would naturally make more offerings.

Even with all this, the work of excavating and constructing the tanks could not be completed because of the early death of the Guru and the work was finished by his son—Guru Arjun Dev.

The laying of the foundation of the city of Amritsar is a step of far-reaching importance. "In founding the town of Amritsar at the most convenient and fertile centre, he laid deep the foundation of the future greatness of the Sikhs as a nation." The reasons are not far to seek.

Firstly the city, being situated in the heart of the tract and occupied by the sturdy peasants, enabled the Gurus to secure followers from their ranks, who ultimately proved the bulwark of their warlike successors. Secondly the people were able to gather at a common place of worship so well-situated. The Sikhs who followed the simple and pure tenets prescribed by the founder of their faith, now learnt to unite together and to foster those feelings of brotherly love which eventually strengthened the national tie and paved the way to the formation of a commonwealth on true patriotic principles. Thirdly, with construction of the city, the people abandoned visiting Hindu places of pilgrimage. Fourthly, the city, because it was surrounded by fertile lands, grew into a very important centre of trade in the Punjab. The merchants developed connections with far off countries such as Bokhara, Kabul and Kashmir and contributed a lot towards widening the outlook of the Sikhs. Fifthly, the commercial prosperity of Amritsar ensured a rich revenue to the Sikh Gurus in the form of offerings. Sixthly, the city was free from all traces of communalism and symbolised in itself the secular way of life—which was the need of the times. Seventhly, the city, being a new colony of the disciples radiated dawn-light and no-wonder the people embraced Sikhism in a large number.

Masand System

Another step which contributed a lot towards organization was the setting up of Masand System. Two reasons prompted the Guru to bring this organization into existence. There was genuine need for building a rapport between the Guru and ever-swelling number of the Sikhs; and secondly the regular collection of the offerings was to be ensured.

Under this system the Guru sent his trusted Sikhs to spread Sikh faith and collect offerings to be remitted to the Guru. The Sikhs, commissioned to do the aforesaid job were allotted a definite area, and were known as Masands. Masand seems to be a corruption of 'Mas Nad' shorter form of Masnedi-Ali or his Excellency, the title which the Moghul Governors often held. The exact number of Masands and their respective areas are not known to history, but this much is certain that very many Sikhs famous for integrity and piety were asked to act as Masands. Some scholars, such as Mohsan Fani the author of "Dabistan-i-Mazahib" and some other modern historians are of the view that Masands system was introduced by Guru Arjan Dev and not by Guru Ram Das, Macauliffe, however, states that the system was originated under Guru Ram Das.

We have examined the contemporary records and reached the conclusion that the system grew up during the pontificate of Guru Ram Das, although it was elaborated in its details during the time of Guru Arjan Dev. In the support of our view, there is a concrete evidence in Panth Parkash, whose author calls "Masands" Ramdasias. On our further probe, nowhere in the contemporary records or other relevant records, the word 'Masand' has been used. Hence under the circumstances, it will not be wrong to conclude that the word 'Masand' came into use during the Guruship of Guru Arjan Dev.

Connected with this system, a pertinent question can be asked as to what was the need of this system when 'Manji' system was already existing. There seem to be two reasons for setting up the fresh organisation. In the first instance, the persons holding Manjies were so much engrossed in their work that it was not possible for them to keep in touch either with the Sikhs or with the Guru and consequently they were not in a position to appreciate the difficulties of the Guru and also the new challenges, he was confronting. Secondly, some of the holders of the Manjies had fallen under the influence of Bidhi Chand, the son of Handal who was vehement in his propaganda to denigrate the personality of the Guru and hence all the Manji Holders then could not be relied upon. Thirdly with the lapse of time, the Manji holders had grown lax and lazy.

Under the circumstances there was dire need either to invigorate the existing institution of Manji or to set a new one. The Guru chose the latter path.

Masand system played a great role in consolidating Sikhism. It injected into the body social of the Sikhs the requisite cohesion and tried to develop in them the habit of remaining in discipline. In times to come, this habit of theirs helped them a lot to save themselves from the onslaught of the Moghul Imperialism. Furthermore, the "Masands" used to remit the money offered by the Sikhs to the Guru regularly and this thing went a long way to alleviate the financial difficulties of the Guru—apart from being the first step towards orgnaising the "Guru's Golak" or "Guru's Treasury."

The Guru was aware of the fact that any organisation unless its followers have full faith in its organaisers, is sure to meet its doom. To safeguard Masand system against this, the Guru repeatedly impressed upon the people in so many hymns that without abject faith in Guru, salvation was not possible. In Var Gauri, the Guru explained his point of view in full length and with candour. He advised his opponents to have faith in the Guru and in his words, instead of indulging in blasphemy by introducing an edge of disunity among the sikhs. He condemned the people who were scheming to denigrate the exalted personality of Guru Amar Das.

In keeping with the policy of his predecessors, the Guru asked his followers to avoid singing filthy songs on occasions such as marriage, child-birth and instead he composed hymns which were akin to 'Ghori' or Sithnian in their form, to be sung on the aforesaid occasions. He composed four hymns known as 'lawan' in Suhi Rag and asked the Sikhs to recite them to solemnize marriages as the 'lawans' embody in themselves a lesson for the pair to develop true love for each other and lead a life of equipoise. Besides, the following hymn was made obligatory for the Sikhs to recite before starting any work.

Ask thy Lord if thou wantest thy work done
Through the true Guru's word, He accomplisheth thy tasks
In the society of the holy, drink thou then the Nectar, the treasure of Good
O Thou, the Dispeller of fear, O Merciful Lord save my Honour
Nanak, by singing thy praises, on knoweth the unknowable thou

In this way a distinct social code of the Sikhs began to emerge which considerably separated them from the common mass of the Hindus.

Baba Sri Chand, the eldest son of Guru Nanak Dev, was the leader of a religious sect of his own known as Udasis. He roamed over the country as a mystic of great repute. In his travels, Baba Sri Chand came to Amritsar to meet Ram Das. On seeing Ram Das, long flowing beard, Baba Sri Chand asked him jocularly why he grew it. "To wipe the dust from thy holy feet," replied Ram Das. Sri Chand replied "It is this magic that has made thee so great and me so small." Thereafter in the discussion, Sri Chand made frank confession of the superiority enjoyed by the Sikh religion and promised to extend co-operation to him. Indeed, the Udasis, after the re-approachment, spared no pains to serve Sikh religion. After the death of Banda Bahadar, it goes to the credit of the Udasis that, when Moghul rulers decided to destroy the Sikhs root and branch, they who could not easily be distinguished from the common mass of the Hindus, kept the divine spark of the Sikh Faith alight.

Like his predecessors the Guru carried on the work of free kitchen with vigour and zeal characteristic of him. He made the arrangements more elaborate, more elegant and more methodical. Proper amount of emphasis was laid on 'Pangat' in the 'free kitchen' and anyone, irrespective of caste, creed, clime, and colour could partake of the food without any hesitation. The caste system and pilgrimages were decried and superstitions of various types were denouned.

Apart from the steps of the Guru enumerated above which contributed a lot so far as the dissemination of Sikhism was concerned, he sent many of his trusted disciples to different places to spread Sikh faith. He is said to have converted one Handal of Jandiala whom he asked to go and settle in his native village to propagate the new faith. Similarly he sent Bhai Gurdas to Agra to spread the Guru's Gospel. Sri Chand, the eldest son of Guru Nanak and progenitor of the Udasi sect was won over by the Guru and the age-long rivalry between the two sects of Nanak-Udasis and the Sikhs—actually ended in the truimph of Sikhism. Besides this, Maya, Japa, Kanahaya, Tulsa Dharam Das, Jetha Sansari and Tirath having convinced of the greatness of Sikh mission embraced Sikhism and dedicated their lives to its dissemination.

This is an admitted fact that Akbar disliked the quarrel between different religious. He, through his experience had known that every religion had grain of truth and true religion lay in the transcendence of self. No wonder the Sikh faith which regarded 'love' as the key-note of its ideology was much liked by the emperor. He paid homage to Guru Amar Das and was much impressed by the institution of 'free kitchen' run by him. Guru Ram Das was also held in high veneration by him and in token thereof, he gave 500 bighas of land to him. It is said that at the instance of the Guru. Akbar remitted the land revenue for full one year. Consequently, the Guru grew very popular among the people in general and peasantry in particular.

The Guru's work during his pontificate of seven years was remarkable in asmuch as it lent initial impetus to the work of the spread of Sikhism under his successor. The Guru consolidated the Sikhs by giving them a sacred tank, named Amritsar, a distinct organisation, Masand system, and a central treasury by advising the Masands to collect a part of the income of the Sikhs of their respective diocease and then to send the same to the Guru.

Cunningham, however feels that inspite of the fact that Guru Ram Das commanded esteem of the people, he could not attract very large number of converts because after forty-two years of the Sikh movement, the number did not even double. The aforesaid view is unwarranted in view of the fact that in the ministry of Guru Ram Das, Sikhism made its headway at far off places and various sangats were organised to keep the torch of Sikh faith alive.

Guru Ram Das, seeing his end approaching nominated his son Arjan Mal as his successor. This choice of the Guru was much resented by his eldest son, Prithia, who charged his father for having ignored his right to the 'Gaddi' and did not hesitate using even indecent words. At this, the Guru felt annoyed and rebuked him "Be off with you. Never show me your face. You are mean. My Sikhs will never obey thee and will never associate with thee." As a matter of fact, it was Arjun Mal's intelligence, far-sightedness and fore-sight, organising capacity, love for the Divine and spirit of sacrifice that qualified him for the exalted office.

The Guru, having nominated, Arjan Mal, left Ramdaspur (Amritsar) and retired to his old headquarter, Goindwal. After a few day's stay in Goindwal, Guru Ram Das expired on September 1, 1581. Though the period of his Guruship was that of seven years only, yet his achievements occupy a unique place in the history of the evolution and consolidation of the Sikh faith.

The succession of Arjan Mal is of tremendous importance. The fact, that Guru Ram Das appointed his youngest son. Guru Arjan as his successor, decided once for all that succession to Guruship would be decided on grounds of heredity and merit. The succession became "a family and personal concern and claims to it were paralleled with those to throne. In Latif's views "this changed the very character of Guruship and materially contributed to the growth of Sikh power, for henceforward the Guru was looked upon by his disciples no only in the light of a spiritual guide but also as a wordly lord and a ruling sovereign." According to Dr. Narang "The Guru now become such—a Padshah or the true king." The true king ruled his followers not only in the present life but also in the times to come. The orders of the true king were of greater importance than those of a false ones; and herein lay the difference which prepared the Sikhs later to challenge the authority of the Moghuls. In this way, the establishment of hereditary principle in the Gurship proved a step of far-reaching consequences in transforming the character of the Sikhs. The principle of deciding claims to succession on principles of heredity and merit, also minimised the chances of quarrel over the succession to Guru Gaddi.

4

Guru Hargovind

(b. 1595 A.D. — d. 1645 A.D.)

Guru Arjan had only one so, Hargobind. He was born on 21st Har Sambat 1652 (June 1595 A.D.) at Vadali in Amritsar District. He ascended on the 9th Har Sambat 1663 (June 1606 A.D.) at the age of 11 years. At the time of his accession, the *Masands* or Tithe collectors, according to the old custom, presented a *manji* (bedstead), a *seli* (a woollen thread worn by Faqirs), a hat, a religious book and a rosary. The Guru returned them with the remark that he was destined to change the doctrine of the rosary to that of the sword: his mission was to protect the faith of the Lord and the necessary protection could not be afforded without the aid of arms. Therefore he proclaimed his intention of wearing arms; and he wore two swords, one on each side, right and left, abandoning the *seli,* and *topi* (tokens of a *faqir*) for good. He explained that one sword represented *faqiri* and the other *amiri,* the proper exposition of which expression is yet a mystery. The most probable construction is that he combined the qualities of a warrior and a saint. He became a military leader as well as a spiritual leader. He took delight in hunting and was the first Guru who organised a military system, armed his followers, and prepared them for action in the field. He engaged the services of the brave and drilled them in arms. In a very short time he formed a handsome group of combatants and those Hindus, who had proposed to embrace Islam under coercion of the authorities, began to look to him for comfort and protection,

On 5th Har Sambat 1666 (June 1609 A.D.) Guru Hargobind constructed Akalbunga (the house of God) in front of the Sikh temple at Amritsar. In that temple he began to convene assemblies to preach his gospel. He said that as long as he continued in Harminder, he should be reckoned as a saint and in Akalbunga he should be looked upon as a King. He dressed himself in costly and princely attire and issued an edict to the Sikhs to present him with arms on their usual visits of pilgrimage.

He became very famous for his charity and spiritual power. The home *(langar)* was maintained on a much larger scale than before and thousands of Hindu and Muhammadan poor were constantly waiting for a food and clothing. Psalms were ever being recited in the temple and the formulas of morning and evening prayers were more rigidly observed. The Guru toured through the country on various occasions preaching the mission of Guru Nanak. He constructed many gardens and established many public institutions. He obtained a lease from the Emperor and founded Hargobindpur on 17th Assu Sambat 1677 (October 1620 A.D.).

On seeing the prosperity of the Guru, his cousion Mehrwan, the son of his paternal uncle, Prithi Chand, grew very jealous and conspiring with Chandu Lal, complained to the Emperor Jahangir, that having abandoned the practice of his ancestors, the Guru had buckled on the sword, and organised a regular army, and had begun to dispose judicial cases like the King's law-courts. He also represented that these facts were injurious to the interests of the State and prayed the Emperor to adopt measures to stop them. Chandu Lal reminded the Emperor of the imposition of the Fine of Rs. 100,000 on the deceased Guru Arjan and suggested its recovery from his son. The Emperor deputed two Sardars to fetch Guru Hargobind.

On his part also the Guru was seeking an opportunity to have an interview with the Emperor, so that Chandu Lal might be chastised for his cruelty. On the arrival of the Sardars, he at once made necessary arrangements for his household and the Temple at Amritsar, and started on 3rd Jeth Sambat 1673 (May 1616 A.D.) to Delhi with 100 horse and foot. When by convenient marches he reached Delhi, the Emperor received him with due marks of honour and respect and during the interview he was very much pleased by what he saw. He granted Rs. 500 for the *langar* and issued orders for the necessary supply of grain and fodder for horses. At the same time he gave him permission to attend the Court daily. On several occasions the Guru accompanied the Emperor to his sports. The Guru's rising in the estimation of the Emperor grieved his father's enemy, Chandu Lal, who made several unsuccessful attempts to injure him. However on an occasion when the Emperor was attacked with high fever for three successive days, the old snake. Chandu Lal, found opportunity to bite. He bribed the royal astronomer to attempt the removal of the Guru from the royal presence. The astronomer told the Emperor that an evil star *(Sarh satti)* had appeared which fore-boded evil to His Majesty for 7½ years, unless a pious faqir like the Guru, should repeat holy hymns for 40 days in some suitable place in the south. Then Chandu Lal came in and pretended to praise the Guru much and suggested that the Fort of Gwalior was the most suitable and convenient locality for the purpose. The Emperor was deceived and a message was sent to the Guru accordingly. The latter did not think it proper to enter into a discussion at the time and carried out the royal wishes at once and left for Gwalior with 5 Sikhs. When he had been there for some days, Chandu Lal sought an opportunity to explain the prosperous condition of the Guru and the advisability of levying the fine of Rs. 100,000, and suggested that until the amount was paid in, the Guru should be told to remain in the Fort as a State Prisoner. His Majesty agreed and orders were issued accordingly. Some months later, the news of the fact reached Amritsar and the Guru's mother deputed Baba Budha to procure his release on payment of the fine. About 2,000 Sikhs accompanied him. They gathered round the fort and bowed before its walls in worship of the Saint undergoing persecution there. They asked for permission to pay the fine, but the Guru frobade them on pain of curse and excommunication, and it was never paid in.

The Guru was ever busy in contemplation and did not care about his imprisonment, but the Sikh Nation was deeply concerned. At the time the famous Faqir, Mian Mir, happened to visit Delhi, and obtained an interview with the Emperor. During the conversation the latter stated the troubled nature of his dreams, which the former attributed to the incarceration of the innocent Guru. At the same time he showed the Emperor how Chandu Lal had been cruel and hard upon the deceased Guru Arjan on account of a private grudge and how for that same reason he was bent upon doing mischief to the Guru. He added that for such acts, though the Subordinates were directly responsible, the Rulers were also lable to suffer. By these remarks the Emperor was much affected and ordered the immediate release and return of the Guru to Delhi. On his arrival there precious presents were sent to him, and His Majesty apologised and sought forgiveness for his past treatment of the Guru.

At the Emperor's request the Guru halted for some time at Delhi. His Majesty found in him an excellent sportsman and a talented combatant. He accompanied the imperial camp during His Majesty's tour of Rejputana and raised himself much in the estimation of the Emperor. His Majesty deputed him to subdue Raja Tara Chand of Nalagarh who had continued for a long time in open rebellion and all efforts to subdue him had failed. He was vanquished and brought before the Emperor in Sambat 1675 (1618 A.D.). Owing to this, new honours were conferred upon the Guru, and he was made Honorary Commander of 7 Guns and 1000 horse and foot. He was also invested with the powers of control over and of hearing appeals against the decisions of the authorities in the Punjab. His decisions in judicial cases were received and accepted by the parties with gratification and his tuition in spiritual knowledge and moral courage raised his followers much higher in social and moral standing. His popularity as spiritual leader and temporal judge largely augmented his power and fame. He was termed by the people "Sacha Padshah Sodhi Sultan." (True King, the Sodhi Sultan).

When the Guru was about to leave Delhi for home, he had a parting interview with the Emperor. The former was wearing a very beautiful and precious *Simrna* (a miniature rosary of 28 beads) of pearls and *Kapurs* (a sort of gems) and His Majesty asked for one of those pearls to serve as a top-head of his royal rosary as a token of the Guru's friendship. He placed it at His Majesty's disposal with the remark that his father had a rosary of 108 pearls much superior to those, and that now it was in possession of his Diwan, Chandu Lal. These remarks reminded the Emperor of the story related by Mian Mir and he asked for its details, which were duly given. Then the Diwan was immediately sent for, and Guru Arjan's rosary and seal which were in his possession were demanded. The Diwan denied all knowledge thereof, on which his house was searched and both of these articles were found. On this his whole property was confiscated and Chandu Lal, being considered as the murderer of Guru Arjan, was handed over to Guru Hargobind to be dealt with as he deemed proper.

The Diwan was put in charge of the dog-keeper and orders were issued that every Sikh should deal five blows with a shoe on his head every morning. Enduring that treatment he was brought to Amritsar in Magh Sambat 1675 (1618 A.D.). During the next month he accompanied the Guru's camp to Lahore where he was dragged through the streets with irons on his feet. He was so abused and taunted by the public and so oppressed by the sense of his own sins that life hung heavy upon him and eventually on 27th Phagan S. 1675 (March 1619 A.D.) one Gurditta Bharbhunja (grain parcher) ended the Diwan's miserable life by pouring hot sand upon his head as he was passing by his shop. It was a very good moral for the public that one whom the tyrant had employed to supply hot and burning sands for paining the Guru, served similarly to execute and end the life of the tyrant.

In 1677 S. (1620 A.D.) one Bhag Mal, a Sikh, was taking a fine Turkistani horse from Kabul for presentation to the Guru. It was seized at Lahore by the officers of the King and presented to Prince Shahab-ud-din (afterwards Shah Jahan). He was struck with its beauty and ordered its price to be paid and the horse to be sent to the royal stable, notwithstanding the vehement protests of the owner. The fact was reported to the Guru who said that it must eventually come to him. The horse became lame and was made over to Rustam Khan, the Chief Qazi of Lahore. He properly treated and cured it and then sold it to the Guru. At the time of which we are speaking the Guru was encamping at Muzang in the vicinity of the town of Lahore and halted there for five months. The house of Qazi Rustam Khan was close by. He had one 'Kaulan' in his harem. She used to hear the hymns which were constantly chanted by bands of musicians in the presence of the Guru. She admired them but the Qazi was greatly offended to know that a Mussalman woman should have any like for the hymns of infidels. He began to maltreat her and contemplated her murder but she contrived to escape and took protection with the Guru. She was treated by him very kindly, and was lodged in a separate building with necessary arrangements for her safety. Eventually the tank named Kaulsar was constructed by the Guru in her memory as a true devotee. It is close to the grand and secred reservoir at Amritsar just in front of Baba Atal. It took 7 years in its construction and was completed in Sambat 1684 (1627 A.D.). She died in Sawan S. 1686 (1629). A.D.).

In Sambat 1682 (1625 A.D.) the Guru accompanied the Emperor Jahangir to Kashmir *via* Chaprar, Wazirabad and Mirpur. From Srinagar he went to Tibet and Ladakh. When His Majesty left Kashmir for Kabul, the Guru returned to Amritsar *via* Muzaffarabad, Abbotabad, Hassan Abdal, Rawalpindi, Gujrat, Hafizabad, Talwandi, (Guru Nanak's birth place where he founded the present Nankana

Sahib), Manak and other places. The famous Shah Daula and Jahangir faqirs met him at Gujrat,

On his way back from Kabul the Emperor fell ill and died at Bhimbar on the morning of 28th October, 1627 A.D. (S. 1684). He was succeeded by Shah Jahan, his son. During the life time of Jahangir, as could be expected, the power and authority of the Guru had engendered jealousy among the king's officials. The faith of Guru Nanak was already disliked by the priestly classes on account of its all equalising tenets. Chandu Lal's relations and Prithi Chand's descendants were all lying in wait for an opportune time to renew their complaints. Rustam Khan, Qazi, was seeking on opportunity to claim the restoration of Kaulan. Many attempts to injure the Guru failed during the lifetime of Jahangir, but when the young and inexperienced Emperor ascended the throne, the malicious attacks were renewed and many complaints poured in. Although, before his ascending the throne, Shah Jahan was a great friend of the Guru and held him in high respect and used to pay him visits during his stay at Lahore, yet on receipt of these multifarious complaints his views changed. Immediately after he became Emperor, the selfish and jealous Muhammadan officials advised him to withdraw the powers with which his father had invested the Guru. The latter did not care a bit for it.

The Guru in Sambat 1684 (1627 A.D.) was invited by certain hill Rajas to visit their country, but he sent Baba Gurditta, his eldest son to Dun and Hindu. The young prince founded Kiratpur on 13th Maghaa Sambat 1684 (December 1627 A.D.).

At about the same time, the Guru was sporting near the village of Gumtala, and Shah Jahan also chanced at the very juncture to be sporting in the vicinity of Kuhala. A hawk belonging the Emperor joined those belonging to the Guru, who proposed not to part with it. On this various past complaints were brought again to the notice of the Emperor and induced his Majesty to send an armed force with a view to seize the Guru and disperse his followers. Gulam Rasul Khan was deputed from Lahore at the head of 7,000 troops. The Guru encountered him with 1,000 men. On 17th Chet Sambat 1685 (March 1629 A.D.) a severe battle was fought at Vadalo near Amritsar. The King's army was signally defeated and returned to Lahore after sustaining a heavy loss in killed and wounded. Two leaders were killed and the commander was wounded in the engagement. An enormous quantity of stores and magazines fell into the hands of the victor, and this was the first battle in the annals of the Punjab which was fought between the Muhammadans and the Sikhs.

When the news of this discomfiture reached the Emperor, he was inflamed and burned with anger. He immediately despatched Mukhlas Khan, Naib Subadar, at the head of 15,000 men to fight the Guru. The Guru had anticipated this and made necessary arrangements. He had by this time 4,000 combatants under his banner. He added 5 more to the number of guns in his possession by boring holes in wooden logs, which he mounted on the Lohgarh Fort. A pitched battle was fought on 11th Baisakh Sambat 1986 (April 1629 A.D.). The issue was undecided when the fall of night stopped operations. However during the night the Sikhs inflicted a heavy loss on the enemy. Next morning the king's force was on the eve of breaking down when Mukhlas Khan very bravely stormed the fort. Then the town of Amritsar was plundered. When the imperial army was busy with the spoils, the Guru, who was not present during the storming of the fort, was preparing for another encounter. He personally led the combat, both sides lost seriously in killed and wounded, and Mukhlas Khan was killed by the Guru himself. The imperial army suffered a disastrous defeat and returned to Lahore. In order to avoid further and immediate attack by the imperial force, the Guru went to Jhubal. He halted there for a few days and then left for Kartarpur *via* Tarn Taran, Khadur and Gondwal.

When the news of the defeat reached the Emperor, he was extremely enraged and proposed to despatch a large army again, but Wazir Khan, Governor of Lahore, dissuaded him, explaining how the Guru, who was a mere faqir, had roused the spirits of the people, and how he was fighting with wooden guns. He represented that nothing good would come if he were captured or conquered and the proposal was thus, after the consideration, dropped.

Owing to the somewhat prolonged absence of the Guru from Hargobindpur, one Bhagwana, a relation of the well-known Chandu Lal, had taken wrongful possession of it. When in S. 1686 (1629 A.D.) the Guru went there, Bhagwana refused to deliver its possession. He thought that since the Emperor was not on good terms with the Guru, he would be able to hold the village for ever. He therefore, resisted and fought with the Guru, but was slain in the encounter. Rattan Chand, the son of the deceased, then hastened to Jalandhar and, after consulting with the relations of Chandu Lal and others, who were unfavourably disposed towards the Guru, induced the Governor of Jalandhar; Abdulla Khan, to seize the Guru as a fugitive, and present him before the Emperor. The Guru was stated to have only 200 men with him. Abdulla Khan then marched on Hargobindpur at the head of 5,000 men. The Guru also made necessary preparations and a heavy battle was fought for three days. Both sides sustained serious losses, and the Muhammadan Commander with many high officers fell in the field. Victory remained with the Sikhs, and many trophies of war fell into their hands.

When fate decided against the invader, Bhagwana laid his case before the Viceroy of Lahore. A thorough and sifting inquiry was made into all his allegations and a detailed report was submitted to the emperor at Delhi. On perusal of this report all the suspicions which Shah Jahan had long entertained in regard to the Guru, were effaced from his mind, and thereafter he took no action on any complaint against the Guru.

Things then went on smoothly for about two years until fresh incidents necessitated the disturbance of the peace. In Sambat 1689 (1632 A.D.) a Sikh house-dealer brought from Kabul two very fine horses for the Guru. The Governor of Lahore forcibly took them for the King and paid for them against the owner's will. He protested against the bargain, but in vain, and intimated the fact to the Guru, who remarked that the Governor had no right to seize horses which were intended for the Guru. One Bidhi Chand volunteered to feth them for the Guru. In a very curious way he took one animal from the fort of Lahore and presented it to the Guru. At that time the river Ravi was flowing under the fort and the animal being made to swim therein for some distance, no track was left by which it could be traced. Then the same Bidhi Chand appeared as tracker and pretended to find out the stolen animal. After some preliminaries he rode the second horse in day light and in presence of king's officers, jumped into the river just in the same way as he had done before, and then, giving them full particulars of himself and his destination, he challenged them to follow him. All were astonished at it and a detailed report was submitted to the Emperor. He flew into violent anger and deputed Mirza Kamir Beg Khan, a leader of the army, with 22,000 troops to capture the Guru. The latter entrenched himself on the bank of a pond at the village of Lahr. and a serious battle was fought on the 17th Poh, Sambat 1690 (1633 A.D.). It continued for several days and the loss, especially of the King's army, was enormous. It suffered extremely from the difficulties of the march, and the want of provisions had a disastrous effect upon it. It was signally defeated and leaving its commanders slain on the battlefield, it fled to Lahore. The Guru duly respected the dead of the enemy. The Hindus were collected and burnt according to the Hindu custom, and the Mussalmans were duly buried. He took the wounded along with himself and adopted necessary measures to properly dress their wounds and feed them. When their wounds were cured, he sent them to the Emperor with necessary travelling expenses. On their arrival at the imperial court they greatly praised the valour, charity and liberalty of the Guru. It is said that the loss of the imperial army in this battle amounted to about 16,000 men or 73 per cent. of the total.

After that, the Guru toured through many villages preaching righteousness, and visited Raja Tara Chand's territory. Then he came back to Amritsar in Sambat 1692 (1635 A.D.). For some time there was quiet until the disloyal Painda Khan induced the Emperor to attack the Guru again.

Painda Khan was a Pathan. He was employed by the Guru on Rs. 5 per diem and was mostly liberally treated. He had long been in his service. Once many valuable presents, which were brought for the Guru, were stolen by his son-in-law, Asman Khan. The Guru told him to restrain the young Pathan from committing such acts again, but Painda Khan, who was arrogant and overproud, took no notice of it. On the contrary he went on encouraging Asman Khan. Again a valuable hawk, which chanced to have flown to his house, was seized by him and misappropriated. Similarly he was guilty of many more misdemeanours and denied each and every offence. Many of the stolen articles were then recovered from his house and he was disgracefully dismissed from the service for misbehaviour.

Painda Khan thought that it was he alone through whose powers the Guru was ever victorious in the field of battle. He went to the Governor of Jalandhar for help, which was refused. Then he came to Lahore, and on various pretexts and false assurances, the Emperor furnished him with a powerful army, and in Baisakh Sambat 1693 (1636 A.D.) he marched upon the Guru who, at the time, had about 3,000 men. There was desperate fighting at Amritsar for three days, ending with a miserable and complete defeat of the imperial army. The Guru exhibited many feats of bravery and killed many of the enemy with his own hands. Painda Khan directed his attack upon the person of the Guru and thrice endeavoured to injure him with his sword, but it was dexterously warded off. He then dismounted from his horse and the Guru, desiring to try a duel with him, followed his example and immediately alighted from his horse and challenged him to shield himself against his blow. The very first blow served him a fatal stoke, and he lay strewn on the earth.

Then the Guru told him "O Painda Khan, repeat thy Kalmah." he replied "Thy sword serves me as Kalmah, O Lord." The Guru had great pity on him and sat by him. The hot rays of the sun fell upon his face, and the Guru protected him with his shield until he breathed his last.

When the Guru was shading Painda's face, Asman Khan, the root of all the mischief, rushed towards the Guru. Before he reached him, he saw the Guru's son and shot an arrow at him, but it missed him. The Guru's son replied to him with an arrow which pierced through his forehead and he fell dead.

The Guru and his son had some little conversation when the battle was raging at its height and prayed God to bless the souls of Painda and Asman Khan when they had just despatched. After this the Guru killed many more with his own hands and the majority of the Commanders tasted their death at his hands. The fight ended with the defeat of the imperial army.

While the fight was going on, a brave soldier rushed on the Guru with sword. The Guru warded off the blow and returned him a fatal stroke exclaiming "You have not knack of using the sword; this is the way to wield it.

The loss of the enemy in dead was estimated at 5,000 men, and that of the Sikhs at 700.

Soon after gaining this victory, the Guru started towards Kiratpur. As soon as the Guru left Amritsar, the scattered army of the enemy rallied again and after sacking Kiratarpur followed him. A severe battle was again fought at Phagwara in Jeth Sambat 1693 (1936 A.D.) and the Imperial force was routed in disaster. Then the Guru continued his march to Kiratpur.

One almost, an Udasi faqir, who was in change of Nanak Matta in the district of Naini Tal, complained that Jogis had expelled him from the shrine and burnt down the Pipal tree under which the Guru Nanak had carried on his religious discourses with the followers of Gorakh Nath. Therefore in Katak S. 1693 (1636 A.D.) the Guru started for that place *via* Najibabad, Nagina, Muradabad, Chandosi, Bareli, and Pili Bhit. Almost was restored to the possession of the shrine and the Pipal tree was resuscitated by sprinkling water mixed with saffron, and the leaves of the tree have, sincs then, peculiar marks on them. After that the Guru returned to Kiratpur through Aligarh, Bulandshahr, Delhi and Karnal.

Raja Tara Chand of Hindur had some boundary dispute with the Nawab of Ropar upon which a fight ensued in Phagan S. 1698 (1642 A.D.). The Guru joined the Raja, and the Nawab was completely defeated.

During the following month the Guru started for Kurukshetra with an escort of 1,000 sowars. When he came to Baman Majra the Pathans of Ropar, Sangholi, Bahlolpur and Kiri surrounded him with enormous troops. The Guru defended his position very valiantly and admirably until reinforcements were received from Kiratpur when the Pathans were dispersed.

Nothing of importance took place during the next two years. The Guru spent his last days at Kiratpur and breathed his last there on Chet Suddi 5th S. 1701 (March 1645 A.D.) after nominating his grandson Har Rai, as Guru. He died at the age of 48 years, 9 months and 4 days and reigned as Guru 37 years, 10 months, and 1 day.

The Sikhs had great love and respect for him and were ever ready to rally round his banner, on the approach of danger, at the shortest notice. His death was considered a national calamity and the author of the Dabistan Mazahib, gives as an eye-witness, a very pathetic account of his death and of the cremation of his body. Many of the Sikhs volunteered to burn themselves on his funeral pile. Two of his followers, notwithstanding remonstrances, actually jumped into the burning pyre and expired at the feet of the Guru. Many more including Raja Ram Partap Singh of Jaisalmer, were ready to follow their example but were strictly forbidden by the young Guru Har Rai. Such was the estimation in which the deceased Guru was held by the Sikhs, and it appears to be and unprecedented and unparalleled instance in the religious world. He was respected by Hindus and Muhammadans alike. Between Hargobindpur and Amritsar he had constructed at convenient stages, Masjids and *dairas* for Muhammadan travellers who were also fed there at the expense of the Guru.

5

Guru Har Rai

(b. 1644 A.D.—d. 1661 A.D.)

Of Guru Hargobind's five sons, two had survived him. The elder Surajmal was a worldly man and the youngest Tegh Bahadur was a recluse. The Guru's deceased eldest son Gurditta had two sons, Dhirmal and Har Rai. The former not being a sincere devotee of the Guru, the latter, a lad of fourteen years, born at Kiratpur on January 30, 1630, was chosen as his successor. He was strongly advised to retain the existing contingent of 2,200 mounted soldiers as his body-guard.

The material about the pontificate of Guru Har Rai is scanty. Mohsin Fani, who had been so helpful to us for the period of Guru Hargobind, asserts that he was a great friend of Guru Har Rai, but he does not tell us much about him. The reason is that the author had closed his account in 1645 when Guru Har Rai left for Nahan, and the two do not seem to have met each other afterwards. Mohsin Fani returned to his home in Kashmir and spent the rest of his life there. He writes: "Har Rai spent one year at Kiratpur. In 1645 Najabat Khan, son of Shahrukh Mirza, led an expedition under orders of Shah Jahan, conquered the country of Tarachand and took the Raja prisoner. Guru Har Rai retired to Nahan in the country of Raja Karam Prakash not far from Sarhind."

Guru Har Rai lived at Nahan for twelve years. He devoted all his energy to consolidate the Sikh religion, and went frequently on short tours to inspire the Sikhs by personal contact. At Nathana he blessed a poor and hungry Jat boy, Phul, who became the founder of the famous Phulkian family comprising the erstwhile states of Patiala, Nabha, Jind, Faridkot and others.

Prince Dara Shikoh, the eldest son of Shah Jahan, was in the habit of visiting saints both Hindu and Muslim. He met Guru Har Rai though he was fifteen years younger than the Prince. Dara was noted for his liberal views and was popular with Hindus. "The Punjab was strongly attached to Dara," writes Sir Jadunath. "The province had long been his viceroyalty." Shah Jahan fell ill in September 1657, and civil war was imminent among his sons. Dara seems to have called upon his friends and supporters to get ready for his help. This brought Har Rai back to Kiratpur in the winter of 1657. In the war fought in April-May 1658 Dara was defeated by Aurangzeb. Dara fled to Agra and then to Delhi. He crossed the Satluj at Rupar where Har Rai joined him at the head of 2,000 troops. The Prince and the Guru reached Lahore on July 3, 1658. Dara spent a month and a half in making preparations for war. "But Dara was utterly broken down in body and spirit." "He despaired of success, and his despair infected his troops." Finding the Prince in an indecisive mood and Aurangzeb in hot pursuit of him, first Raja Rajrup of Nurpur (1646-61) left Dara on the pretext of bringing reinforcements. Har Rai followed suit afterwards.

After having firmly established himself on the throne, Aurangzeb summoned Guru Har Rai to his court. The Guru sent his 14-year-old eldest son Ram Rai. He was instructed to concentrate on God and reply to the Emperor patiently and carefully. He was reminded of Guru Arjan's conduct when Jahangir ordered him to modify hymns in the holy Granth. He was warned to avoid flattery and behave with dignity. The led being over-zealous and ambitious, and perhaps out of fear for his life, tried to win over the Emperor and his courtiers. He was asked to explain why the following verse in the holy Granth abused the Musalmans: *"Matti Musalman ki pere pai kumhar; Ghar bhande ittan kian jalti kare pukar."* [The dust of a Musalman is kneaded by a potter into a dough, and he converts it into pots and bricks, which cry out as they burn.] The hymn was uttered by Guru Nanak to show that cremation and burial differed little. Ram Rai was overawed by the splendour of the court. In order not to offend the Emperor, Ram Rai just in his early teens, replied that Nanak's actual word was *'Beiman'* or faithless, and not Musalman which appeared in the text by the mistake of the scribe. He had forgotten that he being the Guru's son and employed on such a delicate mission had upon him a tremendously heavy duty and that he should be ready for death. His answer naturally pleased the Emperor but offended the Sikhs of Delhi who reported the matter to the Guru at Kiratpur.

Guru Har Rai was deeply distressed at his sons behaviour for having insulted Guru Nanak and the Granth Sahib. The Guru declared Ram Rai unfit for Guruship and immediately excluded him from succession. Har Rai observed: "The Guruship is like a tiger's milk which can only be contained in a golden cup. Only he who is ready to devote his life thereto is worthy of it. Let Ram Rai not look on my face again." His decision was conveyed to Ram Rai as well as to the Sikhs at Delhi. Ram Rai was detained at the Mughal court where he conducted himself as a faithful courtier. Shortly afterwards Guru Har Rai died at Kiratpur on October 6, 1661 at the young age of 32.

Guru Arjan was a great statesman, a peaceful organizer, philosopher, social worker, and poet. His themes are love, devotion, and union with the Beloved. His "Twelve Months" *(Barah Mah)* and his *"Sukhmani"* rank among the best of his literary works. His poems are the most extensive among the immortal poets whose work is included in the Adi Granth.

Fifth Phase—Military Action and Organization

Sikhism was organized into an army in the hands of the Sixth Guru. Har Gobind was Guru Arjan's son and became the Guru at the age of 11. He was brought up by Bhai Buddha, and as per his father-Guru's instructions he at once enrolled a small army and a personal body guard of armed men, sending messages to the *masand* that the usual gifts of money should now be replaced by weapon and horses. He took to hunting and instilled martial spirit among his Sikhs.

The Guru's explanation was that the extreme non-violence would only encourage the enemy, and sword was necessary for whose who oppressed and impoverished the poor people. Har Gobind maintained a great state having over 800 horses and a splendid retinuê of well-equipped soldiers. According to Fani a contemporary of Guru Har Gobind, in his Dabistan-i-Mazahib the Guru had 700 horses in his stables and 300 cavalries and 6 artillery-men were always in his service. This was the first corps of Sikh volunteers raised by the Guru Amritsar. It was near the site of the Khalsa College that the Sikhs fought in 1628 their first battle again the Moghul forces of Emperor Shahjahan.

Har Gobind — Both a Saint and Soldier

Guru Har Gobind, although he adopted military means, was a Divine teacher for the Sikhs and instruct them on the spiritual path as well. He was, as is known in Sikhism a "soldier-saint," which the Tenth Guru later created on a mass scale and influenced the leaders of the Maratha nationalist movement.

Guru Har Gobind was a bold reformer. The Sikh institutions of sangat (Common congregations) and *pangat* (common Community lunch or *langar*) had gone a long way towards demolishing caste. But the existing differences in the social level of the low caste *sudras* and the high born *Brahmins* and *Kshatriyas* were further reduced by enlisting in the Gurus' army.

The Battles. At the instigation of Chandu Shah, a meeting was arranged between Har Gobind and Jahangir in Delhi in 1612. Jahangir welcomed him with respect and joined him in hunting, where the Guru saved Emperor's life from a tiger. Chandu was constantly working for destroying the Guru and did not rest until Jahangir had the Guru interned on false charges in the Gwalior Fort. The Guru was so kind to other captives that he won all their hearts. In vain did Chandu try to get him murdered there, while the Sikhs outside were working for his release. Twelve long years went by, and the Guru would not go free till he had all the other royal prisoners freed first, himself standing surety for them. This was finally accomplished. The Emperor handed over Chandu to be punished by the Sikhs in whose hands he met his death.

The long threatened trouble with the Moghul Empire began in 1628. Some Sikhs captured Emperor's hawk and killed a few of his soldiers. Mukhlis Khan was sent with troops by Shah Jahan to arrest the Guru. Shah Jahan had now succeeded his father and was an enemy of Har Gobind and the Sikhs. There was a fierce battle with the Moghul troops at Wadali; the Guru himself fought like a tiger, and the Moghuls were driven off.

The Guru built a new city on the bank of the river Beas, which he called Hargobindpur. His enemies brought here an army of ten thousand men and attacked, but were driven back with great slaughter. Bhai Buddha after this battle came to the Guru, took his leave, drank water from his feet, and passed away, more than a century after his first coming to Guru Nanak.

For some time Shah Jahan sought pretext against the Guru, while Wazir Khan, an old friend of the Sikhs, persuaded him that a man of Har Gobind's stature was no enemy of Islam. But in 1631 an incident over the stealing of horses and recovered for the Guru by Bidhichand from the imperial stables, led to a punitive expedition, which was defeated at Gurusar, though at the cost of 1,200 Sikhs. In 1634 when an envoy of Emperor came to the Guru at Jullundur and began to insult Guru Nanak, a quarrel developed which ended in a great victory for the Sikhs.

Historical Perspective. In self defence the Guru fought these battles during his life and changed the character of the Gurudom. The Seventh, Eighth, and Ninth Gurus adopted the policy of non-violence according to circumstances, but the Tenth Guru again took sword to correct injustices and defend the country from aggression.

This change in the methods of using violence or non-violence should not mean that the Sikh philosophy of Guru Nanak changed entirely in the hands of Guru Har Gobind and Guru Gobind Singh. The Sikh spirit started with Nanak and was developed to its zenith by Gobind Singh which now permeates in the heart of every Singh. The philosophical basis of Guru Nanak's, Guru Har Gobind's (and later Guru Gobind's) action rests on this principle—the propagation of truth and establishment of peace. The methods change according to circumstances. This should indicate that Guru Gobind Singh was as peaceful as Guru Nanak or Guru Arjan. The view held by some that the philosophy of Guru Har Gobind (or Guru Gobind Singh) was entirely different from Guru Nanak or Guru Arjan is misplaced and misjudges the objectives of the Gurus.

SIXTH PHASE—AESTHETICS, SOCIAL WORKS AND RETURN TO NON-VIOLENCE

Guru Har Rai (1630-1661)

Guru Har Gobind retired on March 31, 1664, and the spirit of Guru Nanak changed bodies once again. Guru's grandson, son of Guruditta, Har Rai was seated to the Guru's gaddi. Har Rai's elder brother, Dhirmal, was considered unfit for this high office.

Har Rai was only fourteen when he ascended the Guru's gaddi and developed into a man of gentleness and love. For most of his reign he lived at Kiratpur and was a popular teacher of religion there.

Political Involvement. Guru Har Rai had once cured the Prince Dara Shikoh of poison administered by Aurangzeb, and Shah Jahan vowed eternal friendship with him on this account. As soon as Shah Jahan died in 1658, Aurangzeb drove his brother Dara away, and the Prince sought the Guru's help. The Guru promised him salvation but did not promise victory for the crown. When Dara Shikoh had to retreat from the River Beas, the Guru sent a small Sikh force there to cover his friend's flight, but eventually Dara was captured and executed.

The Emperor sent for Guru Har Rai to know why the latter had helped his enemy. The Guru sent his elder son Ram Rai to represent his case at the court. This young man worked miracles there to display his own greatness, and adroitly changed a line in the Guru Granth Sahib reading "Beiman" (Faithless) instead of "Musalman." The verse is: 'The clay of Mussalman may find its way into the hand of a potter who makes vessels and bricks out of it; it cries out as it burns." Ram Rai was banished by the Guru on this account. Guru Har Rai passed away on October 6, 1661 and installed his younger son as the eighth Guru of the Sikhs.

Guru Hargobind had three wives of whom he had five sons. (1) Baba Gurditta born S. 1670 (1613 A.D.), (2) Ani Rai born 26th Magh, S. 1672 (1616 A.D.), (3) Suraj Mal, born 11th Har S. 1672 (1615 A.D.), (4) Atal Rai, born 22nd Katak S. 1676 (1619 A.D.) and (5) Teg Bahadur born on the 5th day of the dark half of the month of Baisakh, Sambat 1679 (A.D. 1621). The traditional account of the death of Baba Gurditta and Atal Rai is very curious and interesting. In S. 1695 (1638 A.D.) Baba Gurditta restored to life a cow which had been accidently killed by a Sikh. When Guru Hargobind heard of it he was very angry and told him that he had been unable to contain his spiritual power and might within himself, and indicated that his behaviour proved that either the son or the father must live and that both of them could not live at the same time. Thereon the son encompassed his father and went straight to the tome of one Budhan Shah, a Mohammadan faqir. Close to that tomb he spread a bedding of grass, lay down and gave up his soul. The father was rather glad to hear of it and his funeral obsequies were duly performed and a tomb erected on the very spot where he died in the vicinity of Kiratpur.

As regards Atal Rai it is stated that one day when he was about 9 years old, he was playing with boys of about the same age. He won the game but owing to its getting late in the evening he said that he would play the next morning. The next morning the playmate who had lost the game, was bitten by a snake and died. When Atal Rai went to his house to call him to come out and play, he found his parents lamenting for him. Atal Rai kicked and called him out as if he were pretending to sleep in order to evade his turn. The boy at once arose and began to play. When he came to know of this, the Guru was very angry and when Atal Rai came to him, he said "Thy act shows as if thou art an equal with and antagonist to the Lord. Thou art vying with and disobeying Him. He causes one to die and thou reanimatest the dead.

To work miracles in this way is strictly prohibited and thy conduct in this respect is reprehensible." When thus reprimanded, Baba Atal Rai very submissively and meekly went out and lying down on the ground, spread his sheet over himself and breathed his last. His tomb was erected on the spot at Amritsar. It is close to the holy reservoir on the bank of Kaulsar. It is the highest building in the town. At the time when Baba Atal Rai died the locality was a dense jungle.

Guru Har Rai travelled in different parts of the country. In 1710 She went to Malwa and halted for some time at Dowali in the Parganah of Bathinda. The ancestors of the Phuls, a subdivision of Jats, resided there as tenants-at-will and the landlords would not even allow them to sink a well. One day Chaudhri Kala brought his nephews, Phul and Sandhi, whose father was, during the time of Guru Hargobind, killed in a battle. Phul, who was then 5 year old, struck with his hands, at the instance of his uncle, his own naked belly like a drum in front of the Guru. When asked why he did so, Kala explained that he was hungry and wanted some thing to eat. The Guru replied that his descendants would lord over the country between Satluj and Jamna. This prediction was fulfilled shortly afterwards, and the Rajas of Patiala, Jind and Nabha are descended from that very Phul. Having obtained the above reply and returned home, Chaudhri Kala related the whole story to his wife. She rebuked him because it would not benefit him, or his own progeny, and remarked that if Phul's descendants became rulers of the country, it would be better to be lorded over by a Muhammadan than their own *shariks* (agnatees). She advised him to get some blessings in his own favour. He therefore appeared again before the Guru, with his own sons. The Guru said that the lot of Phul's descendants was unalterable whereas Chaudhri's descendants would enjoy free grants of land. Kala's descendants are now Jagirdars and are called *Land gharie Sardars.*

Guru Har Rai had, as already stated, no taste for war, and as soon as he assumed the Guruship, he discharged all the troops which were maintained by his grandfather, except 2,200 men, who were either foreigners or refugees from the Muhammadan oppression, whom it was considered not advisable to disband. Nevertheless the military spirit of the Sikhs which was fosterred during the time of Guru Hargobind did not abate but continued to flourish. Guru Har Rai took particular precautions to avoid any intermeddling with politics, but circumstances were not wanting under which the Sikhs were compelled to exert their power and energy for their own defence. In S. 1713 (1656 A.D.) when from his tour of Malwa and Doaba the Guru was coming back to Gondwal, Muhammad Yarbeg Khan (son of Mukhlas Khan who was killed by Guru Hargobind in battle) who chanced to be on the way with 1,000 men, attacked unawares the baggage and the laides who were following the Guru at some distance. The Guru knew nothing of this attack, but the little escort defended themselves admirably and drove the enemy away with considerable loss. Bhai Garra, whose descendants now rule the Kaithal State, was the most prominent, and was rewarded by the Guru for his courage and bravery. The Raja of Kahlur became troublesome and was reduced by the Sikhs to submission.

The Emperor, Shah Jahan, like his ancestors, Akbar and Jahangir, lay under the course of rebellious sons. He suffered from the intrigues and rebellions of his family. When in S. 1714 (August 1657 A.D.) he was seized with a severe sudden illness, his sons began to quarrel for the throne. In June 1658 A.D. Dara Shikoh, the eldest son, was totally defeated at Chambal and compelled to fly to Delhi with a handful of followers. The governor of that place closed the fortress against him and he was obliged to march rapidly on Lahore. Aurangzeb sent troops in pursuit of him and they had reached close to him, when he came to the Guru at Gondwal, and implored him to take measures to delay the crossing of the Bias by the pursuers, so that he might gain time to elude the pursuit. The Prince had always maintained a close alliance with the Gurus, and through the effectual assistance of the Guru with his small contingent of 2,200 men and three Guns, the enemy was kept at bay and obliged to return towards Delhi.

After a treacherous conflict with his brothers. Aurangzeb deposed his father, making him a Statt prisoner in the fort of Agra, and proclaimed himself king in S. 1715 (June 1658 A.D). He cleared the field by disposing of his rivals by death or dungeon, and Dara Shikoh also being betrayed into his hands by the Chief of Jun, was, by a mock tribunal, pronounced to be an apostate and doomed to suffer death. After the establishment of his rule and the strengthening of his hands, the hypocrite Aurangzeb embarked upon his grand but wicked enterprise of religious crusade against the Hindus. In connection with that crusade his Majesty summoned Guru Har Rai to Delhi on a certain pretext but, the Guru foreseeing his intentions submitted on 7th Baisakh S. 1717 (1660 A.D.) a mild petition to him, representing that he was a mere faqir and that he had no business at the imperial court and hoped that his presence would be excused. Ram Rai, the eldest son of the Guru, took this letter to his Majesty. Aurangzeb was satisfied on the receipt of that letter, and was highly pleased with the conversation he had with Ram Rai whom he kept at his Court for a long period and treated with marked distinction granting Rs. 500 daily for his langar (public kitchen) Ram Rai had strict injunctions from his father to be true to his faith and never to swerve from it whatever the circumstances might be. His Majesty used to hear much from him about the Sikh religion and highly reversed the Holy Granth. He deemed the faith to be practically on all fours with the tenets of Islam. One day his Majesty came across a sentence in the Sikh Scriptures in Rag Asa, and asked Ram Rai about its meaning. That sentence related to the sufferings of the body of a Mussalman after his death, and Ram Rai thinking that it would offend the Emperor, who was very bigoted, substituted the word "beiman (faithless)" for "Mussalman" in order to please him. When the report of the fact reached him, the Guru was exasperted with anger and remarked that no mortal could change the sayings of Guru Nanak,and that the mouth which had dared to do so should never be seen by him. He was charged with falsehood and disinherited with a perpetual injunction that no true Sikh should on pain of excommunication from Sikhism, maintain any intercourse with him or his progeny. Ram Rai asked for forgiveness and personally waited upon his father at Kiratpur. Pardon was not granted and the request for an interview was rejected with the order that he should instantaneously leave Kiratpur for any direction he willed. He thereupon, went to Dehra Dun and founded a shrine there, to visit which the Sikhs are strictly forbidden.

At the age of 31 years, 8 months and 22 days, and, after a reign of 17 years, 6 months and 9 days, Guru Har Rai died at Kiratpur on 9th Katak (Suddi) S. 1718 (1661 A.D.). He nominated his youngest son Har Krishan as Guru.

6

Guru Har Krishan

The Child-Spiritual-Head

Guru Har Krishan, the tiny child was the unique proof of spiritual greatness. Guru Har Rai, the father of this great child was the seventh Guru of the Sikhs. Guru Har Krishan was born at Kiratpur Sahib on the 7th of November, 1656 A.D. and was named after the name of his mother, Har Krishan Kaur. He had an elder brother named Ram Rai who was deeply devoted to meditation but became a seeker of occult powers which made him selfish and proud, and took him astray from the true path of spirituality which is a balanced combination of humility to serve humankind having dauntless courage to uphold truth. But a man lost in acquiring "sidhis" or occult powers and their display and use for his personal ends, falls with a thud from the ladder of spiritualism. It happened to Ram Rai, though he was elder to Har Krishan by many years.

Guru Har Rai was a very brave man but was also known for love and compassion for all. He often used to say that to hurt one's is to offend God and thus he preached uninversal love and service not only with words but also running a free public refectory or "Langar" and a charitable hospital, at Kiratpur Sahib. He also had a cavalary of 2,200 brave soldiers and expert horse-men for self-defence as the fanatic Muslim rulers never saw religio-spiritual and patriotic teachings of the Sikh Gurus with tolerant and friendly eyes and could attack the Sikhs, any time.

The spiritual grace and miraculous mettle of Har Krishan were realised by his parents and many other devotees, right in his toddling age. Of course, the showy and shallow demeanour of Ram Rai was disliked by his parents as well as by the people. Anyhow, inspite of being a learned person, he grew like a magician, absorbed in his occult powers.

Guru Har Rai saw his end approaching fast. So, fully realising the divine wisdom, effulgence, inspiringly peaceful personality and healing sight, word and touch of Har Krishan, he made him the 8th Guru of the Sikhs, just at the age of 5 years 2 months and 16 days. To Ram Rai, the news of the succession of Guru Har Krishan as the 8th Guru of the Sikhs and admonition by his father, was a bolt from the blue. He became a spineless tout of Aurangzeb who bestowed on him the land on which the City of Dehradun is situated. He also concocted his own Granth or Holy book which could never be accepted by the Sikh Gurus and the

Sikhs. However, he kept Aurangzeb inciting against the Sikhs of the Punjab and filed petition to call Guru Har Krishan to Delhi, so that he might be deprived of his Guruship, and he himself could become the 8th Guru of the Sikhs, by his right of primogeniture. Aurangzeb was in league with Ram Rai. Therefore, he decided to call the child—Guru to Delhi to plead his case, expecting that the very summons would perturb the child. He expected that the child-Guru would never dare come to Delhi and then this offence of default could be easily construed as a revolt and he could be dethroned or disclaimed for reinstating Ram Rai who after becoming Guru would be a great help to make his Sikh followers the faithful slave-subjects of the State.

The King and his advisers did not know the spiritual age, wisdom, power, prudence and clairvoyance of Guru Har Krishan, the child spiritual head of the Sikhs, far beyond his physical age, Hence, on receiving the orders of Aurangzeb through Paras Ram, the Minister of Mirza Jai Singh, the cowed down Rajput supporter of Aurangzeb from Jaipur, the child Guru smiled and calmly became ready to go to Delhi. His mother, relatives and Sikhs, all were afraid of going to Delhi but the only one who had no fear at all was the child-Guru himself.

Here I feel to mention that Guru Gobind Singh, the 10th and last Guru of the Sikhs has invoked his preceding nine Sikh Gurus in the very first hymn of his great poetical composition called "Chandi Di Vaar," the epic poem of goddess Chandi, the Sikh prayer or Ardas begins with it and says about Guru Har Krishan, "Sri Har Krishan dhiyae jis dithey sab dukh jai" (concentrate on Har Krishan the great whose very sight removes all sufferings). Such was the bewitching beauty and divine influence of the "darshan" or vision of Har Krishan.

It was nothing short of miracle that a child of just five expounded the hymns of religion and spiritualism and spoke to the audience in a matchlessly impressive manner. Anybody who faithfully had his darshan or touched his body was blessed with health, happiness, love and peace. Once the child-Guru was being taken in a palanquin for an outing. A leper approached him weeping, crying and cringing for his mercy and bliss to remove his misery. The child-spiritual-head was deeply touched by his suffering. So, he lovingly and smilingly gave his handkerchief to that leper and asked him to gently wipe his face and body with it. So, as he did it, his leprosy vanished spontaneously and that leper became a great devotee of the Guru. The child-Guru did to that leper what Jesus, the Christ did to Lazarus.

Guru Har Krishan and his mother asked some Sikhs to accompany them to Delhi, for which the required persons started for Delhi by the horse-coaches then in vogue. They took with them all the necessaries needed on the way. The people flocked to them in large numbers at all the places of their night-stay. Truly, they realised what they had heard about him that his sight, nectarous and divine words could console soul and cure ailments. He went preaching love, humility, unity of humanity, unicity of God and the Holy Name to all who came to him.

Many people came to have his darshan at Kurukshetra where he stayed for some days. The Brahmins became jealous of him ridiculing him and saying to the people, "Is it not a joke that a child of five is the spiritual head of the Sikhs? To add another joke to a joke, his name is Har Krishan. How can he bear the name and greatness of Lord Krishan? How can he understand and expound the depth of the shlokas of the Holy Gita, as uttered by Lord Krishna? They are fools who go to him for any spiritual enlightenment and peace of mind." The head of those Brahmins was Pandit Laloo Chand who went to the Guru, with the Gita to test the justification of his being a spiritual head. Many people accompanied Laloo Chand and many more were already there to hear the discussion between the Pandit and the Guru. The Pandit approached the Guru with a diehard attitude of vanity and said to him, "I cannot believe that a child of your age could be spiritual Guru and that also in the name of Lord Krishna who uttered the Holy Gita, the summit of spiritual philosophy. Do you know the Sanskrit language and the Gita? Can you explain and expound the Shlokas in Sanskrit which I will read out to you? If you do it and satisfy me, then I will believe you to be a true Guru. Can you accept my challenge"?

Prejudice which sees what pleases it, cannot see even what is plain and self-evident. They say all looks yellow to the jaundiced eyes. Prejudice is that mist which during our journey in the world, dims the brightest and obscures the best of all the glories which meet us on our way because when the judgment is frail, prejudice is strong. So much so that ignorance is far less remote from the truth than prejudice. The prejudiced Pandit Laloo Chand went to the Guru grinning his teeth of prejudice.

The exceptionally beautiful, calm and peaceful Guru smiled and politely offered a seat to him. Then he said to Laloo Chand, "Pandit Ji, if I explain the meanings of the shalokas of Gita in Sanskrit to you, you will simply say that I have done it as I have been taught by some Pandit like you. Please, bring some absolutely illiterate and ignorant person of your village whom you and your people know well since his very birth. I will ask him to expound the Shalokas of the Gita in Sanskrit." Laloo Chand was amused by the suggestion of the Guru and said, looking at the people around, "See, this child has really talked childishly. He cuts impossible jokes on me." Then the Guru emphatically and seriously pressed him to bring somebody as he was asked to do and see the wonders of the Lord Almighty.

A water-carrier or Jheewar named Chhajoo Ram was standing nearby. He was an illiterate person and dumb by birth. The pandit and all other people knew him well. Therefore, the Pandit offered him to the Guru, considering that he was retaliating the joke of the Guru and by doing it the Guru would be exposed.

Laloo Chand recited the verses of his own choice from the Holy Gita as the born-dumb Chhajoo Ram sat before the Guru. The Guru placed his walking stick on the head of his medium and exhorted him, "Brother, Chhajoo Ram explain the

Shalokas of Gita in Sanskrit." Spontaneously, Chhajoo Ram began to speak in the most articulate and impressive words expounding the meanings of the verses, pointing out with his finger, emphasising certain points with his forceful gestures. Then what? Chhajoo Ram, Pandit Laloo Chand and all others who were present there became the most faithful devotees of the Guru. They loudly sang in ecstasy the praises of the Guru as the true-child-spiritual-head or Sacha Bal Guru.

The Guru, his mother and other companions reached Delhi after some nightstays on their way. They stayed there in the house or bangla (bungalow) of Mirza Jai Singh. Thousands of people came to pay homage to him. Mirza Jai Singh himself tested the telescence of the Guru by disguising his Queen, sitting amidst scores of other women who were gaudily dressed and every one of them looked like a Queen. He watched all of them with his divine-enlighted eyes and smilingly sat in the lap of the real queen just like her child. The queen was issueless and the Guru blessed her to have a son. In course of time, she was actually blessed with the birth of a son.

Aurangzeb kept hearing about the spirituality, piety, nobility and gentility of the Guru. He was very anxious to see him personally as even his son Muazzam highly praised the Guru after coming, paying homage and talking to him. But Guru did not want to see Aurangzeb at any cost as he had told Diwan Paras Ram at the time of leaving Kiratpur Sahib. The divine faith and force in the body and soul of the Guru were invincible. Faith boisterously laughs at the shaking of a spear but unbelief timidly trembles at the rustle of a leaf. Thousands of people used to come to the Guru and their sufferings were cured even by the use of his feet-wash water. As God willed, the city of Delhi was attacked by epidemic of small-pox and cholera. Consequently numerous entire families were wiped out.

Aurangzeb certainly had reached the highest pitch of eagerness to see Guru Har Krishan but hearing about his spiritual power, was afraid of going to him without his consent which he would not give for any appeal or under any amount of oppression. God's will helped the wish of the Guru. He was also acutely attacked by small-pox. He asked the Sikhs to take him to some open place outside the city, beyond the crowd and din of Delhi. So, he was taken to the east of delhi, on the eastern bank of river Jamuna. High fever and attack of small-pox became worse and worse. His bed was kept in a tent where his devotees kept seeing him. He saw his death closely hovering over his head. The Sikhs and his mother clearly understood it also.

It was the mid-night of the 30th of March, 1664 A.D. when he had not completed even the 8th year of his age. The Sikhs appeared before him with their folded hands and requested, "Reverenced Sir, right from Guru Nanak the founder of Sikhs faith, every Sikh Guru has been appointing his successor before leaving his mortal body, but who will become the Guru after you to guide the Sikhs?" The Guru, still calm, peaceful and smiling in divine joy, pointed his finger towards the Punjab and uttered only two words, "Baba Bakaley" and breathed his last, closing his eyes from the earthly light and mingling with the divine light of the Lord, the Origin of all origins and Endless End of all ends.

He was cremated there on the bank of Jamuna where at present the Sikh shrine or Gurdwara Bala Sahib (the tomb of the reverenced child) stands. The Bangla of Mirza Jai Singh where he stayed at Delhi is called Gurudwara Bangla Sahib from the weli of which even today millions of devotees get holy water and the faithful are cured of incurable diseases.

The 9th Sikh Guru, Tegh Bahadur was discovered at 'Baba Bakala' in the district of Amritsar, as told by the eighth Guru.

Now millions of Sikh devotees all over the world, daily recite or invoke in their prayer or "ardas," "Concentrate on Guru Har Krishan whose very sight removes all sufferings."

Annexure

ANNEXURE—I

GURU HAR RAI (1630-1661)

9.1 Birth and Ancestry

Guru Har Rai was born on Saturday, 16 January 1630 at Kiratpur, district Hoshiarpur. His father was Baba Gurditta, the eldest son of Guru Hargobind, and his mother was Mata Nihal Kaur. He was the second grandson of Guru Hargobind, the first being Baba Dhir Mal. The Guru, like his grandfather, was a saint-soldier, well built in body and very strong in mind and heart. Being a direct male descendant of Guru Ramdas, he was of a Sodhi clan.

9.2 Childhood and Education

Guru Har Rai spent his childhood at Kiratpur. All his education, both in weaponry and languages and religious studies took place there. He was brought up under the direct care of Guru Hargobind. He was very tender-hearted, compassionate and a loving person. One day, during his childhood, when he was walking in a garden his robe got tangled with a bush and broke stems of some flowers which fell to the ground. The sight was too much for him and brought tears to his eyes.

9.3 Marriage

Guru Har Rai was married to Mata Krishen Kaur, daughter of Baba Daya Ram, of Buland-shair, Uttar Pradesh, on 18 June 1640, when he was about ten years old. He had two sons, Ramrai born in 1646, when Har Rai was sixteen years old and Harkrishan, born in 1656, when the Guru was twenty six years old.

TABLE

GURU HAR RAI—SEVENTH GURU OF THE SIKHS
1630-1661 (31 YEARS)

Father-baba Gurditta — Mother - Mata Damodri

GURU HAR RAI

Place of Birth - Kiratpur — Date of Birth - 16 Jan. 1960
Religion - Sikh

MARRIED TO MATA KRISHAN KAUR
DAUGHTER OF BABA DAYA RAM
MARRIAGE DATE — 18 JUNE 1640 (10 YRS.)

Son-
Ramrai (1646)

Son-
Harkrishan (1656)

EDUCATION

Place — Kiratpur
Period — 1635-1644

Subjects - Punjabi, Religions

CONFLICTS

1. Elder Brother — Dhirmal, who
   a. took possession of Guru Granth Sahib
   b. Declared himself guru and took over the residence at Kiratpur

2. Mehrban (Son of Prithi Chand), who
   a. took possession of Harmandir and
   b. declared himself guru at Amritsar.

INVITATION OF AURANGZEB
1661

Time Period — 1661

Reasons — a. Aurangzeb had complaints from Dhirmal and Muslim fundamentalists.

Result — a. The Guru sent his elder son Ram Rai

b. Ram Rai dared to change a line of Guru Nanak's hymn to please the Emperor

THE GURU PERIOD

Place of residence-
Kiratpur-Nahan

Period of Guruship-
(8-3-1644 — 6th Oct. 1661) (Age - 14)

TEACHINGS

1. Unity of God 2. Daily prayers 3. Love of God 4. Love for man 5. Correct pronunciation of Gurubani

CONTRIBUTION TO SIKHISM

1. New concept of langar (langar at home); 2. Dispensaries and clinics (free for

all); 3. Unique/first zoo; 4. Opening of 3 new missionary centres at Barmaula, Bihar and Kasur; 5. Consolidation of administration 6. Teaching by parables.

RELATED GURDWARAS

Total = 13
Location = Amritsar 4, Gwalior 1, Srinagar 1, Gujrat 1, Wazirabad 1, Kartarpur 2, Lahore, 1, Kiratpur 2.

HYMNS

Total = None

SAKHIS/SOURCE

1. Gurbilas Path Shahi Dus — Koer Singh 1751
2. Bansiwala Dus Patshahian — Kesar Singh Chhiber 1769
3. Mehma Parkash — Sarup Das Bhalla

IMPORTANT NAMES

Aurangzeb

THE DEPARTURE

Place of death — Nahan

Date/Year — 6 October, 1661

GURU HAR RAI — SEVENTH GURU OF THE SIKHS

		Guru's Age
1630	Born at Kiratpur, younger son of Baba Gurditta	
1640	Marriage with Mata Kishen Kaur	10
1644	Anointed as the seventh Guru of the Sikhs	14
1645	Moved to Nahan to avoid confrontation with elder brother, Dhirmal	15
1646	Birth of Ramrai	16
1656	Birth of Harkrishan	26

1657	Moved back to Kiratpur	27
1658	Dara Shikoh (eldest son of Shah Jahan) visited Guru Har Rai	28
1658	Aurangzeb became the Emperor of India, after killing all his brothers and capturing his ailing father, Shah Jehan	28
1661	Aurangzeb invited Guru Har Rai - Ramrai sent to meet Emperor Aurangzeb; Guru's declaration of dis-owning Ramrai	31
1661	Died at Kiratpur	31